ret
st

UFFA FOX

A PERSONAL BIOGRAPHY

June Dixon

Foreword by
HRH The Duke of Edinburgh

ANGUS & ROBERTSON · PUBLISHERS

ANGUS & ROBERTSON · PUBLISHERS
Brighton · Sydney · Melbourne · Singapore · Manila

First published by Angus & Robertson (UK) Ltd,
16 Ship Street, Brighton, Sussex, in 1978

Copyright © June Dixon 1978

ISBN 0 207 95827 0

Printed in Great Britain by
Ebenezer Baylis and Son Limited, The Trinity Press,
Worcester, and London

ACKNOWLEDGEMENTS

I would like to thank the following for their help and guidance:

    Madame Yvonne Fox
    Miss Elfrida Fox
    Peter and Murray Dixon, and
    Mrs Lucy McQueen-Mason
    Sir Max Aitken
    Mrs Kelly Cooper
    Mrs Dorothy Hounsell
    Mr and Mrs Norman Terry
    Mr and Mrs W. T. Waight
    Mr Charles Willis

My especial thanks to Tony Dixon for his very great contribution in the form of technical advice and drawings.

My thanks are also due to the following publishers, from whose books I have quoted: George Newnes Ltd (*Joys of Life* by Uffa Fox); Nautical Publishing Co (*More Joys of Life* by Uffa Fox); Peter Davies Ltd (*Sailing, Seamanship and Yacht Construction* by Uffa Fox); William Kimber and Co (*Britannia: Rowing Alone Across the Atlantic* by John Fairfax).

ILLUSTRATION ACKNOWLEDGEMENTS

The author wishes to thank the copyright holders of the following photographs used in the book.

Sir Max Aitken: 32
Daily Telegraph: 20
Dumfries and Galloway News: 21
Giles (*Daily Express*): 24
Tom Hanley: 27
Keystone Press Agency Ltd: 26, 31
London Express News & Feature Service: 18
The Press Association Ltd: 19
Roger M. Smith: 22, 23, 25
Norman Terry: 29

Title page drawing by Michael Eldridge.

FOREWORD by
HRH the Duke of Edinburgh

It seems to have become a common belief that all people can be put into some arbitrary catalogue or other; Uffa defied this rubbish with relish. His life was one long campaign for the freedom of the human spirit and against the foolish, the stupid and the self-important, the whole conducted with a cheerful breeziness that disarmed all but the hardest cases. All the qualities of his nature were over life-size but neither malice nor dishonesty were among them.

In conventional terms Uffa was eccentric, but it always struck me that even his more bizarre ideas had a way of exposing how irrational some of our most cherished conventions can be.

June and Tony Dixon have made a splendid job of what is really the hopeless task of capturing this mercurial character between the covers of a book. According to the epilogue St Peter admitted Uffa because of his Goldfish Club Certificate, but even without that certificate, I think St Peter would have been justified in letting Uffa through the Pearly Gates simply as a prized addition to the heavenly collection of exceptional souls.

1978

To Mahala

[1]

Uffa Fox was a man consumed and controlled by the basic elements: earth, air, fire and water. The earth, air and water surrounded and became an integral part of his being; the fire was within. Loved, hated, but seldom ignored, he was born on 15 January 1898, within the tight structure of late Victorian society, and yet manages to emerge as a 'one off' in an ever-increasing age of mass production.

His boyhood, particularly for those around him, was traumatic in the extreme and it says much for his parents, Arthur and Lucy Fox, that they succeeded in channelling his thought and energy along practical and constructive lines without destroying the inherent spark.

One of the earliest incidents to emerge involving Uffa discloses an interesting psychological pattern which has amused, intrigued or downright annoyed those around him throughout his life. This particular event concerns his younger sister, Elfrida. The infant Ellie, sickly and ailing, was the delicate one of the remaining three children and not expected to live. Consequently the household tended to revolve around her struggle for survival, perhaps sometimes to the disgust of Uffa and his elder sister, Mahala. Uffa may have felt particularly neglected for, until Ellie's arrival on the scene, he had been the baby of the family.

Uffa, who was some seven years old at the time, was despatched to the local chemist at East Cowes in the Isle of Wight, where he had been born and spent most of his childhood, to purchase talcum powder for Ellie's *toilette*. Mrs Fox's face on being presented with a toy pistol instead of a box of talcum was, from all accounts, a joy to behold; and Uffa's explanation – 'I thought it would be kinder if we shot Ellie like the animals and put her out of her misery' – completely took the wind out of her sails.

Had Uffa been unable to resist the temptation to purchase the toy pistol and thought up an alibi on the way home – if so full marks for the courage to take such a gamble and heaven help those who were to pit their wits against him in later life? Was he so resentful of the demands of the younger child in the home that he would really have enjoyed seeing her shot? Or was he, as so often happened in later life, stretching authority to discover just how far he could go? In the event his strategy paid off. Ellie (who as Uffa and Mahala jokingly said she would, survived them both and lives on) managed without her talc and Uffa kept the gun.

Environment plus family background play major roles in the evolution of us all. In the case of Uffa Fox, his childhood, surrounded by the water and the breathtaking beauty of the Isle of Wight, a stable and happy home life, plus the sea in the bones of his ancestors, led as naturally as summer follows spring to the essence of his character and his deep love of the sea.

Lucy Fox came from the farming branch of an old Suffolk family, the Cobbolds; and it is here, in his mother's family, that one finds periodically recurring the names of Uffa and Mahala. Genealogical records in England do not exist from as far back as the Viking invasions of the eastern counties but there is no doubt that, over the centuries, invaders from the Scandinavian countries came, saw and conquered. Their kings were called Uffa and the king's eldest daughter, Mahala. We have no means of knowing, one way or the other, if these unusual names were passed on from generation to generation because their original seeds were bedded in the loins of the Viking kings, but it is an interesting thought. It would also indicate a background of sea and adventure on his mother's side.

On the Fox side, however, we have factual evidence of an ancestor so famed as a seaman in his day that his exploits were captured for posterity in the pages of the *Illustrated London News*. Most families can produce from their background a legendary, larger than life figure whose achievements are passed on by word of mouth from parent to offspring through the years. Grandpa Miller was such a person, the difference being that his deeds of daring and courage were time-capsuled in print on Saturday, 29 January 1848. He would have been proud of his great-grandson, Uffa Fox.

William Miller had style. Tall for his day and well built, bursting with amiable charm, he was a man amongst men. No wonder, descending like a bombshell on the small port of Cowes, he caused a flutter and a beating of the feminine heart; but it was the beautiful Miss Elizabeth Roberton who finally captured and married him and bore him two children.

Their times together were few but idyllic for William Miller was first and foremost a seaman. Breezing in after a long voyage he would say to Grandma Miller, 'Hold out your apron', and, with a flourish, rain a glitter of gold sovereigns into her outstretched pinny. She never got over his untimely loss at sea and mourned him until the day she died. Mahala remembered her as a very sad old lady dressed in black.

Extract from the *Illustrated London News*, Saturday, 29 January 1848
WILLIAM MILLER
Boatswain of Her Majesty's Steamer *Avenger*

Amongst the unfortunate persons who lost their lives in this ill-fated
vessel, was William Miller, her boatswain, better known by his
fund of anecdote, as Joe Miller. A finer fellow never stepped on a
vessel's deck. To his herculean frame, born to brave the fiercest
storms, was added a heart that was made of the right stuff to set
off to advantage his iron frame; and in his short but perilous life,
he had need of it. 'Joe' was, in fact, the very beau ideal of a British
sailor. We feel, therefore, some interest in his chequered life,
tracing his varied course of daring peril and mishap. All who knew
him must lament that such a life should have been brought to such
an end.

William Miller was born at Warrington in Lancashire, about the
year 1802; he was of Scottish parents, in humble life, and by his
own account was the youngest and smallest of the family; but our
Correspondent adds that he has never seen a finer stature of a man.
In height he was about 5 feet 11 inches, and weighing about 17 stone;
he possessed amazing muscular power; his arm was 19½ inches in
circumference, and he possessed a frame of equal proportions. In
his early youth he had a predilection for the sea, and at the age of
eleven went on board a merchant ship, apprenticed to the late
William Mellish Esq., bound to the South Seas.

He then entered the American Navy; and was next on board an
ill-fated whaler, which was cut off by the Natives, at the Society
Islands. The narration of his exile and his many miraculous escapes,
if told in his own language, would fill a volume; how he was sold
from one tribe to another, until he engaged in the *Patriot* service.

He subsequently became Coxswain to Lord Cochrane (now
the Earl of Dundonald) when on board the Chilean States ship the
O'Higgins and was present at the memorable capture under the
batteries of Callao, of the Spanish flag ship *Esmeralda*, by his
Lordship, on the night of the 5th of November 1820. Miller was the
first man on board; he drew the first blood of the sentry who
attempted to oppose his progress and by one blow of his sword
from his powerful arm, Miller laid his antagonist headless.

Miller accepted the command of the British schooner *Daring* of
Cowes, which was then open and was engaged in the Mediterranean
and foreign trade. On that vessel being sold, he was engaged, for
about twelve months, by Mr. Pitcher, the shipbuilder of Blackwall
and Northfield, as rigger, in the equipment of several steam vessels
for the Neapolitan Government; he was subsequently employed,

in the same capacity, by Mr. Laird of Birkenhead, and he sailed as mate of the East India brig *Clyde*, built by that gentleman. This vessel was wrecked at the Cape de Verde Islands, on her voyage out; when Miller having lost his all, returned home, and made application for a petty officer's berth in the Navy.

He succeeded (through Admiral Sir George Cockburn) in getting made acting boatswain's mate of H.M.S. *Daring* and sailed in her with the Experimental Brig Squadron. During the past year we find him acting boatswain of the *Scourge*, from which he was lately transferred to the *Avenger*, and joined that ill-fated vessel but a few days before the melancholy catastrophe which terminated his eventful life in the 45th year of his age.

Although education had not done much for our hero, nature had amply endowed him with practical abilities; and in justice of his memory, be it said that he was a most excellent naval draughtsman, a good navigator, a thorough seaman and a first-class rigger and disciplinarian; and, though his herculean figure might inspire terror to the timid, his mild countenance and amiable disposition would instantly disarm it. He was also a good father and kind husband. He lived at Cowes and was much respected by all who knew him. We regret to add that he left a wife and two children.

'Joe' Miller's daughter, Mary Jane, was to grow up and marry John Fox, who had departed his native Lincolnshire to take up employment at Osborne House, East Cowes, which was being built to the design of Prince Albert, the Prince Consort, and which for many years continued to need the services of skilful carpenters.

Although in later life Uffa filled out to a rather stocky build, he was a weedy youngster and nicknamed 'Skinner' by his contemporaries – this despite the undoubted cooking skills of his mother who, after leaving her parents' farm in Suffolk as a young girl, had been trained in the culinary arts, graduating in the course of time to the position of housekeeper to Queen Victoria in one of the annexes to Osborne House. Here she had the responsibility of caring for the creature comforts of the overflow of Queen Victoria's royal and diplomatic guests from all over the world, the accommodation within Osborne House being totally inadequate for the influx of visitors clustered together on the numerous large family and state gatherings. The housekeepers of the annexes were often in need of the tact and skill of a five-star hotel manager to keep their pampered guests cosseted and happy.

It was while working for Queen Victoria that Lucy Cobbold, Uffa's mother, first met and fell in love with Arthur Fox. Arthur had inherited his Grandpa Miller's love of the sea and it was no surprise to his parents when, after serving his apprenticeship as a boatbuilder and joiner at John Samuel White's Shipyard at Cowes, he opted for a seaman's life, spending many happy hours travelling the world as ship's carpenter aboard the beautiful ships of the Peninsular and Orient Line. He brought home many exciting souvenirs of his host of voyages, which were later to enchant his children: exotically shaped shells booming with the sound of the seven seas when placed to little ears; a Japanese lady in porcelain holding a movable fan in her right hand, the merest touch of a childish finger setting the fan in seductive motion from side to side. Listening to his father's stirring tales of the great oceans with one ear, and the roar from the seashell pressed to the other, the young Uffa would be inevitably drawn by the lure of the sea.

No more separation, begged Lucy, when she became Mrs Arthur Fox: so he said farewell to his life on the ocean waves and they took up residence in London where Arthur's woodcarving skills were employed to full advantage in Westminster Abbey; but the pull of the Island is strong, and when there was a call for volunteers skilled in woodcarving to undertake a special task for Queen Victoria at Osborne House, they returned to the open spaces and tranquillity of the Isle of Wight. This is a frequently repeated scenario. Today's youngsters still leave their Island nests in search of the greater dimension and action of London and beyond only to find, with the passage of time, that there is a part of them which will belong for ever to the Island.

The special task at Osborne was the creation of the incredible Durbar Room, which was to become such a favourite with Queen Victoria. The Durbar Room was previously a lawn on which, in the early days, a marquee was erected for the larger receptions which could not be accommodated in the state apartments. Queen Victoria chose the Indian style of the interior herself, and for its designer John Lockwood Kipling, father of Rudyard, the famous author of books set in India. J. L. Kipling had worked for many years in the Indian Educational Service and was Curator of the Lahore Central Museum. The actual work was carried out under the direction of an expert in Indian decorative techniques and is a masterpiece of wood and plaster carving.

Lucy and Arthur, both hard and conscientious workers, were, by dint of careful budgeting and living well within their means, soon in a position to purchase their first home at East Cowes and settle down to the serious business of raising a family. Their little house was cleverly located within walking distance of Osborne House, the seashore and the floating bridge which takes one across the River Medina to West Cowes. Their one great sadness was that, of their five children, only three lived beyond childhood; Herbert and Dorothea succumbed to the dreaded disease of the day, diphtheria, a killer before the salvation of mass inoculation.

Mahala, the eldest of the three surviving children, was the closest to Uffa until her marriage, there being but two years difference in their ages. She and Uffa, the unholy twins, were the wild ones within the home, seemingly getting away with every mischief imaginable provided they did not make Ellie laugh or cry. Sadly, if Ellie became excited, she fell into a paroxysm of coughing. Uffa swore that she did it on purpose to get him into trouble, and many were his cries of 'I only looked at her'.

Outside the home Uffa was even more the wild one. Either barefoot or in hobnailed boots caked with mud from his rabbiting, with a dog at his heels and a nasty-looking ferret poking out of his pocket, he was the scourge of the neighbourhood.

While some mothers tried to keep their sons away from the local terror, others wore a path to Mrs Fox's front door complaining of Uffa's fighting and intimidation; but their protests fell upon deaf ears, Mrs Fox refusing to hear one word against her only remaining son. She was a quiet and philosophical woman who believed that kindness and gentleness in the home, combined with a solid religious upbringing, would in time soften the character of the unruliest of small boys. In truth Uffa was much influenced by her.

[2]

The death of Queen Victoria in 1901 was the end of an era in British history; but for the people of East Cowes, which had swelled and prospered under royal patronage, it was also a time of deep concern and anxiety for their future livelihood.

With the sorrow and tension all around it is little wonder that, although only three years old, the young Uffa was to retain so vividly the memory of those dramatic days. He was profoundly moved by the pomp and ceremony of the funeral procession as it passed his grandfather John Fox's house in York Avenue; but mostly he was affected by the sight of the royal yacht *Alberta* as she sailed from Cowes carrying the Queen on her final sea voyage.

From his vantage point in the grounds of Norris Castle he witnessed a brilliant ray of sunlight pierce the sombre sky, select the *Alberta* from her surrounding escort of ships and merge and become one with her as they crossed together to the entrance to Portsmouth Harbour. Speculating that the ship and clouds must be travelling in the same direction at exactly the same speed, his young brain recorded the first of many cause and effect impressions of wind and cloud.

Amongst the many legacies left by Queen Victoria can be counted the charming little village school at Whippingham, designed by the Prince Consort and commissioned by Her Majesty to the finest specification and standards of the day for the children of the employees in the royal household and on the Osborne Estate. The site was carefully selected, two miles from East Cowes, in the heart of the countryside with a view south-westwards across open land to the River Medina and beyond.

The schoolhouse was set down within a large field surrounded by pine trees, and teachers chosen from amongst the most able and qualified in the land. It was here that Uffa and Mahala, and Ellie when she was able, merrily walked and ran and hopped and skipped their way to school each day. The distance was no great hardship, the Isle of Wight being renowned for its mildness of climate, and in those days tiny legs were used to walking. On the rare occasion of truly inclement weather, the thoughtful Princess Beatrice, who was Queen Victoria's youngest daughter and became Governor of the Island, supplied them with a brake.

The children carried their lunches to school in satchels, in summer eating them on the grass or in the miniature make-believe houses they had constructed out of long grass and pine needles, and in winter in one of three snug classrooms. By eleven o'clock Uffa, the forever impatient the and hungry one, was to be observed surreptitiously groping in his partially opened desk drawer until his grubby fingers alighted upon an edible morsel which he hastily crammed into his ever-open mouth.

One day, catching him *in flagrante delicto*, the master confiscated the remains of the feast, and uttered the words dreaded by every schoolboy, 'See me after class.' The seething and panic-stricken Uffa, only too aware that he was in for six of the best, on the first stroke of the bell denoting the end of morning lessons was away like a stag, running, running, running until, wide-eyed and breathless, he regaled the normally placid Mrs Fox with the tale of the dreadful teacher who had robbed him of his midday meal. Now if there is one thing guaranteed to make the adrenalin run in the Fox family, it is the thought of being deprived of food.

Mrs Fox sat her ill-used son down in front of a meal so huge that even Uffa was hard put to stagger, let alone run, back to school in time to slip into his seat just as the afternoon session commenced. Then, having washed-up and hung her tea towels over the gooseberry bushes in their sunny back garden to dry, Mrs Fox changed into her best dress, put on her hat and gloves and, breathing fire with every step, set off on the two-mile walk to Whippingham School.

By the time Mrs Fox reached her destination and demanded to see the headmaster she had worked herself up to such a pitch that the poor man was quite terrified. The interview was lengthy and heated and accorded Uffa enormous satisfaction for, although in later life he agreed that the many canings meted out in his youth had been richly deserved, there is no doubt that he was extremely bitter and resentful at the time.

Behind the schoolhouse the headmaster had his own living accommodation and well-stocked garden where he kept chickens and all manner of exciting things. One Friday evening Uffa's heels dragged heavily as he slowly wended his homeward way, for he was carrying a most serious letter personally addressed to his father, and he was only too well aware of the contents. Mr Fox was sad and angry when he read the letter. Not only had his son thrown stones at the headmaster's chickens, an inhuman enough act in itself, but he had attacked them so viciously that he had succeeded in killing one. Furthermore, the letter continued, it was expected that Mr Fox would do the honourable thing and pay for the bird, and the account was enclosed.

A heavy pall hung over the Fox household for the whole weekend, and not solely on account of Uffa's cruelty. Arthur Fox was, not to put too fine a point on it, careful with his money; and the cost of a chicken in those days before the coming of the mass-produced plastic battery hen was, by comparison, comparable to the price of a large joint of roast beef today. One only ever had chicken on extra-special occasions, and here he was having to pay for a fowl that he wasn't even going to taste. It was too bad of Uffa. He and Lucy had been much too soft with the boy, he really would have to be taken in hand. Arthur brooded the whole weekend.

Finally, late on Sunday night a faint smile crossed his lips. Taking out pen, paper and ink he sat down and composed a letter to the headmaster apologizing for his son's cruel behaviour, and adding that he would willingly pay for the bird if he could have it. If the headmaster would kindly give Uffa the chicken to bring home from school on Monday, the account would be settled by return. Needless to say, Uffa returned empty-handed, the headmaster's wife having roasted the chicken for Sunday lunch – refrigerators being, of course, unheard of in those days. Arthur Fox was well pleased, and the incident closed.

Always fighting, climbing, tumbling, Uffa was constantly in the wars. In addition to the multiple scars and bruises, he broke an arm falling from a gas lamp post in Osborne Road, East Cowes. Then, by way of an encore, broke the same arm climbing over the church wall. He was rather proud of this particular break, and something of a hero amongst the boys, since his elbow was now held together with silver wire.

He repeated the double in later life when he took to the saddle again. Having hardly mounted a horse since riding as a child at his Grandfather Cobbold's Suffolk farm, he naturally expected, when he bought Puckaster Manor during the Second World War, to continue where he left off. The horses had other ideas, Uffa spending more time on the ground than in the saddle. During the course of these periodic battles between man and beast, he twice broke the same ankle.

On one occasion after being thrown he was taken to the East Cowes Cottage Hospital as an emergency and placed in the public ward, managing *en route* to alert his employees at Medina Yard to rendezvous at the hospital. When the hospital sister returned with the X-rays she found Uffa sitting up, grey-faced and drawn, surrounded by his entourage, his voice booming instructions which reverberated to the four corners of the ward and back, his bed completely obscured by plans and drawings which overflowed and cascaded to the floor where they unrolled in a snake-like procession on the polished surface. The convalescent patients sat up, thoroughly enjoying the pantomime, the sick and dying just groaned.

'Will this day never end!' cried the sister, clutching her head. It was eleven o'clock in the morning.

Notwithstanding his constant childhood clashes with authority, the teachers at Whippingham school were aware of an outstanding quality in Uffa and spared no effort to help him – Uffa's basic problem being that, finding in his early schooldays the answers coming too easily, he ceased to make the effort. In other words, he thought he knew it all, continually larking around in class, or reading books which he tried to conceal in his half-open desk drawer, instead of paying attention to the words of wisdom beamed in his direction. The masters tried all in their power to bring him to his senses, from corporal punishment to encouragement and praise for work well done, but all to no avail.

When Uffa failed to take the scholarship, in those days the yardstick deciding whether one left school at fourteen or transferred for further education, and in his case college for training as a naval architect, it was a bitter blow for parents and teachers alike.

Years later, when he had calmed down sufficiently to take an inward look at himself, he came to realize that he was severely handicapped by lack of formal education, particularly the inability to transfer ideas from his head to the drawing board: so, at an age when most men have their feet established firmly on the first rungs of the success ladder, he had to come to terms with the need to catch up. This entailed working all day followed by evening classes and study at night.

One cannot help wondering into which stream his life would have flowed had he gone away to college and studied naval architecture instead of working as a boatbuilding apprentice at Cowes. Would he have gravitated towards larger ships and been lost to the world of the pleasure craft? Instead of the airborne lifeboat, might we have been presented with the first flying submarine?

In those early years at Whippingham school Uffa's great love was cricket. Dr Rogerson, the headmaster, was a fine cricketer and wonderful coach, but firstly he was an extremely good musician, organist and composer; and a man wise enough, while teaching the young tearaway to bowl and bat, to capture a part of his soul and create in him a desire to devote a little more of his treble to singing and a little less to screaming and shouting. He also succeeded in awakening an interest in and love of music that remained for life.

Before pollution the River Medina, with its mildly sloping banks and warm and gentle water, was a child's paradise, and it was here, near the old East Medina Mill, that Uffa, when only six years old, went alone and taught himself to swim. Later, when swimming lessons were added to the school curriculum, Bob Savage, the instructor and licensee of the Folly Inn on the river's edge, allowed Uffa and other experienced swimmers (after the initial session when their rumbus-tiousness so terrified the beginners that the whole project was all but abandoned) to go off on their own and do as they pleased.

One of their favourite pastimes was to swim across to Werrar Brickyard on the west bank, where swallows nested in the brick-drying sheds. Removing an egg from each nest until sometimes they had three or four they would return with the eggs in their mouths, not daring to laugh or speak for invariably, if they broke one, it would be addled and the vile taste would have to be endured, for fear of losing the whole clutch, until they touched bottom on the east bank.

Old Bob Savage was a firm favourite with the boys. In addition to swimming he taught boxing, and spoke of life in the world outside, having spent many years in the Royal Navy where he had been Heavy-weight Boxing Champion. His rugged personality counterbalanced the more aesthetic teaching of Dr Rogerson, and at one period Uffa all but became his shadow, hovering spellbound listening to the never-ending source of yarns. The Medina was to play an important role in Uffa's life, and through the years he grew to love every twist and turn, bank and eddy as it wound its course through Newport to Cowes.

The only time of the year when anything resembling peace descended upon the Fox household was when school broke up for the long summer holiday. Then, like a couple of uncaged lions, Uffa and Mahala would bound up to Suffolk to the never-to-be-forgotten life on Grandfather Cobbold's Woodhouse Farm. Mahala, being two years older, was given frequent admonitions to keep Uffa in order and not let him worry his grandparents; all this went completely overboard the moment they set sail from the Island, Mahala, for all her blue-eyed innocence, being something of a madcap herself, and the Cobbolds, like grand-parents the world over, content to let them run wild, safe in the knowledge that they would be returned only too soon to the steadying influence of parents and teachers.

Uffa and Mahala started looking forward to their next holiday in Suffolk the day after returning from the last, and the threat of not being allowed to go was one of the few things that quietened Uffa when he was particularly unruly. In retrospect those Suffolk summers were always dry and sunny. When not horse-riding they helped to feed the animals and collect eggs and generally enjoyed themselves as only children can on a farm. Above all they cherished the long days of harvesting when they would be up at the crack of dawn, their refreshments tied up in drawstring bags just like the grown-ups', Uffa plundering and nibbling at his whenever he felt the pangs of hunger, with never a fear that authority might be looking over his shoulder.

On one of these early holidays Uffa made his first boat out of a galvanized iron bath, using bean sticks for mast and sprit, a shovel lashed to the handle for rudder and a couple of Grandma's old tea towels for sails. He launched her, amid great hilarity, into the murky waters of the duck pond and was more than half-way across before, in the tradition of the best sea captains, bravely going down with his ship. While Grandpa retrieved and cleaned the bath, Grandma Cobbold boiled up great pans of hot water on the old black kitchen range, and the stinking Uffa was soaped and scrubbed until he came up smelling of roses.

Sometimes they would pop into the local village of Thorpe Morieux to call on Aunt Mahala who kept the sub post office, and while Mahala stayed and played with her cousins, Uffa would wander off and give the blacksmith the benefit of his thoughts and advice or watch the carpenter at his toil; and on market day they might even go as far afield as Lavenham or Bury St Edmunds. Then home to early dinner and bed, for trying to make a living from the soil was hard work in Suffolk in those days and Grandfather Cobbold, rising each morning at daybreak, was only too thankful to fall exhausted into bed directly he had eaten.

Little did Uffa know that there were guiding forces at work behind the scenes. When he returned from Suffolk in the year of his tenth birthday he found himself all but enrolled as a member of the St James's Church choir. His parents, with the strong backing of Grandfather John Fox, who was a leading light in the church, believed his character to be in sore need of the steadying influence of the church and sweet music; and his father hoped additionally that the older boys would put him down if he became too obstreperous.

St James's Church was designed by the famous architect, John Nash, when he lived at nearby East Cowes Castle, the church itself rising on land that was once part of the castle grounds. Although Uffa attended his first interview with a certain amount of fear and trepidation, he had no cause for alarm at the prospect of failure as the trap had been carefully laid and there was no way, short of cutting his vocal cords, by which he could possibly have been rejected.

Uffa had a beautiful clear treble voice and, as with everything he considered worth doing in life, he put his heart and soul into his singing. When he hallelujah-ed he hallelujah-ed until he nearly burst a blood vessel and his whole body shook with joy and exultation, while his solo rendering, brown eyes raised innocently heavenwards, of 'O For the Wings of a Dove' swelled his mother's heart with pride and brought a communal lump to the throat of the congregation.

Sometimes after his solos he was so moved and drained of emotion that he was forced to bury his head in his hands to hide the tears.

This depth of feeling was a part of Uffa unsuspected by casual acquaintances who knew only the extrovert, bright and breezy, life and soul of the party Uffa. Conversely, one of his contemporaries recalls him as 'a boy chorister with a ferret showing beneath his cassock singing in a very high key as though all the devils in hell were after him'.

Uffa was also sent to music lessons. He did not fare too well with the piano or violin, but enjoyed a minor success with the one-stringed Japanese fiddle, and at the concerts held at the East Cowes Town Hall performed with gusto in Japanese costume and make-up. He enjoyed these theatrical evenings and for one fleeting moment, before his voice broke, thought he might enjoy life on the stage.

Although the choir boys skylarked and fooled around as choir boys will, his four years as a chorister with St James's Church strengthened his religious belief, and taught him the Christian pleasures of helping and giving, and being kinder and gentler to those with whom one comes in contact. In addition he acquired a knowledge and feeling for music which soothed and helped him through the turbulent years ahead.

The 'teenager' had yet to be invented in those days before the First World War. One left school a child of fourteen and commenced work the following Monday an adult: so when Uffa began his apprenticeship with S. E. Saunders, builder of fast motor boats, hydroplanes and flying boats, he became immediately in greater control of his own destiny, earning his own money and living in a mature world.

One of his first decisions concerned the choir. His voice was about to break and, faced with the choice of continuing as an alto or leaving and perhaps returning later as a tenor or bass, he decided to cut the cord completely. He enjoyed singing, but the discipline of four years devoted to practice three nights a week, plus twice-daily services on Sunday, had been quite enough.

The working day was long, with a six a.m. start, three-quarters of an hour for breakfast at eight-thirty, and an hour for lunch before the long-awaited knocking-off signal at five-thirty; but, having eliminated choir practice Uffa was compensated by greater freedom and more spare time to indulge in the water sports on which he thrived, and from midday on Saturday he could be observed afloat in one boat or another.

The formation of the Cowes Sea Scouts by Harry and Eric White of the John Samuel White Shipyard gave Uffa and other boat-crazy young apprentices the opportunity of a lifetime, the opportunity to learn seamanship and generally mess around in boats. Uffa was in with a head start as he could already swim, row and tie most of the knots and, thanks to his father and his own basic instincts, he understood the complexity of the Solent tides and currents.

Harold Lidstone, Thorneycroft's chief designer, tested them for their badges, Uffa passing at such a rate that his delighted mother was hard-pressed sewing them on in time. He was exceptionally kind to Uffa and his unruly friends and, appreciating Uffa's natural sailing ability, frequently loaned him his ten-foot rowing and sailing dinghy. On one occasion during his first summer after leaving school, Uffa and a friend capsized the boat skylarking around in a gale of wind in the Medina. No damage was done and they managed to retrieve all of the gear, clean her up and restep the mast, but it frightened Uffa sufficiently to hammer home the necessity at all times to treat the sea with the utmost respect.

Harry White was the perfect scout master. An educated man and a fine seaman, the boys looked up to and emulated him. Consequently their manner and speech improved along with their seamanship, although Uffa was never to lose his broad Isle of Wight accent.

The Isle of Wight is an enchanting diamond sparkling off the southern coast of England, separated from the mainland by a strip of water some thirty miles in length which varies in width from four miles to half a mile. The area to the west near Cowes is the Solent and the eastern part, opposite Portsmouth, is called Spithead. Sailing conditions are challenging and can be hazardous to the unwary. The general strength of the tide is four knots, and the currents strong and varied. Add a sprinkling of sandbanks, rocks, estuaries, liners in and out of Southampton Water on the twice-daily tide, cargo boats and large naval vessels to be manoeuvred, and it becomes easy to grasp that a person who has learned to sail in and around the Solent has survived one of the finest testing and training grounds and is fit to stand up to most sailing conditions to be found anywhere in the world.

The boys were fanatically keen and took tremendous pride in their boats which, in time, included a sailing dinghy, a rowing and sailing gig and a seven-ton cutter; and they were eternally grateful to a member of the Royal Yacht Squadron who put up £100 towards these purchases. Graduating from rowing, at which they achieved an almost machine-like precision, to sail, by degrees they extended themselves further and further into the Solent and beyond, although the smaller boys were not allowed on the very long camping trips. On Saturdays, when they were free from work at midday, they would rendezvous at the clubhouse, an old yacht store at East Cowes on loan from George Marvin and Son, with their food and camping gear, and set off for the weekend.

The initial cruise set a pattern for the many joyous trips to follow. Leaving the Medina westabout they made their way past Gurnard, Thorness and Newtown to Yarmouth, seeing their beautiful Island for the first time from a new dimension, and continued between the narrows of Hurst to Colwell Bay. Here, after beaching and tidying the boat, they sat around the camp fire laughing, yarning and singing in happy exhaustion while the tea brewed and their sausages cooked. Unless it rained, the tents that accompanied them were neglected, the boys preferring to sleep, wrapped in a blanket, under the stars.

Colwell Bay became first base. Sometimes, on the ebb when the tides were right, they would visit the lighthouse keepers at the Needles with letters and parcels of food from their wives at Cowes, slipping back on the young flood tide into Colwell Bay to camp for the remainder of the weekend. Then, as they grew more confident and adventurous, and setting their sights on the mainland ports beyond the Needles to the west, they would make camp in Colwell Bay overnight, and from there they could look out at the wind and weather before making the decision to continue next day into the open Channel and on to Lulworth Cove and Weymouth.

Throughout most of his life Uffa was in a perpetual rush. No time to stop. Everything at the double. He left work at five-thirty a grubby apprentice and, especially on the long evenings of summer, reckoned to quit the house a clean and well-fed sea scout by six-thirty; so Mrs Fox moulded her domestic routine accordingly: they all ate at six o'clock. Furthermore, having no idea when he would return, every night she made a rice pudding, thick and gooey the way he liked it, which he gobbled up cold out of the dish in about ten seconds flat before going to bed; and woe betide anyone who dared to touch Uffa's rice pudding.

The scouts never planned their evening rowing excursions until they reached the mouth of the Medina, and then it depended upon the tide and the weather. With the tide on the last of the ebb, someone would say 'What about going down to Colwell Bay for a lemonade?'; and they would row down and quench their thirsts with a lemonade or beer, returning on the young flood; often arriving back well after dark, young limbs aching after the twenty-four-mile row. Or perhaps they would go across to Lee on Solent for an ice-cream.

In August 1914 the Cowes Sea Scouts, with troops of sea scouts from all over the country, were encamped up Beaulieu River. Though small in number compared with the mainland troops, and showing a certain lack of discipline in marching and parade work, they were in the forefront when it came to sports, especially rowing, swimming and sailing. Their only serious rivals were the Portsmouth Troop, under W. L. Wylie RA, who had also benefited from Solent training, and they were looking forward to pitting their skills one against the other; but it was never decided which was the better team, for war was declared and the lads despatched post-haste to their respective homes.

Uffa soon found himself engaged on war work with S. E. Saunders who had obtained large government contracts. He was not the easiest of apprentices, being fiery-tempered and resentful of authority, always the ringleader if there was trouble and, as at school, believing he knew all the answers. Appreciative of fine workmanship, he hardly endeared himself to some of the tradesmen, most of whom were hand-picked and first-rate craftsmen, by drawing attention to flaws if he felt their work fell below the exceptionally high standard he was used to seeing at the homes of his father and grandfather; and his unsolicited advice was particularly unwelcome if it was something they should have determined themselves and were about to do anyway. Uffa's thought processes usually being one jump ahead of the rest of the field.

During the early days of the war Uffa was tempted to lie about his age and volunteer for the Army, but his father was able to dissuade him from such a course. Mr Fox felt that Uffa's time would come soon enough, and that it made more sense for his son to hold fire until sent for when, hopefully, he would be placed in a unit able to make use of his particular skills rather than being taken into the Army as gun fodder.

Meantime Uffa was of the opinion that he had acquired sufficient practical knowledge to build a boat of his own. His father's pride and joy was a large well-equipped carpenter's workshop at the bottom of the garden, and Uffa thought it would be a good idea if he took over the workshop and built his craft there. When he put the plan to his father, together with a request for financial assistance to purchase wood, his father regarded him silently for a few moments. Then, beckoning him outside, pointed to a fine oak tree growing some seventy-five yards from the house.

'It's all yours,' he said, 'provided you grub it out by the roots and don't disturb it until the winter when the sap runs down.'

Turning on his heels Mr Fox returned to the house leaving Uffa gazing up into the branches.

Mr Fox had been advocating evening classes for some time and, within days of the tree episode, Uffa had enrolled for naval architecture and mathematics. The man in charge of naval architecture was Archer Brading, chief draughtsman of John Samuel White and Company. He added an abundance of patience to his natural teaching qualities, and displayed infinite tolerance when confronted with Uffa's outspoken and aggressive ways. The tree-boat project fascinated him, and he devoted many hours to guiding Uffa's thoughts until they took shape on paper; for, of course, Uffa had already carved out a twenty-foot water-line centreboard cruiser in his mind's eye the day his father presented him with the tree.

Uffa studied and planned all through the autumn. The butt would be the main keel through which the centreboard would work, and the stem shaped to suit the great curved branch. The various crooks would be hanging knees, and the main deck beams could come from the more gently curved branches.

When winter came, with the enthusiastic help of his friends, Uffa started digging out the roots and lopping off the branches above them, his father having told him that if a branch is removed from a tree, the root forging beneath should be cut and dug out to balance the tree; the roots of an oak can extend as far below ground as the branches above.

This readiness to assist on the part of his companions is an early example of Uffa's charisma. Throughout life he was to attract people towards him like moths to a flame. He was never alone. There were always those within his orbit eager and waiting, without thought of favour or reward, to drop everything and serve at his altar.

With a sweat of superhuman effort the tree came down, and pit saws were borrowed to saw out the keel, stem, horn timbers and so on, until finally the main frame was ready to set up; but by this time Uffa had lost interest. All was not lost, however; the main keel was sawn in half to make two useful gate posts, and Mr Fox regained the use of his workshop.

Uffa's next venture, many moons later, was more successful. He had the golden opportunity of purchasing the first hydroplane S. E. Saunders ever built on condition that she was broken up. This time, secretly impressed by the way his son had tackled the old oak tree, his father agreed to help financially. He also helped physically, and between them over a period of several months, working evenings and weekends, they built a sixteen-foot by two-foot-nine-inches sailing canoe for cruising, Uffa having accepted that the twenty-footer he had previously attempted was over-ambitious at that stage.

This first little boat of Uffa's gave him such happiness and contentment that he knew he would never forsake the sea. If only, he hoped and prayed, I could earn my living doing the thing I enjoy most in the whole world.

Shipyards and factories engaged on government contracts could exempt employees attaining the age of call-up by the simple method of adding their names to the reserved occupation form submitted periodically to the appropriate ministry. Someone, somewhere, omitted to include Uffa on the list and suddenly, when he was happily and cosily settled and beginning to enjoy life, to quote his own words, 'I was in the Royal Naval Air Service like a shot out of a gun.' Ironically, Uffa was to make use of the same expedient himself during the Second World War when confronted with the odd workman who made waves or otherwise did not contribute to the smooth running of the firm.

After the trauma of his initial training at Blandford, Uffa was posted to the Royal Naval Air Service Station at Great Yarmouth, where he felt more at home helping to repair and maintain seaplanes and flying boats which he understood, and in some instances had even helped to build. His adventurous spirit yearned to fly, and when he was repeatedly turned down, he felt shackled and frustrated.

Uffa believed that the period of his life spent in the RNAS was, for the most part, a waste of time. He buckled against discipline and had frequent clashes with authority. He did not enjoy being a small fish in a large pond, and when he did not make the first teams in cricket or football took up cross-country running. One of his proudest possessions was a medal he won with the RAF (the Royal Naval Air Service amalgamated with the Royal Flying Corps during Uffa's service to form the Royal Air Force), racing against teams from the Army and Navy. He thought nothing, when he had a free pass, of cycling from Great Yarmouth to Wing in Buckinghamshire to spend a few hours with his sister Mahala, once even breaking away from his cross-country team mates to reappear on her doorstep, a wet, dirty and dishevelled figure in running shorts.

There was also a spiritual side to Uffa. An organist, one of Uffa's service friends, had a card which invited him to play on any of the organs in churches and cathedrals throughout the country. He, Uffa and two other music buffs would enter a place of worship and, sitting beside the organist on the long seat, the three non-players would listen to the recital and dream their cares away. Sometimes they would join in and sing, and people from the outside, attracted by the music, would stop in their tracks, then steal quietly into the church to eavesdrop from the pews at the back.

The sergeant at Great Yarmouth probably said it all as far as Uffa's service career was concerned when he escorted him personally to the station to put him on the train back to Blandford and early demobilization, remarking that he wanted to be sure with his own eyes that Uffa was really on the train.

Uffa was a great practical joker, but somebody in the Royal Air Force had the last laugh, for he was documented on his discharge papers as a coal miner and as such placed on the Royal Air Force Reserve.

[4]

There were changes afoot in the Fox *ménage*, the twenty-year-old Uffa returning from the war to find the family installed in a new and larger house at Mayfield Road in East Cowes. Split-level, with two storeys in the front and three at the back, the centre floor was set aside for paying guests who, in the main, would be instructors from the Royal Naval College at Osborne. Mr Fox's carpenter's workshop had been taken from the old homestead and re-erected at the bottom of the garden where, slightly extended, it covered the whole width.

Uffa, like so many of his contemporaries whose lives had been uprooted, found himself restless and unsettled. He suffered from two basic problems. Firstly, he was too strong-willed to accept orders from others, and secondly, he could not keep away from the water. He could not resist the temptation, when asked to crew, of downing tools to go sailing. Wherever he worked the foreman would finally lose patience and suggest that he might be happier elsewhere.

Over a period of three or four years Uffa exhausted the local job opportunities, and his father's patience, and spent several periods at sea. He even tried London, returning after six months at the Thames Iron Works hotly pursued by a young lady called Margaret. Mrs Fox was not at all amused at the prospect of Margaret for a daughter-in-law, considering her far too 'forward' by Island standards; this trait finally proved the young lady's downfall when she made the tactical error of tracking Uffa down on one of his sea scout camping holidays.

Throughout military service Uffa had remained a sea scout, spending most of his long leaves messing around in their various boats; and when he was twenty-one he achieved one of his major ambitions the day he was appointed Scout Master. He decided there and then to create the finest sailing and rowing crew in England, and his leadership was such that he could command INSTANT OBEDIENCE. Any boy caught misbehaving or not pulling his weight felt the knotted end of a piece of rope or was excluded from their expeditions for an appropriate period of time, the latter being dreaded more than the rope's bruises.

The scout premises later on became almost an extension of Uffa's workshop; three of the scouts, Bill Waight, Bob Dickerson and Stan

(Spike) Crews, becoming the nucleus of his business as it gradually mushroomed; and in assessing Uffa's early beginnings it is vital not to overlook the importance of the sea scouts as they were a connecting and intertwining thread.

The boys were overawed and mesmerized by Uffa, held in his power by a strong love–hate relationship, never knowing if he would react to a given situation with gentleness or violence. On one occasion Uffa decided on a purge of the clubhouse, setting the boys to cleaning and painting until everything shone like a new pin. Several days later Spot Smith drew an amusingly lifelike caricature of Uffa, using a stick and tar, on one of the blank walls. The boys hooted with laughter, and sat back in joyous anticipation for Uffa to join in the fun when he arrived. It was so lifelike, the hair standing on end, the large bushy eyebrows, the mouth twisted up one side and the dark staring eyes.

Uffa took one look at the sketch and stormed out. Picking up a large iron bar, with one mighty swoop he thrust it through the window frame, shattering wood and glass alike. His action stirred the boys to such a wild frenzy that, within minutes, the clubhouse was almost completely demolished. One of the former sea scouts said that there appeared to be some uncontrollable force within Uffa which periodically exploded and unsettled the boys, making them temporarily as bereft of reason as he was.

In the summer of 1920 Bill Nutting, a member of the staff of the New York magazine *Motor Boat*, sailed his thirty-five-foot waterline ketch *Typhoon* into Cowes from Nova Scotia. Crossing the Atlantic in a small boat was a rarity in those days, and Uffa and the sea scouts were yearning to get aboard to see her and the crew; but it was not until the end of August, when they heard that *Typhoon* needed two more to make up her complement for the voyage home via the trades to New York, that an excuse presented itself. Uffa wished to be one and Charles Hookey, an eighteen-year-old patrol leader, the other; so, whaleboat loaded to the gunwales with sea scouts, they luffed alongside *Typhoon* and presented themselves.

Bill Nutting had seen and admired the boys in the Hamble River the day before, and in his book no excuse was required to come aboard other than a love of the sea. He was overtly impressed with their precision and the way they brought the whaleboat in with the snap and skill of an American Coast Guard crew, and delighted in the enthusiasm with which they examined every last detail of *Typhoon*'s equipment.

When Uffa broke the news to his family that he planned to sail to America aboard *Typhoon* all hell broke loose. His father, with his vast knowledge of the sea, begged him to abandon the idea for two important reasons. In the first place he considered *Typhoon* an unbalanced boat with a hollow weak bow and broad stern, and secondly, bearing in mind that they planned to cruise down the French and Spanish coasts and the Azores before crossing the Atlantic, they might well run slap into the equinoctial gales. He believed the project was tantamount to suicide, and said so in no uncertain terms. The altercation was fiery and hurtful, and when Uffa rejected his father's advice the breach was so grave that he knew he could expect little help from that quarter should he run into trouble.

Uffa's gear was at Hamble aboard his favourite schooner, *Black Rose*, in which he had been crewing; so he quickly organized his galley slaves to accompany him in the whaler the fourteen miles there and back, returning to *Typhoon* at three in the morning to be met by Bill Nutting with welcoming bowls of hot soup. Three hours later Uffa crept into his home to collect the remainder of his bits and pieces, for they were due to sail on the noonday tide.

There was a small crowd of wellwishers to bid farewell as *Typhoon* set sail on the last day of August, not least of all the Cowes Sea Scouts who turned out in force to cheer their leader on his way.

William Washburn Nutting was a popular figure, and made many friends during *Typhoon*'s brief sojourn in Solent waters. His meeting with one man in particular – Claude Worth, Vice President of the Royal Cruising Club and author of *Yacht Cruising* – was to have far-reaching effects. Impressed by the whole concept and range of services offered by the Royal Cruising Club, Bill Nutting had a vision of forming a similar body in America. On his return to the States a meeting was set up at 'Beefsteak Joe's' in Greenwich Village, and from this early acorn the Cruising Club of America grew.

Typhoon's crew comprised Bill Nutting and Jim Dorset from America, and Charles and Uffa from Cowes. After cruising for six weeks along the French and Spanish coasts and across the Bay of Biscay to the Azores, they took Manson Dillaway, an Admiralty lawyer from Boston, aboard at Ponta Delgada, bringing their number up to five.

Despite the overwhelming personal kindness shown by the people of Ponta Delgada they were of little help when it came to victualling as there was an acute shortage of food in the Azores, with soldiers on every ship and along the quays keeping watch lest food be passed between the vessels. Consequently, with the concentrated effort required to obtain food and smuggle it aboard, and the general maintenance needed to withstand the rigours of the days ahead, they were not equipped to set sail for New York until the night of 19 October.

It was more or less plain sailing until 2 November when they were hit by a squall full of heavy rain, which practically knocked *Typhoon* over on her beam ends even though the mainsail was half down, and for some days the squalls followed in rapid succession, slowing them down considerably. By 12 November they had reached an area where heavy gales could be anticipated in the month of November, added to which most of the good food had been eaten.

They were down to making all sorts of weird cakes and unleavened bread with the remaining flour, but could no longer use the coal stove which had kept the ship warm and sweet below, and the motion was so violent that they had to cook by primus in gimbals with the cook lashed to the job.

On 13 November they were hit by a really fierce squall, and for more than two hours *Typhoon*, with only her jib, had all the sail she could stagger under. The wind blew with great force from the west, then south-west, then north and finally settled into a hard north-easter. The rapidly growing seas were confused and agitated, the shifting winds having blown hard enough to cause cross seas.

Towards sunset the glass started to rise, and by morning the breaking seas gradually became less formidable; and, because it had turned so cold, they re-lit the stove in an attempt to dry out and warm *Typhoon*.

The moderate weather proved but a breathing spell between gales, for 16 November came in with a staggeringly hard blow from the east, even stronger than the previous one; so, anticipating the worst, they put extra lashings on the dinghy, stowed sail and generally prepared for the worst. *Typhoon* was flying through and under seas that were heavy and strong, and Charles had to hold Uffa in a vice-like grip while he stowed and lashed sails. Although he sometimes caused pain through the excessive force of his grip, it gave Uffa confidence to continue and lessened his fear of being washed overboard.

Typhoon began careering along too fast for safety. On top of the seas she would begin gathering way and then rush down the face of the wave at an alarming speed, every sea that caught her lifting her elevated buoyant stern high in the air. Mid-way through the afternoon she lurched so alarmingly to port that her masts hit the water. Uffa was below at the time, and managed to grab the table and Dillaway's bunk, while Jim fell from his upper berth onto Bill Nutting who was stretched out on the port seat.

The cockpit filled with water, and empty kegs floated around mixing with the remains of the salt beef. Uffa chose this dramatic moment to start up a heated argument with the skipper on the subject of boats' sterns. Uffa, echoing his father's warning when he advised against the voyage, now believed in pointed while Bill Nutting advocated broad sterns.

Conditions were so harrowing by the 17th that, with everything stowed except the storm trysail set on the mainmast, they could only steer for two hours on end as they were rushing along too fast for the violence of the waves and motion of the ship: this despite towing two great warps astern, one with a heavy iron bucket attached to its end. The wind continued to increase, the sea became more and more confused, the tops of the waves were blown off and the valleys were streaked with foam like snow before a gale; and they could feel the sting of the spray whip their bodies as it lashed against their oilskins.

Fearing the worst, the skipper decided there was no alternative but to heave-to. They prepared the Voss type drogue, or sea anchor as it is commonly called, in the comparative quiet of the cockpit below. The Voss varies from the Board of Trade type in that, whereas the latter is a round, tapered canvas funnel with its large end extended by a hefty, galvanized steel hoop and shaped like a dunce's cap with the point snipped off to allow the water to flow through, the Voss is square and held open by a wooden St Andrew's cross, giving an advantage in that the cross can be folded and stowed below, and the drogue itself rolled into a small compass.

Even in the cockpit rigging the drogue was not easy, Charles sitting and lying on it to hold it down as the wind fought to lift it out of the boat. Once rigged, the problem was to get it aft, drop it over and get the sail down.

Dillaway was to pump bilge water and oil with the bilge pumps. Jim and Uffa were to lower and stow the sail, then make their way aft and help Charles stream the anchor. Bill Nutting, who was at the helm, ordered Uffa and Jim to put lifelines on, but they disobeyed his command, feeling it would impede their progress. Uffa made his way forward and signalled Jim to follow. He had just climbed out when a giant sea came. Jim held onto the mizen and Uffa clutched the mainmast for that one, which turned out to be the forerunner of a sea which broke upon them with ton after ton of water from an enormous height, towering cathedral-like above them.

Looking heavenwards at the wave it appeared to be perpendicular, with its top bent over like an overhanging cliff, and the summit seemed thirty feet above at a time when they had already climbed fifteen feet from its base.

Suddenly *Typhoon* was over. Her masts hit the water and failed to stop. She went on down and over for another twenty degrees. She had gone down on her beam ends and beyond, and was now over at an angle of 120 degrees to the vertical.

Jim, who was half-way between the two masts, with only the handrail along the deckhouse to hold on to, had no chance at all and was swept overboard. Uffa wrapped his legs around the main mast, clutched belaying pins in each hand, and managed to hold on for a fraction of a second. Then he felt swept miles and miles until like a bolt from the blue the mainmast came down and hit him: so he clung on for dear life.

Slowly at first *Typhoon* righted herself. Uffa was lifted clear of the water and found himself clinging to the hounds, three-quarters of the way up the mast. Sliding to the deck he gave a heave at the trysail, which he had expected to be troublesome, and to his heartfelt relief it came down as sweetly and easily as if there had been no wind at all.

Jim, meantime, had managed to grab one of the ropes trailing astern and was dragged alongside as *Typhoon's* way slackened with the release of the trysail. It seemed hours before they could haul him aboard. Bill, Charles and Uffa succeeded in getting him up under the counter, but as the stern rose out of the sea Jim lacked the strength to hold on and kept sliding back down the rope; and it was not until Bill Nutting succeeded in getting a heavy boathook under him and prised it down, using it as a handspike to raise him to the level of the rail, that he finally slid to safety. They pushed him below and streamed the sea anchor. In the log next day Jim wrote, 'I would like to say right here that I owe my life to the coolheadedness and quick work of my friends.'

Down below *Typhoon* looked like the wreck of the *Hesperus*. The inside ballast had burst through the floorboards while she was almost upside down and, striking the chart case, had fallen into the corner of the coach roof where it was joined by the ashes from the stove, a fair indication of how far she had rolled over. Dillaway, who had found himself trapped, a helpless prisoner, when she keeled over, said she lay there for several terrifying seconds suspended in time, debating, before making the decision to right herself.

Spreading towels over the floorboards to keep the broken glass from their bare feet, they made themselves as comfortable as possible before ceremoniously opening their last tin of soup, their last small can of beef and their last tin of mixed vegetables, which had been put by as an emergency ration. They had come so close to missing their last meal they they determined to make sure of it. Washing the feast down with a bottle of cognac that had been mercifully spared, in the dimly lighted cabin midst the wreckage they made merry and sang their bawdiest songs; Uffa, despite bruises and a broken toe, joined Dillaway to lead the choir until, exhausted, they crawled into their bunks.

The seas crashed down at regular half-hour intervals, shaking the ketch as a terrier shakes a rat; but by this time, and fortified by the brandy, they were immune to it. They could not sail, the wind and the seas were too much. They could not eat as they had consumed virtually the last of the food. So they slept.

Next day was bitterly cold; but the wind, though still blowing, had eased and the seas were not thundering so heavily or so often. Charles lit the stove, and finding some porridge that had fallen into Dillaway's bunk from the stove, fried it for breakfast with a thimbleful of left-over soup. By two p.m. the seas eased sufficiently to work on deck again, and a tiny land bird came aboard, rested for an hour and flew on. They were about two hundred miles south-east of New York, with the wind north-west dead ahead.

The seas might have eased slightly, but the days and nights that followed were shiveringly cold, and with little or no food they were less able to withstand the rigours of the continual icy showers. Existing mainly on flour and water, with no fats at all, they survived on small pancakes. The cooking trick was to put five little dabs in the frying pan, turn them over when they began to solidify but before they stuck to the pan, eating one each as the next batch cooked. Operation pancake took three men; the skipper coupled to the stove, with another lashing to hold him off it and Charles steadying him with one hand, while Uffa mixed the batter wedged between the companionway and the oilskin locker. The meals lasted for hours without satisfying their hunger.

November 20th came in fine and with a lessening of the wind, and at eleven a.m. a ship travelling east was passing their bow within a quarter of a mile. Uffa semaphored with log book in one hand and frying pan in the other, 'Please report *Typhoon* of New York thirty-one days from the Azores'; but she was a Spanish ship and could not read the message. Stopping her engines she hove-to while *Typhoon* luffed under her lee. She was the *Guillem Sorolla* of Barcelona, and her generous Captain Soler, upon recognizing their plight, rained food like manna from heaven onto the little ship's deck. A leg of mutton, beef, sugar, bread, rice, a keg of lard, fresh and tinned fruit, salmon and two bottles of cognac.

Letting go *Typhoon*'s warps and falling away from the steamer, the adventurers gave three cheers for the Captain and crew, and saluted on their foghorn; the *Guillem Sorolla* responded with a succession of deafening blasts from her powerful steam whistle.

Trimming the sails so that he could join the others below, Uffa looked down and beheld the skipper with a thirty-pound chunk of beef on his lap, fondling, stroking and patting it, as he carved off king-sized portions which they fried and ate with new bread, cooking and feasting for hours. Then, fearful that their stomachs might burst with such overloading, they ended up with fruit and five cascaras apiece.

Early next morning Dillaway at the helm sighted a flashing light on the port bow; but instead of the expected Montauk intervals it showed what turned out to be the triple flash of the Shinnecock Light, which is on Long Island, thirty miles to the west of their estimated course. With a north-easterly breeze they headed straight for New York, running alongside the outer edge of Long Island, finally anchoring for the night off the Atlantic Yacht Club in Gravesend Bay, thirty-two days from the Azores.

When the shouting and heroes' welcome had died down – for they had been reported overdue in the gales which had already claimed five victims, and their survival attracted world-wide interest – Uffa found himself alone in New York. Charles was already on his way back to England, having obtained a passage as trimmer aboard the *Celtic*, while the remainder of *Typhoon's* crew, after the trauma of their dice with death and the variance of five individual characters within the confines of a thirty-five-foot boat, were only too thankful to return to the security and peace of their respective homes.

Without friends in America, and too proud to contact his father after their angry parting, Uffa booked a cheap cubicle at the Seamen's Institute near the docks hoping, like Charles, to work his passage: not an easy task as there were some two thousand seamen out of work in New York alone. He passed his days wandering round the docks looking for a passage and doing odd casual jobs of work, and the evenings he spent in the reading room of the New York Public Library, for the most part living on one meal a day that consisted sometimes of only a five-cent bowl of rice. The days of winter were dreary and miserable, and Uffa's one thought was to get away from New York which he found cold and inhospitable.

At last Uffa was taken aboard the *Roman Prince*, bound for a Spanish port, as third cook. His job did not entail any cooking, only the endless washing of pots and pans and the peeling of potatoes; so, when two Spaniards who were working their passages home as deck hands were taken to hospital, Uffa applied for a job on deck. He saw the skipper, but for reasons best known to themselves the skipper did not want Uffa aboard, and he lost even the job of third cook, and returned to the Seamen's Institute.

Most of the casual jobs Uffa obtained were helping to load ships. He was far from happy with the work. In his opinion he was continually being picked upon and bullied because, as he put it, he looked young and innocent and was the most inoffensive. One day he felt he could put up with it no longer and 'sailed in' at the big Dutchman in charge. Uffa caught him a left on the chin with the full force of his fury behind the blow and, taken by surprise, the Dutchman crumpled to the ground. Uffa further released his pent-up emotions by jumping upon the unconscious man and banging his head up and down on the steel floor until he was dragged off by two big black men. Uffa was paid off immediately, and his chances of ever working in the docks again became increasingly slim.

Uffa had less and less money for food as the days dragged on, and one night in the depths of despair, he stood on a small swing bridge at Brooklyn so low in spirit that he contemplated jumping into the dirty water below to put an end to his life. A kindly keeper on the bridge, believing Uffa to have lost his hat, came over and said, 'Here you are, sonny, here is the cap,' and the moment was saved. Next day he had the good fortune to obtain a job as deck hand aboard the *Vauban* bound for Liverpool; and soon he was home in the Isle of Wight, with his feet under his father's table, and no desire to wander ever again.

After regaling the scouts with tales of his adventures – for although they had heard most of the *Typhoon* story from Charles who had arrived home earlier, no one could tell it like Uffa – they settled down to the peaceful pastime of preparing their craft for the summer. The most loved of their boats, certainly as far as Uffa was concerned, was *Valhalla's* whaleboat. In addition to the many happy hours spent aboard her, she had a special significance for Uffa, as his Great Grandpa Miller had done whale harpooning at one point during his chequered career. Though 30 feet 6 inches overall, she had a beam of only 5 feet 6 inches and a hull weight of 850 pounds. In her prime she had hung proudly in *Valhalla's* davits, suspended high above the water ready to be lowered like a streak of lightning directly a whale was sighted when, filled with gear, harpoons and a crew of seven men, she would speed after her quarry, rowing or sailing according to the weather.

Uffa believed that the time was ripe for his scouts to be 'blooded'. In those days 'going foreign', even by conventional means, was virtually unheard of; so when he reached the conclusion that they were sufficiently experienced to sail and row their way to France and back he proceeded with the utmost caution. He thought it wiser not to let the parents know for they would only worry or perhaps even forbid the voyage. No, far kinder to keep the older generation in ignorance than cause unnecessary worry, he reasoned. He made his plans quietly and carefully, and the air of secrecy surrounding the whole operation added to the boys' sense of excitement.

They would be ten in number, their ages ranging from fourteen to eighteen, except for Scout Master Uffa and ASM Bill Waight who were older. The object was to take their two-week summer holiday cruising as usual; but instead of heading north to England, they would cross the English Channel to Le Havre and make their way up the Seine to Rouen and, time permitting, on to Paris.

Uffa, who enjoyed going barefoot, forbade shoes or socks in an effort to keep the weight down. For drinking water they carried a large wooden breaker from which they were each allowed six sucks, and the food was stowed in square biscuit tins sealed with black sticky tape. The boat was open, without comfort or convenience, and she invariably collected sufficient water in the bilges when under way to warrant a boy on permanent duty with hand pump or bailer.

Setting sail from Cowes on the last Saturday of July 1921, on the tail end of a strong south-westerly wind which had been blowing some days, with a fair tide they beat down the Solent, putting into first base, Colwell

Bay, for the afternoon. By seven-twenty in the evening the conditions were right to continue, and they set sail for France.

Uffa steered throughout most of the night, and the boys were divided into three watches of three; their jobs being look-out, mainsheet man and bailer. Taking an hour at each, they all three performed for an hour at each operation during the three-hour watch. Those not sick or on duty slept fitfully, huddled in oilskins under tents attempting to keep out the worst of the spray; mostly hanging like hammocks with their necks on one thwart (an oarsman's bench placed across the boat) and the backs of their legs on the next. Two of the luckier ones found some shelter under the dodger, with just their little cold feet sticking out.

With the dawn the look-out was allowed to turn in and Uffa, Bill and Spike sailed on into the steadily improving weather until eight a.m. After breakfast Uffa, likening himself to Napoleon who, upon retiring, left orders that he was only to be called in the event of bad news, slept until mid afternoon. He woke to find the sea quieter and the spray no longer flying over the weather bow, and soon there was a flat calm.

Delaying rowing until the cool of the evening, at eight p.m. they split into two watches, both to take four hours rowing. Uffa joined in the first watch. Although the fifteen-foot oars were long and heavy for short arms, Uffa did not think the four-hour shift excessive as the boys had had plenty of practice, and the youngsters accepted his decision as a matter of course. At four-thirty in the morning, half an hour after Uffa's watch had commenced its second spell at the oars, a breeze started up from the west, and for the next three hours Uffa and Bill sailed under dipping lugsail while the remainder of the gang turned in. Suddenly, at seven-thirty a.m. the fog which had come up with the dawn lifted and, as Uffa yelled 'Land ho', the boys opened salt-weary eyes for a first thrilling glimpse of La Belle France.

Cruising gently towards Le Havre they washed and smartened themselves and the whaler before showing the flag in a foreign port and, forty hours after setting forth from the Needles, sailed proudly into the harbour on what proved to be the hottest day of the year. Exhaustion forgotten, they tied up their valiant ship and, fascinated, savoured the wonderful new sights and smells as they explored the sea-front and town; followed by football on the sands until, overcome by the heat, Charles collapsed, giving them all an excuse to adjourn to the nearest café-bar for refreshment.

At six-thirty in the evening, with a fresh breeze and strong flood tide, the intrepid lads set off on the first leg of their journey up the Seine and, after two hours' good sailing, reached La Roque breakwater where they settled for the night, some sleeping in a rat-infested mud hut, others under the sail stretched over a fence, Uffa lording it in the whaleboat.

Making an early start on the strong rushing flood tide of Tuesday morning, they washed and breakfasted aboard, rowing until eight-thirty when a strong breeze abaft the beam enabled them to hoist sail until the tide turned against them at midday. Putting into the small market town of Duclair, which was shuttered and slumbering in the noonday sun, they tied up at the tumbledown pier and organized sports amongst themselves: tug-of-war, boxing, wrestling and relay racing.

Finally the boys set upon the defenceless Uffa, stuffing grass into his mouth which they forced him to eat: an incident that sums up rather well Uffa's natural ability to retain the comradeship of his willing slaves despite an authority of almost Captain Bligh-like proportion at sea.

In the late evening they slipped away on the first of the flood for a four-hour row, mooring on a small island less than an hour from Rouen, reasoning that the chances of finding a place to camp in Rouen itself would be extremely remote. They rolled up in blankets on the lawn of what to all intents and purposes was an empty house, only to be confronted at seven in the morning by the owner and his wife.

Finding a small steamer from London berthed at Rouen, they tied up alongside, and with several hours before them set out to enjoy one of the most delightful and friendly cities in the whole of France. After tea they set sail again, and were lucky enough to catch up with a tug and tie on astern for, while at one bend of the river they could sail at six knots, they could barely do two at the next: so it was easier to tow at a steady four knots all the way, particularly as the river folk were full of kindness and helpfully disposed towards them. When the tug moored up for the night they sailed on to an island and rolled up in their blankets under the stars.

At six next morning their tug of the previous day came abreast and blew its whistle. They were up in a flash, blankets piled into the boat and rowing out into the river by the time the fourth and last of the barges she was towing drew abreast. Tagging on to the end of the convoy they washed, dressed and breakfasted while being towed at four knots in the direction of Paris. Then, entering their first lock, rose eight feet before continuing on their way.

The first lock only took three-quarters of an hour to manoeuvre, but at the next one there were so many barges and tugs waiting to proceed up and down river that they were delayed for three and a half hours, causing them to reflect for the first time that they might not achieve their ambition and reach Paris after all. In an effort to get ahead faster, when their own tug finished towing at seven p.m. they set off to row to the next lock, arriving at one a.m. and tying behind a fleet of barges waiting to go through.

Sleeping in fits and starts aboard, they were rudely awakened at five forty-five a.m. by piercing shrieks from three tugs' whistles. Tired, cramped and disorientated, they muddled and fell over one another, shouting and abusing, but finally squeezing into the lock and tying up behind the last of the barges for the day's tow.

Towards the end of a day spent being towed in and out of locks they sailed into Nantes where, after visiting the cathedral, they filled their breaker with fresh water from the fountains and bathed before continuing on to the next lock. The friendly lock keeper informed them that they were seventy kilometres from Paris by river although only forty-five by road: so next day they walked into Meulan to talk things over during breakfast, when they reluctantly reached the conclusion that, with both time and money running out, there was no alternative but to turn back without seeing Paris.

Whereas on the outward journey they had been unable to find a single steamer going all the way through to Paris, luck was with them on the return enabling them, after a couple of short tows, to join up with the *Swallow* of Grimsby which was doing eight knots. The skipper was both kind and cooperative. In addition to towing them to Rouen and beyond he permitted them to curl up on the *Swallow*'s after deck at night. At Rouen they shopped in the market place for provisions to last until they reached England and stored them in the whaleboat, leaving at noon on the Monday of their second week's holiday astern of the *Swallow*.

That evening they reached the entrance to the Tancarville Canal where, as there was too much sea due to strong NW winds for the Seine pilot to take the *Swallow* out, she anchored. The sea scouts tied up to the piles alongside the lock gates to await high water, hoping to go through the canal and save the bashing they would receive in the Seine estuary. Keeping a careful watch on the tides they pushed away from the piles at ten-fifteen p.m., for the young flood in the Seine rises so rapidly that if the boat had been caught for only thirty seconds under a notch in the pile, she would have filled.

Entering the canal at midnight they were for the first time asked to show ship's papers and passports. They had made the journey without documents of any kind, so Uffa signed the book 'Cowes Sea Scouts'.

One of the tugs locking with the whaleboat took them through to the Le Havre locks, dropping fourteen feet, and soon they were as free as birds, sailing through the breakwater entrance towards the open sea and home. Before long the strong north-westerly wind faded away, and they tied to the bell buoy Cap de la Hève, an utterly miserable experience for there was a heavy swell rolling in, and the continual tolling of the bell was excruciating beyond belief. Uffa never forgot the ear-shattering misery, and years later at a dinner party during the Second World War, when the conversation veered towards suggested punishments for Hitler on the day Nemesis finally overtook him, Uffa's contribution was that he should be incarcerated permanently within a bell buoy. After a while their warp carried away and they decided to set sail, the wind now coming up from the north.

The relief to be sailing after one and a half hours tied to the rolling bell buoy was immense. At nine-thirty p.m. the flash of St Catherine's Light, seventy-five miles away, became visible, for although the light, one of the most powerful in the world, was below the horizon, it could be observed flashing on the clouds above.

The strong wind continued until one-thirty a.m., gradually dropping until they only just had steerage way. They sailed gently through the night until nine a.m., then rowed until four p.m. when the wind came up with a rushing squall. Stowing oars and setting sail again they headed straight for Ventnor, the southernmost tip of the Isle of Wight, where they were greeted by anxious coastguards who had followed their progress through telescopes believing them to be a shipwrecked crew.

Reaching Cowes that night was out of the question, the tides running against them both east and westabout: so the boys spent their final night in shelters on the sea front while Uffa stretched out in solitary state in the beached whaler.

Two sixteen-year-olds, Spike and Spot, who had to report for work the following morning, set out an hour before midnight, barefoot as they had been throughout the entire trip, to walk the fifteen long and weary miles from Ventnor to East Cowes through the darkness; and despite their hard days at sea, and only two hours' sleep in their beds, they arrived for work on time the next morning. Uffa had the greatest respect for all of his scouts, but he particularly remembered the courage, fortitude and sense of duty of these two youngsters.

Uffa found himself in the headlines again after his Channel crossing, but his glory was short-lived. The parents of some of the boys charged the Sea Scout Committee with irresponsibility, accusing them of placing the boys' lives in jeopardy. After a heated post-mortem the Committee resigned *en bloc*. They said they had been prepared to allow Uffa to take the boys anywhere within reason but not to play God with their lives.

[5]

Mr Fox was on the horns of a dilemma. Uffa was asking his advice, and experience had taught him that whenever his son requested guidance it cost money. 'I thought it would be a good idea', Uffa was saying, 'if I started up on my own. I would need cash for sheds and equipment, but I could soon repay you out of the profits. You might even make a lot of money.' Mr Fox twirled the ends of his handsome moustache and regarded him dubiously. He had no desire to stand in the way of the boy's initiative, though Heaven knows he was no longer a boy; but by the same token he and Lucy had worked hard all their lives, and were still working, for what little they had put by for their old age. He was wary of Uffa's leaning towards an extravagant lifestyle, and was not inclined to part with his life's savings only to see Uffa disappear to some far-flung corner of the globe at the drop of a hat.

'Better to begin quietly,' he countered. 'If I give you a hand we can put up another workshop alongside mine in the garden. In that way you will avoid being saddled with overheads before the orders come in.'

Uffa would have preferred the money, but philosophically accepted that half a loaf was better than no bread.

Nobody consulted Mrs Fox. Up at five in the morning and working through until nine and ten o'clock at night looking after her family and the paying guests, she now found herself with a third of the garden covered by workshops, and a perpetual banging, not to mention the steady stream of visitors through the side passage to the sheds. Sometimes, with Uffa's followers popping in at all hours of the day and night for a yarn or to admire his current project, it was like Piccadilly Circus in the rush hour.

Mrs Fox already knew most of Uffa's boys, as it was not unusual to arrive downstairs in the morning to find half a dozen sea scouts rolled up in blankets on the floor. She would goodnaturedly count heads as she tiptoed over the silent forms on her way to the kitchen, calculating as she went how many extra mouths there would be to feed for breakfast. Uffa could always be sure that, no matter how many friends he brought home, or at what uncivilized hour, his mother could be relied upon to come up with the staff of life.

Arthur Fox had not been erroneous in assessing his son's character for, no sooner was the building programme well under way, than Uffa downed tools and announced his intention of crossing the Atlantic again. This time Mr Fox raised no objection. Apart from enjoying the peace and quiet when Uffa was away, although always worrying and looking forward to his return, he could find fault with neither the ship nor time of the year.

The ship, *Diablesse*, with a 46-foot waterline and beam of 15 feet 6 inches, was a fast and manly vessel, modelled on the Gloucester schooners that sailed and fished on the Grand Banks of Newfoundland, and which were built to withstand the winter gales of the Atlantic. Well known and thought of locally, *Diablesse* had been in Cowes for long periods since sailing over from New York the previous year.

They set sail on 17 June 1922, with the owners, Mr and Mrs John B. Kelley (friends of Bill Nutting, who had no hesitation in recommending Uffa's seamanship after *Typhoon*'s hazardous voyage), as skipper and mate; Bobby Somerset (who so tragically gave his own life attempting to rescue others during an accident at sea not so many years ago) as navigator; Uffa and Bill Waight.

Diablesse was pure joy. She moved through the seas with the graceful ease of a large porpoise and, after two weeks of gentle sailing, they swanned in to Funchal, Madeira. All was not well with the engine, and investigation revealed a broken intake pipe that was letting in water. Uffa was convinced that, by loading her bow down with huge stones off the beach, her stern would lift high enough out of the sea to reach the faulty pipe. When his gallant effort proved unsuccessful, they had recourse to a professional diver. The latter became so annoyed with Uffa, who could not refrain from interfering and telling him how to do his job, that he twice held him beneath the water until he nearly drowned. Some forty years later, when Bill Waight recounted the incident on the television programme *This is Your Life* Uffa was not amused.

On departing from England Bill had been the proud possessor of the princely sum of five shillings, and Uffa was penniless. By the time they were ready to set foot in Madeira Uffa had five shillings in his pocket, and Bill was penniless. Uffa invested the cash on a night of debauchery ashore, and when they left Madeira both were penniless. Uffa never repaid the debt, and Bill never forgot because, at the time, the five shillings had represented the sum total of his worldly wealth.

On 6 July they upped anchor and pointed in the direction of Bermuda. They were happy days, Miss Ann the skipper's wife mixing mint juleps at two o'clock every afternoon, Bobby reading aloud for an hour in the cockpit of an evening, and Bill, Bobby and Uffa harmonizing as they sailed into the sunset.

The one event to mar an otherwise perfect voyage was a fire that broke out as they were leaving Bermuda. John Kelley started the engine to make life easier for the harbour pilot who was taking them out over the reefs, when some oakum resting on the exhaust pipe became red hot, causing a serious outbreak back in the counter. Uffa, who at that period of his life lived only for sail and in his heart would like to have seen all engines abolished, excitedly laid blame at the skipper's doorstep for having started the motor instead of leaving harbour under sail; so, in order to take the heat out of the situation in more ways than one, the skipper detailed Uffa to row the pilot ashore while the remainder of the crew stayed aboard to tackle the fire.

Dropping the pilot, Uffa rowed back as fast as he could towards *Diablesse*, and was livid to find her proceeding to sea without him. Pulling on the oars with all his might he chased her for a long time without making an impression, but imperceptibly the distance between them lessened and at last, in a state of exhaustion, he was able to get alongside and aboard.

The outbreak was still smouldering and, as the only way to the counter was from below, and nobody could breathe down there for smoke and fumes, Uffa started crashing through the cockpit floor using the anchor as a battering ram. Still consumed with pent-up anger at being left behind, though accepting the explanation that the crew's preoccupation with the blaze had left them little time to ponder that every mile sailed away from Bermuda was another mile for Uffa to row, Uffa took wild pleasure in bashing and breaking, and really gave it his all. Then Bobby and Bill set to work, the one aiming a stream of water aft onto the trouble spot while the other pumped. Next day, when Uffa was set the task of repairing the broken floor, he had time to reflect on his excessive zeal and enthusiasm of the night before.

A course had been laid for Montauk Point and, as had occurred in the case of *Typhoon*, they were surprised to find themselves thirty miles out in their navigational reckoning. Uffa was convinced, from these two personal experiences, that the Labrador current running south inside the Gulf Stream can set a small boat much further south than is generally supposed.

At the end of a truly pleasant Atlantic crossing they anchored in New London, then sailed next day to City Island, and loafed around Long Island Sound until midnight on 17 October when John Kelley and Uffa, the remainder of the party having departed, put to sea from City Island to sail *Diablesse* up to Gloucester.

By noon the following day they were off Block Island. There was a great deal of weight in the wind for it was no longer summer, so they handed the squaresail, which eased *Diablesse* considerably, though she was still hard to steer under her four lowers. At two-thirty the jib split right across. Uffa took it in, bending the old one on to the hanks without setting it. The wind continued to pound and, just after dark, she gybed carrying away her main gaff and so the mainsail had to be stowed, for it was sad and forlorn like the broken wing of a bird. The task was difficult as the broken gaff, flogging about, seemed intent on causing damage; but finally both sail and gaff were stowed, and they took in the staysail and hove to for the night under foresail only.

Next morning they put the staysail on her and, managing to set the main trysail, continued on their way until, later in the day, the wind eased enabling them to additionally set and carry the squaresail. Throughout the night John Kelley and Uffa took watch and watch for they were close to the shoals to leeward, and there was real need to be on constant look-out for steamer traffic on such a dirty night.

Uffa repaired the gaff by chopping and splitting down some wood into splints, nailing them alongside the broken spar and binding the whole with wire seizings, which were tightened by wedges driven in after-wards. The repair may not have been the neatest in the world, but the gaff was as strong as ever. The mainsail was rebent to it, but left stowed until the weather moderated.

Towards evening the increasing wind forced them to take the squaresail in. Then, as darkness descended, they entered the Muskeget Channel and under staysail, foresail and main trysail, *Diablesse*, with heavy seas breaking over her, threaded her way through the channels inside the Nantucket shoals.

The night, though dark, was fairly clear and the skipper called the different compass courses from the cabin; or, when not studying the chart, was in the lee rigging watching for lights and buoys while Uffa handled *Diablesse* alone, for even with the heavy wind she steered effortlessly under her present rig; and so they passed the Cross Rip lightship and went on through to Cape Cod. To Uffa, steering *Diablesse*, the hours seemed but minutes and, when they had cleared the worst of the shoals, the skipper asked him to guess the time. Uffa replied 'ten o'clock' when it was in fact three a.m. They were so in love with *Diablesse* on that wild night that they almost fought for the wheel. Uffa, despite steering for some ten hours, was so exhilarated with the roaring wind, the darkness and the flying spray that he, like Kelley, wanted the excuse of steering to stay up.

They wound up by both spending the remaining hours of darkness on deck; but the dawn found them tired, and the wind ahead was driving them off Cape Cod while the steep breaking seas were hitting aboard hard and often. Catching sight of a big Gloucester schooner hove to, they thought it expedient to follow her example; so, taking in the trysail, then the staysail, they put the helm a-lee, and starting the foresheet made for their bunks; for daylight was with them and they were headed off shore to safety and content to spend the day in peaceful slumber.

Making sail at sunset when the wind had eased, setting the staysail and trysail, and sheeting in the foresail, tacking they stood in for Cape Cod, the skipper taking the first half and Uffa the second half of the night. By dawn the wind had eased further, enabling them to take in the trysail and set the mainsail; and later the main topsail and jib, putting *Diablesse* under full sail once again, but the wind fell away rapidly and it was dark by the time they were within two miles of Cape Cod.

At nine p.m. the skipper stood the first watch, and ordered Uffa to bed for five hours, Uffa relieving him at two in the morning for the second watch. Apart from twice almost being run down by steamers which sheered off at the last moment, the night was pleasantly uneventful. Next day, amid light winds and autumn sunshine, and a mist that cut visibility down to two miles, they sailed quietly into Gloucester. That night they went ashore to a riproaring dinner where they met up with, amongst others, Bill Nutting and Chris Ratsey the famous sailmaker from Cowes.

Rating the Gloucester schooners high on his list of the world's finest sailing vessels, Uffa had nurtured a desire to visit Gloucester, Massachusetts, and as luck would have it his arrival coincided with the International Fishing Schooner Races, affording him the additional thrill of watching the duel between *Henry Ford* of America and *Bluenose* of Canada for the championship of the North Atlantic.

The employment situation had eased considerably since Uffa was last in New York, and he experienced no difficulty in securing a working passage home, or at least to Antwerp, as a trimmer. A trimmer, to Uffa, was a stoker's handmaiden; bringing up coal for the stoker to heave onto the fires, and wheeling away the red-hot clinkers and ashes when raked out. Added to the everyday hazards of a trimmer's life, one day Uffa was shovelling away, filling his barrow from what appeared to be an Everest of coal in the hold, when a heavy sea struck the ship causing the coal to avalanche and bury him up to the shoulders.

Uffa inherited an additional chore when one of the stokers developed a rupture – the privilege of stoking the two top furnaces, a task which filled him with boyish delight. Putting his best foot forward, in next to no time he mastered the knack of stoking, deriving enormous satisfaction from pitching the coal exactly where he wanted. He asserted that the pleasure one obtains from swinging a golf club and timing it to a nicety cannot begin to compare with the art and thrill of aiming coal into the exact spot of your choice in the blazing furnace of a large ship.

New Year 1923 found Uffa once more earnestly consulting his father;

this time as to what type of boat he should dedicate himself to building. Governed by the size of the workshop and the width of the passage running down the side of the house, keel boats were eliminated, so it could only be a dinghy; and they settled upon the aristocrat of them all, the National fourteen-footer (the class had yet to be made International).

Watched over and helped by his father, who would accept nothing but the finest workmanship, Uffa set to work. A boat's surface, Mr Fox insisted, both inside and out and whether visible or not, should be as smooth as a baby's bottom. The sight of a jagged screw or crooked nail was pure anathema to him. A master craftsman himself, he insisted that as long as Uffa was under his roof he must strive to achieve the same high standard. This perfection of workmanship was to be the hallmark of the Uffa Fox boats. When nobody else was available to help, Uffa would poke his head indoors and call for his sister Elfrida – 'Come on, Ellie, give me a hand to clench these nails' – and the obedient Ellie would follow him down the garden and into the shed. She and Uffa were the only children at home now, Mahala having married and started a family of her own.

The building of a wooden dinghy, such as a fourteen-footer, entails first constructing a saddle and supports of wood which are secured to the floor to form a skeleton-like upside-down mould. The actual hull is then constructed over, and to the shape of the mould, by adding the centre keel, timbers and planking which are built up to form the shell or hull. The completed shell is lifted off the mould and turned right side up, ready to be cleaned-off and varnished and have the various fittings added; these smaller jobs on a high-craftsmanship boat often taking as long, as if not longer, than the construction of the shell itself.

By the time Uffa had completed and lifted off the hull of the first fourteen-footer the workshop was overcrowded, the mould, of necessity, remaining secured to the floor and taking up valuable space while awaiting the building of the next hull. Gathering his trusty sea scouts around him Uffa solved the problem by organizing a working party to lift the hull out of the shed and up the garden, manoeuvring it sideways through the narrows of the passage, and out on to the road, where it was carried the quarter of a mile to the scout hut, with the care and reverence afforded the most delicate piece of porcelain. The woodworking apprentices amongst the older scouts soon found themselves helping to finish off the boat, while the younger lads, by looking on or rubbing down with sandpaper, received their first lessons in practical boat-building.

While constructing his first two fourteen-footers, Uffa grew to love the class, and to strive for the perfection of the beautiful craft designed and built by Frank Morgan Giles of Teignmouth. He could equal the performance of the Morgan Giles boats when racing, mainly because he was an outstanding helmsman, but he was not content to be equal, he had to be better.

From the days of his apprenticeship to S. E. Saunders, working on *Maple Leaf IV*, the fastest hydroplane in the world and the first boat to exceed fifty knots, Uffa had mulled over the possibility of developing a set of hull lines that, under sail, would hydroplane over the water as *Maple Leaf IV* had done under power. Lately the thought had become an obsession. His concept was against all the accepted laws of sailing lines and, although his first two fourteen-footers had lost money, his father agreed nevertheless to back him in the construction of an experimental boat.

Ariel was Uffa's first attempt at designing a racing hull and he went to work cautiously for, while he had decided views upon the fastest shape within the fourteen-foot rules, he erred on the side of caution, conscious that he was young and was designing for the first time against world-famed designers. He did not feel, therefore, that *Ariel* was a true fulfilment of his thoughts so much as a probe that could not be a failure, but which would let him know how true his ideas were.

Uffa also had very decided views on rigging, and against all advice put the mainmast back almost a third of her waterline length from the fore end. By the time he had added roller reefing gear, once more against the advice of his many critics, heads were beginning to nod and there was talk of 'that madman Uffa Fox'. In the event, during Cowes Week *Ariel*, derided locally as a cockleshell, won every race in her class and gave Uffa the confidence and courage to take his design a stage further.

Meantime, indoors an unusual if not unique event was taking place. Uffa was tidying his bedroom! Mrs Fox, transfixed in the doorway, observed the phenomenon with undisguised amazement. Looking up from his task, and catching his mother's eye, Uffa became flustered.

'I met this girl,' the normally self-reliant Uffa mumbled, 'and I thought it would be a good idea if we invited her round for tea.'

Uffa had in truth known Alma Phillips for many years; her father was a miller, and it was he who worked the Old East Medina Mill where Uffa had gone as a small boy and taught himself to swim. Although very much in love with Uffa, Alma had a practical streak which fought against his lack of stability, and made her seek to escape his influence by accepting a post in Dorchester. He would not let her be, however, and after one particularly harrowing letter in which he threatened to commit suicide if she did not return, she promised to reapply for a post on the Island.

Alma curved generously in all the right places, and the golden hair which was worn up in thick plaits round her head by day cascaded and swayed like a field of sun-ripened corn when she shook out the pins at night. Living on the Medina she was a river person, and enjoyed all the things that were life's blood to Uffa; but she had also a sensitivity which encompassed a love of poetry, music and the arts, and followed what was virtually the only profession open to women of education in those days. She was a schoolteacher.

Although he got along well enough with Mr Phillips, Uffa could make little or no headway with Alma's mother who considered him unreliable and egotistical and not nearly good enough for her daughter. Undeterred by Mrs Phillips's attitude, the young lovers continued to meet, Alma becoming a frequent visitor to the Fox household, eating with them *en famille* three or four times a week. She gave Uffa unbounded help and encouragement with his new thoughts on design and boatbuilding; and when *Ariel* was launched, and Uffa not racing, they used her for day cruising and sailed her round the Isle of Wight, nearly sixty miles for a day's sail.

Winter can be a hungry time for the boat-orientated individualist attempting to go it alone, a period of the year when many an initiative has been stifled by the vision of a regular, trouble-free pay packet. For Uffa, attempting to lure the lady of his choice into the bonds of matrimony, the need to prove that he could obtain and hold down a steady job became of paramount importance. His request for employment to George Marvin and Company of Cowes was so far removed from the normal run-of-the-mill job application that the letter was retained and is still in existence over fifty years later.

> Elmhurst,
> Mayfield Road,
> East Cowes, I.W.
> Jan. 30th 1925

Dear Sir,
This letter may or may not surprise you. Now I have reached the noble age of 27 I am going to steady down and get spliced fairly soon to the little lady from East Medina Mill who is at present headmistress in Dorchester.

When a man as poor as myself gets spliced he has to have a steady job, and that is the reason of this letter. Could you give me a job in your boat shop? There are two and only two firms in Cowes that are decent to work for that is yours and Saunders and yours being far in front of Saunders I am writing to you first.

These are my qualifications for the job. Served seven years apprenticeship at Saunders. Had almost two years in the Royal Naval Air Service repairing Flying Boats on Active Service. Worked as shipwright at the Thames Iron Works. And in J. S. Whites, on the National Life boats. Since when I have been on my own. Building (I built Jack Rabbit top boat of the dinghy class for two years), Repairing, Painting and sailing boats. The last boat I built was a ten foot dinghy and today I sailed her round to Wootton right up Kings Quay and back with full sail. Coming back I own she got half full but that was not in over the lee Gunwhale but from waves breaking aboard over the weather bow. A thing that any boat no matter how well designed and built will do. Now all the 14 footers in Cowes except Papyrus were built from the drawings I made. The design was Nicholsons. I have almost completed a 14 foot design of my own and she would beat all the local Boats the one at Lymington and give the renowned Morgan Giles a hell of a shake up. I shall probably build her spare time for Cowes Week, as I have most of the material for her. So you see besides being able to build boats I can also design them, which might be useful to you if I was one of your men. Then as you know I am able to sail a boat fairly well, and if you should want another man for 'Undine' or 'Pussy Foot' well you would only have to shout 'Uffa' and you would have him.

Now sir I have earnt my bread and butter as a boatbuilder, shipwright, designer, newspaper reporter, trimmer, deckhand, painter and in other ways. Well, my being able to do these things shews that I am able to also use my brain for the purpose it was intended. And as so often happens in repair work a job turns up that no one knows anything about well I reckon that if your foreman turned me loose on it I would find the right answer to it. You see whenever I wrote an article for a paper the editor of the Field or some other paper always reprinted a whole lot of it and generally ended by saying that although I was young I had learnt a lot.

Well I hope I have not given you the guts ache by blowing my own trumpet so much, but if I don't who will, and I want a job in your yard if there is a chance. But Mr. Marvin unless you think that I shall earn my money please don't take me on. I do not want pity or anything of that sort because as I am now working on my own I earn enough to keep myself, four boats, two guns, two cameras, and a typewriter going. In fact I am really quite comfortable.

The jobs I am booked for at present being a scale model of Isme for General Seely. Paint and put windows in a conservatory. Put the engine in a fifteen foot boat. And within a week the Schooner 'Dolphin' is going out for her sailing trials and I am going extra man. Then there is a sailing boat that I may bring round from Wootton. So that you see I am not on the bone of my ass and in need of charity. What I want is a steady job. All these odd jobs pay very well, in fact better than a steady one. But they are uncertain whereas suppose I work for you I am sure of Friday coming every week. Now I shall finish all my jobs by the end of the month and would be ready and willing that is of course if I get the chance to start for you March the first or as Thursday is the fifth and starts I think your pay week, say the fifth. I have the chance of a job in Canada at £3.10s. per week and found for six months, but that leads nowhere and I cannot go on with my study of Naval Architecture either.

Perhaps you wonder whether I am one of those agitators, well I am not even in the shipwrights Union now. I was but had a row several years ago when I went to America the second time. Life is too short to be worried by Trade Unions or politics, I am a member of the Conservative Club but do not worry about Tariffs or Trade. I have my Ideas of course and they are formed on what I have seen in this and other countries and my Ideas are conservative, but I seldom argue about it, because it is such a waste of time. A labourite could talk to me all day and not change my Ideas because I have thought it out so how could I hope to alter his view of life. No I leave all that to those who are paid to argue. I might some day get such a job for myself then the more I am paid the more I'll argue. Still I have wandered away from the yarn I was spinning.

Well today is Friday and an unlucky day so they say but I'll bring this over, leave it with you to read and think over while I walk down to Egypt Light and then come back for your answer. A faint heart never won a fat women. You know there are only two kinds of women. Thin and fat and the fat are far far the better of the two. It is all very well for people to say the nearer the bone the sweeter the meat but dammit there is very little meat on a thin woman to be sweet. And their legs are like canaries.

I do hope your answer will be start March the 5th. I know that some of your men would knock hell out of me as far as Boatbuilding goes and also that I am better than some, and by the time I am as old as your best men I'll be better or anyway as good as they are. I would rather work West than the east side of the river. And if you want to see samples of my work I can bring over two drawings later to-night, and tomorrow I can bring my ten footer alongside Undine before you leave.

Yours sincerely,

UFFA FOX.

Relaxing after an evening meal, Mrs Fox idly sounded Uffa and Alma concerning their plans one weekend. Looking guiltily one to the other, they lowered their eyes without speaking. Slightly embarrassed, Mrs Fox broke the silence.

'My only reason for enquiring was to know whether you would be eating in or out.'

'We thought of getting married at Newport Register Office,' Uffa blurted out. 'I thought we could get it over quietly without any fuss because I want to go sailing afterwards.'

Mrs Fox was thunderstruck, but not dismayed. Alma had her head screwed on the right way, and appeared to have a steadying influence on Uffa.

'Where do you plan to live?' enquired the practical Ellie.

'I thought it would be a good idea if Alma moved in here,' announced Uffa. 'There's plenty of room for two in my bedroom.'

Uffa may have boasted four boats, two guns, two cameras and a typewriter, but he lacked a pair of shoes. Neither did he appear to have the wherewithal to buy a new pair. His wedding morn caused panic within the Fox household as he hunted around for suitable footwear. None of his father's shoes would fit, and he finally caught the bus to Newport wearing a dirty old pair of white plimsolls with a large area of big toenail protruding from ragged holes in each.

He was accompanied by Mr Fox, the only member of the family present, while the bride, when she caught sight of her future husband looking like a fugitive from the workhouse, nearly called the whole thing off. There was no question of a honeymoon. Hastily saying 'cheerio' to his father and wife, directly the ceremony was over Uffa hopped aboard a bus for Ryde where he was due to take part in the day's sailing.

There was a distressing scene at the East Medina Mill that night when they broke the news to Alma's parents. Mrs Phillips was so distraught the family feared she might go berserk and fling herself overboard.

In the autumn of 1925 Uffa's gaze was riveted by an advertisement for the sale of an old steam-driven floating bridge. Cowes and East Cowes are separated by the River Medina, and linked by a floating bridge which travels to and fro across the river on a pair of heavy chains. Once in a blue moon a new floating bridge is built and the old one appears on the open market. Both he and Alma were fascinated at the thought of purchasing the bridge and converting it into a combined floating home and workshop. Uffa's plan was to involve his father in the project, as he lacked the capital to purchase and convert it himself. The flattered Mr Fox opened the negotiations, but the Company turned down his initial offer and it was not until 1926 that a mutually agreeable price was contracted.

The centre aisle of the floating bridge was long enough to take six horse-drawn carriages in line ahead and two abreast; and at either end was a prow, raising and lowering like a drawbridge to allow the vehicles and pedestrians on and off. The centre aisle, currently open to the elements, Uffa intended to cover over and use as his boatbuilding workshop. There were pedestrian cabins on either side of the centre aisle, and between the cabins on the port side was the boiler in the stokehold and coal bunker, while to starboard was the hissing steam engine with great gleaming copper pipes. The Lomore iron hull below stored the water and oil tanks, work benches and spare gear.

Uffa dismantled and sold the engine, boiler and large driving wheels, leaving huge gaping holes, and roughly converted one of the cabins into a makeshift home, where he installed his bride, in order to be on the spot as he planned and carried out the conversion. Moored by the Cowes gasworks, living under the most primitive of conditions with a husband who was regarded as something of a joke locally (Uffa's latest folly of purchasing a floating bridge instead of a house like any normal human being doing nothing to lessen the illusion), Alma carried on working by day and, after preparing and cooking their evening meal, worked side by side with her husband turning her hand to whatever task she was allotted no matter how grimy or unpleasant.

Returning from work one evening, 'the poor girl', as Mrs Fox had taken to calling her daughter-in-law, was astonished to find an empty space where the floating bridge had moored. Standing, a lonely and pathetic figure, in the shadow of the gasworks, she was approached by a workman enquiring if she had lost something.

'Yes, my home,' replied Alma.

Uffa had that morning obtained permission from the owner of Kingston Farm to moor the floating bridge at the bottom of his field between East Cowes and Folly on the Medina. Without further ado he organized a workforce and a tow, and by teatime the floating bridge was settled snugly in her new berth. Alma was exhausted by the time she had crossed from West to East Cowes and trudged through the town and over the fields in her high-heeled shoes.

'You might have let me know,' she reproached, but Uffa was much too excited with his new toy to bother about Alma's pique. She would soon get over it.

Isolated up the river and relatively free from interruption, Uffa was able to superintend and work on the conversion. The left or port side first cabin he transformed into a combined kitchen and dining-room, which became the hub of life aboard as it interconnected with Uffa's drawing office and the bedroom beyond, and all rooms could be additionally reached direct from the central workshop. There was further accommodation on the starboard side, but this was seldom used unless guests were aboard.

No expense was spared, Uffa installing light oak wood panelling and custom-built fitted furniture and fittings of the finest quality money could buy. By the time he was satisfied with the project he was so heavily in debt that even his father could not bail him out, merely allowing him to keep the creditors off his back by overdrawing at the bank against the deeds of some small properties he owned.

There was no piped water, gas or electricity aboard. Rainwater was trickled from the roof and stored in the big tanks below until pumped up by hand into the kitchen sink or wherever as required. The supply was adequate for their needs – even on fine summer nights the heavy dew could be heard running into the tanks; but all drinking water had to be boiled.

Alma, who had been taught the rudiments of cooking by Mahala, soon mastered the paraffin cooker, and the romance of oil lamps and candles far outweighed their nuisance value. When Uffa arrived home with one of the newfangled portable wireless sets they had the additional task of carrying the acid-filled batteries or accumulators by hand to East Cowes for weekly recharging, though in fine weather there was an attractive and exciting alternative – one rowed down the river to shop.

Sometimes they were so poor that they existed almost entirely on the blackberries Alma picked and the rabbits Uffa shot, and many's the time Alma found Uffa waiting to greet her at the bus stop, hand outstretched to relieve her of her salary before he could pay his workmen.

Since *Ariel*'s success the future was looking rosier, even if the good times were a long time coming. Yachtsmen were becoming aware of Uffa, and his boats were selling, but unfortunately not nearly fast enough to cover expenses.

Throughout this period Uffa continued to study and work on his designs, and before long the next experimental boat, *Radiant*, was ready to take to the water. He was not completely happy with her, finding her too unstable for pleasant and careless sailing; but, by teaching him the correct proportions of sails in the fourteen-foot class and confirming his belief that the steep rising floor craft was generally slower than the planing type he hoped to develop and perfect, she taught him two valuable lessons which stood him in good stead; and, although only an experimental boat, *Radiant* was fast enough to take him to second place in the first-ever race for a new cup presented in 1927 which was to become the blue riband of dinghy racing, the Prince of Wales' Cup.

Avenger, the first of the planing dinghies, said it all for Uffa. Named after the ship which had claimed the life of his Great Grandpa Miller, she was the total embodiment of Uffa's thoughts and dreams.

Designed and built in the late summer of 1927 to be ready for the 1928 season, she more than justified his confidence, bringing him fifty-two firsts, two seconds and three thirds out of fifty-seven starts. She was a legend in her own time for, transcending all other consider-ations, Uffa had introduced a new dimension to yacht design and produced a hull shape that was to become accepted and copied through-out the world. In that one set of lines he had doubled the speed a dinghy helmsman could expect from his craft.

Avenger's Vee sections ran down to give her deep chest forward of midships and continued throughout her length, reaching the greatest depth one-third of her length from the fore end, and the last two-thirds made a long clean run. The V-ed sections for the first third gave her an angle of attack to the water. In the same way that a water skier places his skis at an angle to the water to give the lift required, so it is with a planing boat. Uffa likened it to a wedge of ice which, if pinched, jumps up and out of the fingers. Likewise, as *Avenger*'s shaped bow was driven hard through the water, the shape and the angle of attack occasioned it to lift.

By the time *Avenger* had walked away with her first twenty races, the sport became not so much sailing as 'Fox-hunting'. Knowing they could not possibly win, the other competitors ran sweepstakes amongst themselves, betting on the number of minutes by which *Avenger* would romp home ahead of the remainder of the fleet.

Uffa was anxious to see what the French made of his new concept; so when a friend returned from Le Havre with the news that today, Monday, was the first day's racing in the Le Havre Regatta and that there were three more days' racing to come, it triggered one of his snap decisions. Quickly organizing Bob and Spike, and loading *Avenger* with three hundredweight of food, water, clothing, compass, lamps, charts and gear, they sailed away from the floating bridge at four-thirty p.m., cleared the river in half an hour and, going eastabout, picked up a south-west wind so strong that the fifteen miles from Castle Point to Bembridge Ledge were covered in one and a half hours: amazing even by Uffa's standards, bearing in mind the three-man crew plus weight of food and gear.

Knowing that it would be impossible to stand full sail in the wind and sea clear of the Island's shelter, and while still in the lee of Bembridge Ledge, they reefed the mainsail, so that its head came below the jib halyards and pointed for Le Havre close hauled on the starboard tack. Clearing the Island they shipped water faster than two could bail, so Uffa let her off a point to leeward of Le Havre, thus easing the wind and sea sufficiently for one man bailing to keep pace with the water shipped, while two men sat her up.

They spotted a cutter about four miles outside the Wight with three reefs in her mainsail running back to the shelter of the Island. She was also bound for Le Havre, where she finally arrived two days after *Avenger*, the crew explaining that the day on which she had set out proved too rough for her. Uffa considered this a very poor show as she was all of fifty tons.

By midnight the wind and sea had eased sufficiently to allow them full sail, and soon after, the wind easing still more, they changed to the large light reaching jib; they intended to keep her hard at it, even if it did entail changing sails at night, for their target was to sail the hundred miles from Cowes to Le Havre at an average speed of six knots and arrive in time for the second day's race.

Alas, dawn found them gliding quietly over gentle hills and valleys and, enjoyable though it was after the strong wind and rough sea of the night before, it meant that they would miss Tuesday's racing; and from nine a.m. they were becalmed until late afternoon. At six p.m. the high land of Cap de la Hève showed over the skyline reminding Uffa that they must wash and shave and put on a collar and tie before arriving in Le Havre; and by ten p.m. they were wining and dining ashore.

On Wednesday they raced and beat the French fleet, and repeated the success on Thursday. *Avenger*'s lines and achievements, combined with Uffa's daring in sailing her across the Channel, aroused widespread interest and excitement. Uffa, with only the clothes he stood up in, was fêted everywhere. When invited to dine with the Société des Regattes du Havre he claimed to be like the Royal National Lifeboat Institution, entirely supported by voluntary contribution, for, not having a dinner suit, he wore Commander Eldred's trousers, one French yachtsman's dinner jacket and another's shoes. 'It's my own handkerchief though,' he boasted.

Nothing would induce Uffa to return on Friday as it was the thirteenth and he adhered to certain superstitions, always cutting his toenails on Tuesday, for example, although no one ever knew exactly why.

Sailing away from Le Havre on Saturday afternoon with a good north-westerly breeze, it looked like a beat to windward of a hundred miles, so they stood on each tack for four hours. By Sunday afternoon the breeze had freshened to a hard wind, still north-west and dead ahead. The next four hours were hard driving, and the three laid completely out to windward, except for their legs below the knees, and fairly steamed along until the sea made up and they shipped too much water and were forced to reef.

A little before dark they lifted the Island on their weather bow and, continuing on the port tack, later saw the Owers Lightship flashing directly ahead. They stood on until close to the lightship and then came about. There was a heavy sea running for such a small craft as *Avenger* and, through Uffa not easing her over a very steep sea, she shipped a solid wall of water and nearly swamped. The hurricane lamp was put out of action, the electric lamp washed off the thwart into the bilge, and everything was so completely soaked that it was impossible to strike a match or make light of any sort.

Without light, and right in the steamer track, Uffa put her about again hoping to thread his way through the passage between the shoals inside the Owers; but after a while he missed the passage, which is little known and difficult enough to find even in daylight. Finding huge seas breaking on either side and dead ahead, they put about and wove their way back into deep water, where they spent a hair-raising night evading steamers as well as fighting to windward in steep breaking seas.

The light of early dawn found them tacking close inshore of Bembridge and, beating on past Bembridge to Seaview Pier, they made fast and went ashore in search of nourishment, all food having been swamped with the remainder of the gear. Never bashful at coming forward, Uffa presented himself on the doorstep of the first house showing signs of life in the form of a smoking chimney, craving breakfast. While the requested meal was being cooked, the three bedraggled figures fell asleep on the dew-covered lawn, having no cause to worry about the dampness as they could not get any wetter.

Bob and Spike had bailed all night, Uffa had steered for seventeen hours and all three were at the end of their tether. Even *Avenger* had felt the strain and had altered shape forward. Henceforth she was even faster in wind and sea.

They arrived at Ryde in good time for the afternoon's race, only to find that the wind had dropped, and their jaded brains refused to sparkle in the light airs. The most they could achieve was a disappointing third. However, as they sailed wearily on towards Cowes and the floating bridge, with a silver cup and bronze medals from France, plus the knowledge that they had twice crossed the English Channel in a fourteen-foot open boat, they had little to be ashamed of.

After *Avenger* Uffa never advertised. The free publicity was sufficient to last his lifetime and beyond. From all over the world yachtsmen made their way on foot to the floating bridge, for there was no road, and the only postal address required to find him was Uffa Fox, Cowes, England.

Uffa gathered around him a team of loyal craftsmen who could be relied upon to turn out exquisite workmanship whether he was there to bully them or not, and on the whole the operation ran more smoothly when he was absent and the men were free to carry out their allotted tasks without fear of interruption. Additionally, his men were all competent seamen, many of them selected from the ranks of his former sea scouts, and thoroughly capable of handling themselves well in a boat. He had within his workforce trained crews in all shapes and sizes to race with him depending on wind and weather; but mostly he relied upon his heavy weather crew, the reliable and honest Tim Board, and it was Tim who accompanied him to Lowestoft for the 1928 Prince of Wales' Cup race and shared the honours when *Avenger* streaked away and beat the rest of the fleet with five minutes to spare.

Alma continued working as a relief teacher, travelling to the various Island schools to help out in times of sickness and shortage. Still without a car, a useless appendage while there was no road to the floating bridge, she journeyed by bus, changing from sea boots to shoes at the bus stop. Her evenings and weekends were in the main devoted to Uffa's accounts and general office work, and for them both there was infinite joy and satisfaction in building up something together.

A great favourite with the workmen, Alma could be relied upon to reach a sensible decision should any query arise during Uffa's many absences, and she frequently acted as a buffer between Uffa and the men when he was in one of his difficult frames of mind. These moods, which affected everyone within his realm, quite often lasted two or three days until he mentally sorted out and disposed of whatever was currently eating into him. The warm and friendly smell of varnish and wood shavings overflowed into their home, normally shared with two or three dogs as Uffa was not interested in having children; and when Bill Waight, Uffa's draughtsman and second in command, married Alma's sister, Vera, the whole floating bridge operation intertwined and knit together as one large family unit.

Uffa's dinghies travelled by rail, uncrated and unpacked, to havens all over the country. He had faith in the depth of a man's soul and believed that a railwayman's instinct, when confronted with an object of beauty and perfection, was to protect rather than destroy, and only once was his trust betrayed. It was not unusual, in those halcyon days of the old Southern Railway, before the central concourse at Waterloo was defaced with portable cabins and tinkers selling their wares from the backs of lorries, to catch sight of one of his little craft, varnished and sparkling like a pool of sunlight, set out in a place of honour for all the world to admire whilst awaiting onward routing to its final destination.

Uffa had one more serious attempt at fourteen-foot dinghy design when, not appreciating that he had achieved the ultimate in *Avenger*, he attempted to increase the planing ability with *Daring*. Although she won the 1929 Prince of Wales' Cup, the Lowestoft 50 Guinea Cup and, with Tom Thorneycroft as team mate, the Trent Inland Waterways Challenge Cup, he felt that the sacrifice in weatherliness was too much for what was gained in planing ability. Accepting that he could basically achieve nothing further with the class he began to channel his thoughts elsewhere.

Mrs Fox died in the midst of Uffa's triumph, and his father subsequently suffered a nervous breakdown, so the joy was tinged with sadness. Mrs Fox had been a very human person, and her unexpected death had a profound effect upon Uffa, temporarily depriving him of his normal excess of physical and mental energy.

When, to run parallel with his dinghy production, Uffa decided to expand into larger keel boats, he did not have far to look for additional work space. The old Naval College at Osborne, which closed down in the twenties, had its boathouses and slipways at Kingston little more than two hundred yards from the floating bridge, and for the time being he was allowed to use part of these.

Another acquisition was a boat he loved and had crewed in regularly through the years, the twenty-ton schooner *Black Rose*. He kept her moored within spitting distance of the floating bridge so that she would never be far from his ever-loving eye. Built in Stornoway in 1860 for trade amongst the Western Isles of Scotland, she still retained her original hull shape and rig. Uffa changed her from a white schooner into a piratical looking ship with black and white gun ports, and felt and looked like a real buccaneer as, hoisting the skull and crossbones, he sailed her out of the river.

Black Rose proved to be an expensive luxury, and to keep the costs at a viable level Uffa evolved a simple and cheap method of scrubbing and painting her bottom. His men would run her up on the river bank and list her down to starboard, enabling them to get at the port bottom. Then, on the high water, they would raise her dinghy in the davits on the port side and list her down to port and, as her rise of floor was exactly forty-five degrees, it was akin to painting and working on the flat side of a wall.

Naturally this operation took place only in millpond conditions for, if there should be a sea running when the boat was just lifting her bilge clear of the ground, she would easily stove it in, as the heavy solid spars leaning out would drop her down very heavily with each wave.

On one memorable day they beached her on the measured mile within the River Medina and, to Uffa's fury, one of His Majesty's naval vessels began charging up and down the river on full speed trials just as *Black Rose*'s bilge was floating off the bottom. Uffa, who was working inside the hull at the time, became quite deranged. He ordered a young apprentice up onto the stern to shout to the shipyard managers and Admiralty overseers, who were aboard the naval craft, that they must stop the trials until *Black Rose* had been floated. All to no avail, for the powers that be were hardly likely to be impressed by the cries of a young apprentice, even supposing they heard him above the roar of the engines.

The incensed Uffa detailed one of his minions to run like a stag to the floating bridge and fetch his four-bore gun. He loaded the gun quickly and let fly, but the Naval vessel was just out of range and the shots fell short as they passed on down the river. When they came about and sallied forth for the next run Uffa was ready and waiting. He fired one shot across the ship's bows before it was completely in range. Then, quickly reloading, he raised the gun again. To his delight the Naval vessel decided discretion to be the better part of valour and retreated to the more friendly waters of Osborne Bay to complete her trials.

One of the shipyard managers, and spokesman for the Authorities, viewed the incident with extreme displeasure; but Uffa, blending his natural defiance of authority with persuasive charm, succeeded in smoothing things over, and the incident was closed. There was a large school of thought, however, which inclined to the opinion that Uffa should have been prosecuted for firing on a Naval vessel and endangering the lives of those aboard her. He was, they said, under the impression that he owned the river.

Uffa often reflected that the days at the floating bridge were amongst the happiest of his life. There were black days, of course. One of the blackest was when he received a letter from the Income Tax Authorities demanding property tax on the floating bridge. He wrote copious letters of objection to the Authorities, but officialdom was immune to his reasonings, finally putting an end to the correspondence by threatening to issue a court summons.

At the threat of court action Uffa came up with one of his more devious solutions, and one wonders if in this instance he had been aided and abetted by his father who was now the Rate Collector for East Cowes; for, upon discovering that the River Medina was divided into four parts for tax purposes, the Whippingham Parish where the floating bridge was currently moored coming under Arreton, and the Osborne College boathouses two hundred yards away coming within the East Cowes boundary, he piled a team of his boatbuilders into *Britannia*'s five-oared gig and let go the moorings in the parish of Whippingham.

The wind was easterly and the floating bridge blew across the centre of the river, entering the parish of Northwood on the west side. The gig rowed her down river until she entered the parish of West Cowes; and, once they were opposite and in the lee of the sheds at Kingston, she was towed straight to windward across, eastwards into the parish of East Cowes and moored amongst the old Osborne College sheds and slipways, where she remained for a month.

Some ten days after 'operation floating bridge' the court summons arrived. Uffa returned it with this question: 'Is it legal for you to collect taxes from the parish of East Cowes and also from the parishes of Northwood and West Cowes, as well as Whippingham, because my floating bridge has been in these four parishes during the time in question and is at this moment in East Cowes.'

The Arreton Tax Collector was over like a shot and, according to Uffa, almost dropped dead when he saw with his own eyes that the floating bridge was indeed in the parish of East Cowes. He was obviously quite a sensible man who realized that the cost of pursuing Uffa from one boundary to another would involve higher expenditure than the small amount of tax levied on the floating bridge for, apart from a written request some time later asking Uffa to give details of the periods his home had been in Whippington, Northwood, West Cowes and East Cowes, which Uffa ignored, the matter was closed. Having made his stand, Uffa happily returned his home to her original mooring amongst the green fields and woods.

An early venture into keel boat design was in 1930 when Uffa produced the three-tonner *Vigilant*, based on the Skerry Cruiser rules, for entry in the Royal Swedish Yacht Club Centenary Races, Stockholm being the base of many of the famous Skerry Cruisers. With two other crew, including Bob Dickerson from Cowes, he sailed her from Cowes to Sweden, arriving at Sandhamn in time for the last few days of the European Meeting of All Nations, but not in time to get her out of the water for a clean-off and to polish her bottom. Uffa was a pioneer of the shiny bottom, even experimenting with white of egg at one point.

The meeting was a grand affair, a mixture of banquets and racing, with five hundred yachts from all nations both at sea and on the fjords. Accustomed to being King of the Castle in the dinghy world, Uffa had the ignominy of finishing last in the first race, neither did he make the first three on the succeeding days. He was both surprised and delighted, therefore, to be singled out and presented with a handsome silver cup, not for his racing ability, but for what the Royal Swedish Yacht Club deemed an outstanding cruise from the Isle of Wight to Sweden in a boat which is generally looked upon as quite unsuitable for open sea.

Uffa and Bob sailed her home alone, and the return journey included a beat to windward from Cuxhaven to Lowestoft in heavy gales during which they were overtaken at one point by a steamer with her starboard bridge swept away and her lifeboat smashed and upside-down in the davits; so it would seem that, even if she did not revolutionize the Sandhamn racing scene, *Vigilant* was a fine and respected sea boat, capable of more than holding her own in the North Sea gales.

Uffa was rather proud when, in the summer of '31, Paul Hammond invited him to form one of the crew of *Landfall* for the Transatlantic Race. In addition to the honour he felt the invitation carried, he looked forward to crewing in a vessel with an owner who strove for perfection in every detail.

Whether by good luck or design, Uffa's Atlantic crossings appeared to be taking place in boats of ever-increasing size and splendour. *Landfall* was the largest ship in the race, with a waterline length of sixty feet and a fifty-nine-ton displacement. Amongst other refinements she had two washrooms and a swing table which had, in place of the usual lead weight, a small piano. In fact with its gun case, book case, piano and taps dispensing constant hot coffee or boiling water, Uffa thought *Landfall*'s wardroom rather a grand affair for an ocean racer, the list of provisions reading like a food catalogue from Fortnum and Mason's. A far cry from the days of *Typhoon* when they all but starved. She also had a sail area of three thousand square feet which kept Uffa, the sail trimmer, out of mischief.

They had to be towed to the starting line, for there was hardly a breath of wind when they left Newport, Rhode Island, on 4 July. Uffa was set on taking the great circle course just skirting Nova Scotia, believing that, as well as being two hundred miles shorter, it had stronger, because colder, and more reliable fair winds. He petitioned in vain, for the American paper *Yachting* had come out with an article on the best way to cross to England, strongly recommending the Southern and Gulf Stream Course, with its promise of a free and easy ride; and this was to be *Landfall*'s route.

In the event *Landfall* finished third, sailing into Plymouth on the 23rd where she was greeted with the news that Olin Stephens's *Dorade* had arrived two days previous after following Uffa's choice, the Northern route.

Meantime, on the home front Alma was going through difficult times. Her salary was insufficient to pay the men's wages, and Uffa invariably emptied the till when he travelled abroad, leaving nothing for house-keeping or to feed the dogs. Alma's family refused pecuniary aid on principle, but when things were really desperate Mrs Phillips kept her daughter going with food parcels.

The financial reward gleaned from the construction of small wooden craft is not bountiful. Each boat is an individual creation built with many dedicated manhours, such craftsmanship being closer to a cottage industry than a production line.

Uffa was not interested in money for money's sake, merely in what it could buy; and, as he invariably purchased or did whatever his heart desired before he had earned the wherewithal to pay for it, walked a constant treadmill. Something of a hero in the world of small boats, he was acclaimed and accepted by the yachting fraternity everywhere; and, although managing to retain his basic earthiness he, as with so many of the top sportsmen and pop stars of today, tended to get out of his depth and overspend when mixing with moneyed and influential friends.

[7]

If, as has been said, a man's true love is his first love, then Uffa's true love was the sailing canoe he built from the S. E. Saunders hydroplane, and his love of and interest in canoes never diminished. Therefore it comes as no surprise to find him in 1933 actively engaged in designing and building two canoes, one for himself and one for Roger de Quincey, with the sole aim of challenging for the American Canoe Championship and the New York Canoe Club International Trophy; the latter not having left America since it was first raced for in 1866, despite challenges from such eminent canoeists as W. Baden Powell and W. A. Stewart.

Known as the 'Dry Fly of Sailing', the sliding seat canoe demands great versatility as the one-man or -woman crew has to handle jib, mainsail, dropkeel, tiller and sliding seat. Uffa never ceased to be astonished that the sailing canoe had not been chosen by the Olympic Games organizers as the single-hander. No other boat, in his opinion, calls for the sailing proficiency demanded by this lively craft.

Uffa and Roger sailed from Southampton with their canoes, the first deep chested V-ed type planing hull canoes in the world, *East Anglian* and *Valiant* respectively, plus no less than ten spare masts, aboard the *Empress of Britain* bound for Quebec and the Thousand Islands. Uffa, as always, was seasick the first day out. His susceptibility to seasickness was something he both resented and was ashamed of in his youth, and he fought a continually losing battle against the malaise. William Washburn Nutting greatly admired this courage in adversity and in his book *Track of the Typhoon* referred to Uffa as the only man he knew who could sing when seasick.

From Quebec they transported themselves and their canoes, spare masts, suitcases, ropes and gear by train, changing at Montreal and Gananoque Junction, where they finally took the tiny train to the waterfront. Jack Wright, the Commodore of the American Canoe Association, met them with his launch and relieved them of their trappings, leaving Uffa and Roger to approach Sugar Island, which is owned by the American Canoe Association, with its tents, trees, rocks and sandy bays, by canoe. They were greeted by an unearthly yell of

'Whoopahee' from Dudley Murphy, which he had learnt from some Indian canoe men who used it when greeting other redskins. Then, aided by a throng of eager helpers, they pitched tent and put up their beds in what would be home for the next two weeks.

The Commodore, who had taken them under his wing, issued an invitation for dinner in his tent, and afterwards they sailed their canoes in the light of the full moon. The island gleamed with silvery shapes beneath the twinkling stars, the enormous camp fire in front of the headquarters' tent competing with moonbeams to light the way of the shadowy figures moving to and fro, and the sound of their singing wafted across the water joyously breaking into the stillness of the night. Such happiness was infectious, and their hearts nearly burst with gladness to be amongst these delightful people who so generously shared their idyllic surroundings.

After the official ceremony on Saturday, when flags were ceremoniously hoisted and speeches made, they sailed over to Gananoque for the last-minute purchase of tools and odds and ends. Sunday was the day of rest. After church they loafed around for most of the day before attending their first camp fire where Uffa, at the request of the Commodore, sang 'The Bosun's Story'. Later in the week Uffa was crowned King of the Islands, but his reign was short-lived as the Royal family was impeached and a dictator appointed for the duration of the meet. Another fun day was when Uffa attended the fancy dress ball, rigged out in a grass skirt from the South Sea Islands, and barely escaped with his honour.

Wednesday was the first race for the Admiralty Trophy, and it included paddling, which they had not anticipated and never before attempted. One leg of the triangular course was to be sailed, the next paddled and so on, thus alternatively sailing and paddling over each leg of the triangle in two rounds. The start was a paddling one, and things looked black for Uffa. His sliding seat fell overboard at the start, and he had to go back to retrieve it. The second leg was sailing, so he was able to catch up and overtake the fleet. Disaster struck again on the next paddling leg. Uffa had stowed his sails, pulled up the drop keel and stowed the sliding seat, and was leading the other boats with enough in hand to hold back the faster paddling canoes of the Americans, when his jib broke adrift. He walked on the foredeck and fixed it, then, coming aft, forgot the drop keel was up and capsized. By the time he had righted her his paddle had floated twenty yards away, which entailed another swim for the paddle before he could set off again.

When the next sailing leg came round Uffa's sails were wrinkled like a prune, but half-way through the leg, which was fortunately a beat, the creases straightened out and *East Anglian* was first round the weather mark, though not fast enough to hold one of the American canoes on the next paddling section. She passed Uffa half-way down this leg, and he was unable to catch her on the last reach home, so finished second.

The second race for the Admiralty Trophy was pure sailing round three rounds of the triangle. Uffa brought *East Anglian* home a triumphant first, with Roger taking second place in *Valiant*.

The final race for the Trophy was paddling only, and Uffa and Roger were advised to take it very easily, as they could not be expected to beat the faster American canoes, and the first heat of the National Sailing Trophy was to follow immediately afterwards. They both agreed, however, that if they were going to race, they would race to win even if they collapsed in the attempt.

The course was straight along the Island to Stave Island, and there was a strong wind on the weather quarter. Uffa headed *East Anglian* out to sea where, although it was rougher, the wind was stronger and more helpful. He stood up to paddle, and away they went, white water flying off their double paddles, and to everyone's amazement *East Anglian* finished an unexpected second, only thirty yards astern of the champion paddler of Canada. On this placing, Uffa won the Combined Paddling and Sailing Trophy by one point.

With little time in hand, they were towed hastily back to Head-quarters' Bay, quickly rigging their canoes with drop keels, masts, sails and sheets for the first heat of the National Sailing Trophy. There was a strong wind, which was great for the English canoes, helping *East Anglian* to come in first and *Valiant* second.

Uffa also won the second race, with Roger coming in third. The final heat was held in a light wind. *East Anglian* had only to finish fifth to win the American National Sailing Championship, so Uffa sailed a very careful race and, in spite of giving every canoe and buoy a wide berth, came second.

On Wednesday they raced for the Paul Butler Trophy, which was presented by the widow of Paul Butler, the man who adapted the canoe to the Red Indian trick of sitting out to windward on a plank. The Indians measured the force of the wind by men. A two-man breeze was when two men sat out of their canoes at the end of planks, and so on. Paul Butler had been a small man, and crippled, and so light that he stood no chance whatsoever in strong winds until he revolutionized the sport by fitting the first sliding seat to his canoe. Roger, who sailed a brilliant race, won the Trophy, with Uffa, who made a mistake over one tack in the first beat to windward, just twelve seconds behind.

The days at Sugar Island were some of the happiest and most treasured of Uffa's full and varied life and, when the American Canoe Association called an executive meeting at the headquarters tent and made him and Roger honorary members for life, his cup was full.

At the end of the meet Uffa and Roger pointed their canoes in the direction of the United States, and sailed across to Clayton, entering the United States ready for the next stage of their journey and their challenge for the New York Canoe Club's International Trophy on Long Island Sound. While Roger went off to visit his uncle in Vermont, Uffa, ably abetted by Rolf Armstrong and his wife, trailed the canoes plus Rolf's canoe *Mannikin* to New York, where they were met by W. P. Stephens with whom Uffa would be staying.

Uffa and Roger had a few days in which to prepare and tune up their canoes, including organizing the making of new American sails at the Ratsey sail loft on City Island. The Americans were also busy holding eliminating trials to decide the defenders, finally choosing Leo Friede, who had twice before successfully defended the New York Canoe Cup in *Mermaid*, and Walter Busch in *Loon*.

The first race, sailed in light airs, was won by the Americans, which meant that an English boat had to be first home in both of the remaining races if they were to secure the Trophy. That night they held a conference and decided that team work must be their plan of campaign, Uffa to be Mr Nuisance and hold the American boats back while Roger forged ahead. By the rules, only the first boat home counted; so, provided Uffa could stop *Mermaid* and *Loon* from getting through, it would not matter if he finished last. The tactics paid off. Roger crossed the line first in *Valiant*, and Uffa was second in *East Anglian*. Next day, when Roger held back and let Uffa through, their finishing positions were reversed and the Trophy was theirs. When Roger left America two days later he carried in his luggage four cups that had never before been wrested from America.

Although naturally pleased to have beaten the Americans in their home waters, Uffa's joy was tempered with a certain amount of sadness. He was on a natural wavelength with the American people, delighting in their company; the truism that the English are born two drinks behind the Americans in no way applied to Uffa. Quite the reverse – from the manner in which he sparkled and bubbled when on form one could be forgiven the assumption that he had entered this world 'three sheets in the wind'.

The Americans had welcomed them with open hearts, sharing their tents and their homes. They had been the best of friends before and during the races, and now that the excitement was over they were, if possible, better friends than ever. When *East Anglian* swept across the finishing line and won the deciding race for the International Trophy, there was such a shout of joy and tooting from the yachts watching the race that Uffa felt a lump rise in his throat. The cheers, for two strangers in their land, could not have been louder had they been for their own Leo Friede and Walter Busch.

Within two years Gordon Douglas of the American Canoe Association sent a challenge to the Royal Canoe Club for the New York Canoe Club's Trophy. Roger de Quincey was selected, and successfully defended the challenge in *Wake*, a stable planing canoe. Uffa presented Gordon Douglas with a complete set of *Wake's* plans, from which he built *Foxy Nymph* and won all the important American Canoe Trophies. However, whenever the Americans put in a challenge to Britain they appeared with the old non-planing type canoes, and the Trophy remained in Britain for just on twenty years. When it was finally lost and re-crossed the Atlantic another generation had come upon the scene, and the Trophy was defended in a non-Uffa design boat.

Uffa continued to experiment with canoes, and in the autumn of 1935 built *Brynhild*, a two-seater sliding-seat canoe. Having, in a seventeen-foot sliding-seat canoe, reached 16.3 knots over the Medina measured half mile (an achievement which took four months and innumerable attempts to accomplish), he hoped that a twenty-footer with two up might plane at twenty knots, but the most he could wring out of her was fifteen.

The following summer Uffa and Bill Waight took *Brynhild* across to Cherbourg and cruised her along the rocky coasts of Normandy and Brittany, intending to carry on down to Spain. Their plans were thwarted by the outbreak of the Spanish Civil War and, storing her in the cellars of the Hôtel des Bains at Pontusval, alongside the champagne and wine, they returned home by train and the St Malo steamer. Later *Brynhild* was taken up to Paris and shown off in all her glory at the Paris Exhibition.

Uffa was considerably older and pear-shaped when a kayak, the one-man Eskimo paddling canoe made of light wooden framework covered with sealskin, came his way. The exciting and dangerous features of the kayak are that one's legs are completely pinned under the forward coaming; and, should one so desire and sometimes even if one doesn't, the canoe can be hurled over sideways with sufficient pressure to force the canoe and helmsman to perform a complete somersault through the water with neither occupant nor canoe parting company.

Ever anxious to experiment with a new toy, Uffa put her through her paces before an admiring audience of yachtsmen in Cowes harbour. His paddling was faultless, but when he came to the sideways swing he lacked the energy to turn the canoe over completely and found himself trapped head downwards in the water. All Uffa's efforts failed to either free his legs or right the canoe. Two men, witnessing his distress from the deck of a nearby yacht, dived to the rescue. They succeeded in righting the craft, and brought the spluttering Uffa to the surface. With the full weight of his fury behind him, Uffa immediately swung the craft over again, this time with sufficient momentum to complete the full circle.

'I would have done that the first time if you hadn't bloody well interfered!' he yelled at his dripping and open-mouthed rescuers.

[8]

For some months prior to the successful challenge for the American Canoe Trophies, Peter Davies, the publisher, adopted son of Sir James Barrie and the original Peter Pan, had been badgering Uffa to write a specialized book on sailing. Uffa, apart from being too preoccupied with the canoes and other exciting schemes, was not entirely convinced that he was capable of writing a full-length book. Although he had written many successful articles for an assortment of publications he did not believe he possessed the application and self-discipline required to complete a book, once started. With no taskmaster to crack the whip it is all too easy for the writer to wander away in mind or body, or both, from his allotted task; so, surrounded by what to him were infinitely more stimulating happenings, Uffa pushed the book project to the further recesses of his mind.

However, two days before his departure for America there had appeared at the floating bridge, unexpected and uninvited, the one person in the whole world guaranteed to make Uffa's blood run cold: his bank manager. The bank manager put his foot down. Neither the bank nor Uffa's other creditors could see any value or justification whatsoever in an expensive voyage to America at this time and, unless Uffa made arrangements to clear some of his outstanding debts immediately, they planned to foreclose, forcing the cancellation of the trip.

The unfortunate timing of the official visit, teatime, robbed Uffa of his customary ploy of floating the opposition in a sea of alcohol when discussing finance, experience having taught the bank manager not to drink with this particular adversary in any case, so Uffa was with his back well and truly against the wall. In a moment of utter desperation he picked up the telephone and telegraphed Peter Davies, saying, 'Send contract and the advance pay by return and I'll sign up.' He had found his taskmasters.

A habit formed when with the sea scouts, that of logging his voyages and adventures, spilled over into everyday life and was to stand Uffa in good stead when he was compelled to honour the commitment to write. He made a rule of keeping notepads and pencils at his bedside, where he would scribble and sketch his thoughts during odd moments of wakefulness, many of these nocturnal ideas having been already skilfully incorporated into boats and designs, others filed for future use. These, together with the diaries of *Typhoon* and *Diablesse*, plus jottings of the recent American canoe tour, provided a basic outline for the proposed full-length book, *Sailing, Seamanship and Yacht Construction*.

Never in his life was Uffa able to work with so little effort as at the floating bridge where he had his drawing office, works, bedroom and dining-room only a few seconds from one another; and, with Alma by his side to encourage, advise and correct, he settled down with inherent zeal to yet another challenge. In addition to incorporating his own designs within the framework of the book, he wrote to or otherwise contacted famous designers all over the world for permission to reproduce selected designs and, to everyone's astonishment (not least of all his own), so many of them acquiesced that within a few months he had very nearly accumulated sufficient material for a second book.

Later on, when friends marvelled at Uffa's cheek and success in obtaining other designers' plans, he likened it to his approach to women, claiming that the ones who said 'no' were flattered to have been asked and the ones who said 'yes' sweetened life's cup of happiness.

The person who probably exerted the greatest long-term beneficial influence on Uffa's life was Peter Davies, who became a great friend of both Uffa and Alma, as well as a constant source of encouragement and guidance to Uffa. Married to one of the twin daughters of the late Lord Ruthven, who had a home at Bembridge, he was a frequent and popular visitor at the floating bridge; and Uffa was both proud and delighted when he was invited to become godfather to George, one of the Davieses' sons.

When *Sailing, Seamanship and Yacht Construction* made its debut, to ecstatic reviews from the up-market press and yachting journals, Peter was overjoyed as much for Uffa as a friend as for himself as the publisher. Uffa considered Peter Davies his greatest ally, and wrote that to the end of his days he would continue to be grateful to Peter and to fate which threw them together on their voyage through life.

The book, an expensive and prestigious work of art, was to be reprinted over and over again in the years to come, and was a treasure chest of adventure and information, plus a soupçon of Uffa's homespun philosophy, which delighted the hearts of yachtsmen and escapists the world over. Inspired by the instant success of this early effort, and the steady flow of royalties from the books and magazine articles which were also in great demand, Uffa made plans to devote a larger portion of his time to journalistic pursuits.

Another successful venture at this period was the lecture tour. Uffa invested in a magic lantern and, with slides ranging from old-type brigs and the Royal yacht *Britannia* to his own photographs, delighted local audiences with his racy commentary. Garrulous by nature, and thriving on audience acclaim, he soon cast his net wider, catching and holding the attention of audiences at universities and yacht clubs up and down the country, becoming something of a cult figure after the publication of his book, and in great demand. His ribald jokes added a refreshingly welcome salty tang to the lives of undergraduates and the yachting fraternity of the day; though he was to find himself in trouble lecturing to mixed company in the so-called 'swinging sixties' when he made the surprising discovery that jokes he could get away with in top drawer circles became less acceptable as one went down the social scale.

Transcending the lecture itself, Uffa revelled in the subsequent hospitality and conviviality, which all too frequently got out of hand. On one occasion, after a particularly hair-raising session with a group of undergraduates at Cambridge, he was caught red-handed clinging to a wall bracket attempting to put out the street light. He managed to slip through the awaiting policeman's arms and escape; but the wily constable, more familiar with the side streets of Cambridge, all too soon caught up with the culprit, while the more fleet-footed students who had instituted the dare made swift their getaway.

Uffa was marched off to the police station, where he insisted that he was a visiting poet, but truth will out; and to his annoyance the whole hilarious episode was taken up by the newspapers. He was surprisingly conscious of his public image and easily upset by adverse press criticism. Therefore, temporarily subdued, he resolved to manifest a low profile for the time being, and returned to Cowes to re-think his life and assemble material for his next book.

His life was full and interesting, so Uffa did not have far to look for inspiration when the time came to write again. The International Fourteen-footers were still very much his babies, and the previous summer he had found time to accompany the Yacht Racing Association's team of four boats to Toronto to represent Britain against Canada and the United States. The team was young, good and keen with an average age of twenty-one. Stewart Morris was Captain, with Uffa's former canoeist partner Roger de Quincey as crew in *R.I.P.* John Winter and Tom Scott manned *Lightning;* David Beale helmed *Canute* with his friend Oscar Browning, a Cambridge rugger blue; while the fourth and heavy weather boat was *Eastlight*, owned by Peter Scott, son of the famous Antarctic explorer, and crewed by Nicholas Cooke. This boat was named after the lighthouse in which Peter painted his celebrated pictures of wildfowl.

Uffa had been invited by Sir John Field Beale, father of the team, to go out and guide their thoughts as manager, and naturally he accepted with alacrity. He looked upon his assignment as that of court jester, passing off awkward moments with light-hearted banter, and preventing his young charges from getting too strung up and excited. Their combined tactics paid off handsomely for the youngsters sailed remarkably well, and were more than proud to carry off the Trophy for their club, the Royal Norfolk and Suffolk Yacht Club.

The Canadians were warm-hearted and kind and, in addition to their great hospitality, Uffa was impressed by their Junior Club for boys between the ages of ten and fifteen years. They had their own clubhouse, their own Flag Officers, and ran races from their own little island, the shores of which were divided from the parent club's island by a small river or stream some seventy-five yards wide. The boys learnt to sail and race so well that from an early age they became first class helmsmen. Uffa did all in his power to publicize this method of training when he returned to England, and was instrumental in encouraging many yacht clubs to make more opportunity available and provide greater facilities for junior members.

Uffa's spark of originality caused him to be blessed by numerous benefactors, many of whom were or had been themselves adventurous pioneers. One such man was Thomas White Ratsey, in his day the greatest sail maker in the world. He had lost three sons in the war, and when others sought to cut Uffa down to size, he would say 'Quench not the smoking flax', meaning 'Have patience with the impatience of youth'. Uffa spent many happy hours in his company, and made a point of sitting with him during the latter days of his long illness. A true sailorman, when so afflicted that he could no longer stand, old Tom Ratsey passed the last summer aboard his beloved Itchen Ferry type yacht *Dolly Varden*, where he was so admired and respected that the King went out of his way to visit him during Cowes Week.

Another of his legion of benefactors was Alan Colman, who laughingly claimed to have made his fortune from the mustard his customers left on the side of their plates. When he took a gamble and offered Uffa the golden opportunity of designing his new yacht, Uffa was over the moon with excitement; but he quickly came down to earth with a bang for he was a sawdust man and Alan was thinking in terms of steel. Undeterred by lack of more than the most rudimentary training in naval architecture, and clinging to his motto 'Show me a man who has failed and I'll show you a man who has tried', he began scheming his way out of the dilemma, soon coming up with the answer. He must persuade the owner to have the yacht constructed at the John Samuel White Shipyard at Cowes, for then his footsteps would be guided by his former night school teacher and guardian angel, White's Chief Draughtsman, Archer Brading.

Alan Colman, himself a visionary, went into every detail with Uffa, and between them they came up with a wishbone ketch rig yacht with an eighty-three-foot length overall and sixty ton displacement, plus 2,794 square feet of sail. Uffa drew out several different accommodation plans before joining Alan Colman at his Norfolk home where they had the fun of lining out the hull full size on Alan's lawn with a tennis marker. After hours of thought and discussion they settled on a mutually agreeable basic plan; and Uffa returned to Cowes where Bill Waight, his draughtsman brother-in-law, had the gargantuan task of transferring their theories and rough sketches into something resembling a first set of working drawings.

The Managing Director of John Samuel White's was wildly enthusiastic when approached to build *Wishbone*. His Company had been experimenting with new techniques, and put forward the revolutionary suggestion of an all welded vessel. Uffa resigned himself that for six months, for better or worse, except for his writing, he was to be married to *Wishbone* and her builders, for such an ambitious project would take at least that length of time to construct, and he wondered if the builders and owner would be able to stand his critical and exacting nature over such a lengthy period. He wrote that from the very beginning, and throughout the building of *Wishbone*, he endured every emotion from despair to delight.

When Uffa caught sight of the efficient Kelly Coghlan working away on one of his early visits to Whites he asked Mr Billowes, Head of Correspondence, if he would object to his approaching Kelly to do shorthand and typing in her spare time. Mr Billowes envisaged no problem provided Kelly's work for the Company was not impaired, and he even cooperated to the extent of allowing her to use the Company's typewriter when she was unhappy with Uffa's portable; and so began a period when Uffa would either meet Kelly and her parents at home and dictate for hours, or alternatively Kelly would join Uffa and Alma at the floating bridge on Sundays for a day's dictation. In inclement weather Uffa would meet Kelly where the path ended to carry her over the muddy fields and deposit her on the prow of the floating bridge.

Kelly was in the amusing situation of dealing with Uffa's *Wishbone* correspondence from start to finish, typing up the letters and also seeing the effect of their arrival at White's. Uffa's distinctive green or blue linen foolscap envelopes were sufficiently outstanding for Mr Billowes to recognize and remove before his girls could see them. Unable to tolerate crudeness or bad language, he set himself up as an unofficial censor, cutting out any paragraphs that might cause offence before onward transmission to the various departments. He also took his shears to passages in which Uffa attacked members of the workforce with whom he was at loggerheads, referring to one executive, for example, as 'very nice but an old applewoman selling pears'.

Kelly also typed Uffa's everyday correspondence and material for his early books, and the routine would have doubtless continued indefinitely had he not taken more than an employer–employee interest in her. The worried Kelly consulted her mother who recommended that, rather than allow an uneasy and potentially explosive situation to develop, she should relinquish her part-time employment.

Uffa no longer had use of the sheds at Kingston and had purchased an old pub, the Trinity Arms at East Cowes, nicknamed 'The Blood Tub', where his fourteen-footers were now being built, when the firm was augmented in 1935 by a male secretary, Charles Willis, who was to take the strain of the ever-increasing and varied clerical workload; Uffa finally realizing that only a man would put up with the unsocial hours and conditions, not to mention the frequent cussing and swearing.

The twenty-four-year-old Charles was to become Uffa's journalistic mentor and financial conscience. Not infrequently Uffa, in the act of taking up a gun to go shooting or gathering together an armful of sails, would find Charles, notebook in hand, sternly barring his way. More often than not with a 'Right ho, Charles' or 'Ah me', he would reluctantly abandon his more earthly pursuits and follow Charles to some quiet corner of the floating bridge where they would settle down to another chapter of the book or to the ever-increasing backlog of correspondence.

Uffa's mail consisted of two piles of unanswered letters; one batch to be dealt with reasonably quickly as the letters could lead to orders or money. His theory with the second pile was that, if ignored for sufficient length of time, they would answer themselves.

Sometimes, when ravaged by one of his blacker moods and in no way inclined to conform to discipline, Uffa would storm off and disappear without trace. Neither Charles nor anyone else could begin to cope with him on such occasions, the general consensus of opinion being that it was healthier to keep out of sight and leave him to his own devices.

Uffa respected Charles's financial judgement, and in time came to view him with a certain amount of awe. In particular, Charles was able to strangle at birth some of Uffa's wilder financial jugglings, saving him from coming a cropper on more than one occasion. When Uffa was on his beam ends financially, a not infrequent occurrence, a familiar and amusing sight was the spectacle of Uffa lurking or hiding outside the office waiting for Charles to close up for lunch in order to nip in and rifle the petty cash of what was, after all, his own money.

Charles, who had been trained in the more stilted and formal atmosphere of accountants and other normal offices, never quite forgot the first letter Uffa gave him to type, which was typical of Uffa's style. Having finally received the summons to appear before the Magistrates at Cambridge, Uffa replied thus:

Dear Sir,

Thank you very much indeed for the Summons to appear before your Court. I am sorry that as I have another arrangement on that day regretfully I am unable to attend. Will you please thank the policeman who arrested me for being so kind. He did his duty well, being firm as well as kind.

A friend tells me that the charge for putting out lights is five shillings, so I am enclosing a cheque for thirty shillings and would like you to place the balance in the Police Orphanage Fund.

With best wishes, Yours sincerely . . .

The Magistrate read the letter out in Court and, describing it as SUBTLE COERCION, imposed a fine of £2. To this Uffa replied:

Dear Sir,

Thank you very much indeed for the fine, and I enclose a further cheque for £1, which regretfully now only leaves you with a balance of ten shillings to be devoted to the Police Orphanage Fund.

Best wishes, Yours sincerely . . .

Uffa was furious when the SUBTLE COERCION quote was repeated in the press and, although normally an avid publicity seeker, he refused in no uncertain terms a request from Pathé Gazette to board the floating bridge and film him for the newsreel in his natural habitat.

However, as with most of Uffa's adventures, there was a happy ending. When next approached to lecture at the University the invitation was accompanied by a message saying that special bracket lamps would be rigged up for him to put out, with a guarantee of no fines for disorderly conduct.

Charles and Uffa had come together during the *Wishbone* era and, between trying to type up the next book, pacifying other owners whose boats were delayed, selling off lumps of iron from the floating bridge to pay the wages, and tightrope-walking on a plank of wood over *Wishbone*'s deck while Uffa dictated instructions from below to the cacophony of platers and welders in full blast, it is no small wonder that Charles had occasion to reflect upon his own sanity in having shackled himself to such a motley outfit.

When *Wishbone* was finally successfully launched with great ceremony, her evolution can best be summed up with extracts from some of the speeches made at the launching dinner.

F. BILLOWES: I have thoroughly enjoyed dealing with the general correspondence for the contract, as Mr Uffa Fox writes such breezy letters, none of your stilted business type, that they have considerably brightened our usual monotonous round, and altogether it has been a pleasure to deal with this contract; which will have involved upwards of two thousand letters before the job is finished!

G. PARKER: About March of last year Mr Uffa Fox called into our drawing office with an escort of two dogs and produced the outline plans of a yacht for which he wanted an estimated cost. When that was done we thought it was the last of it, as is usual with most estimates. Six months later we were informed by Uffa that the outline of this yacht had been marked out, full size, with a tennis marker on Mr Colman's lawn – a new way of laying down a yacht. On the outline plan Mr Fox had scribbled 'Designed by Uffa Fox for Alan Colman – to be built by J. S. White's'. This showed that the owner had great confidence in his designer, in that he allowed him to place the contract with us without any competitive tenders – a most unusual procedure. From time to time we had to consult our friend the designer as to what we would do. Uffa would scratch his head, utter an oath, take a reef in his trousers and the mystery was solved.

G. SCADDING: On the invitation card I received from Uffa was a note: 'Dear Mr Scadding, Two minutes talk on *wenches* please'. I find that I know nothing about *wenches*. I have been studying the subject very closely only to find tonight that it is the wrong subject entirely and I should have been talking about *mast winches*.

ARCHER BRADING: With regard to Uffa, I have known him practically all his life, and have followed his career right through. When I was the instructor of the Naval Architecture Classes, Uffa was one of my most promising pupils. His quest for knowledge was unlimited, and he was very quick to grasp all that was told him. His big asset is his wonderfully retentive memory.

Later on I entrusted to his care my two boys, who belonged to his troop of sea scouts, which caused me many sleepless nights. On several occasions we had to send out an SOS from the local coastguard station to find out from other stations on the south coast whether they had seen a thirty-foot whaleboat full of boy scouts. He took them on many a hair-raising expedition, including one to France and the Channel Islands, and I am proud to say Uffa always brought them home safely.

Since that time Uffa has broadened his knowledge, and his adventures would put many books of fiction in the shade.

We hoped that he would settle down and become a town councillor or something to that effect, but I am afraid the wanderlust is too strong in him, and I shall not be surprised if before long we hear of him sailing down the Spanish Main and fighting the battles of Drake all over again.

We all know of his wonderful success with his sailing dinghies, and it is quite common knowledge that if you want to win the Prince of Wales' Cup you must have a Fox dinghy.

In Uffa Fox you have a wonderful combination, which is practically unique, for when a man designs, builds and sails his own boats, the knowledge thus acquired cannot but produce the ideal article.

When he came along with his present product, the *Wishbone*, I was very interested, as I have always predicted a great future for Uffa, and dealing with larger material gives his fertile brain more play.

In *Wishbone* we have a unique boat in many ways, and in the preparation of the working drawings, which number about one hundred and fifty, it has been a source of pleasure to work with Uffa. We have come up against many stumbling blocks, but with careful consideration we have overcome them, and I think Uffa will agree with me when I say that every penny spent in the drawing office will save many pounds in the yard.

The result has been a very fine vessel, and it is the hope of everyone who has been associated with the building that she will be very successful and add laurels to the owner's name. We all trust she will lift the Fastnet Cup. That would indeed be a feather in Uffa's cap.

[9]

Lack of privacy can be a penalty of fame, but such was Uffa's gregarious nature that for the most part he accepted it as a reward rather than a penance. There were moments, however, when interruptions annoyed him to the extreme, especially when they retarded his thought processes.

The publication of his books led to invitations from the BBC to broadcast, a medium in which he was never truly relaxed, his heavy breathing into the microphone revealing an uncharacteristic nervousness, and these broadcasts further increased his renown. Thus the ensuing publicity from the written and spoken word enlarged his circle and increased his vexation. Never refusing an order, with its accompanying one-third down payment, he accepted more work than he could possibly cope with and, hampered by petty hindrances, his designing, and writing pledge of a book a year, got further and further behind.

When Isaac Bell commissioned Nicholson's to build the ocean racer *Bloodhound*, being a perfectionist, he asked Uffa to design and build a little tender for her, and this was one of the projects to fall by the wayside. After countless letters and telegrams requesting a delivery date, Uffa finally sent the reply: 'I cannot build the thing because I am disturbed so much at night by the singing of the nightingales.'

The following day a telegram was delivered to 'Uffa Fox, c/o The Nightingales, East Cowes, Isle of Wight. Shoot the bloody birds and build the boat in your own good time. Ikey.'

Unwittingly Isaac Bell hit the jackpot on two counts. Firstly, he appealed to Uffa's sense of humour. Secondly, Uffa had an invincible streak of contrariness, and the suggestion that he had all the time in the world to produce the boat was sufficient incentive for him to drop everything and concentrate on Ikey's dinghy.

Although only eleven feet on the waterline, Uffa went to work with a vengeance, producing one of the sweetest little dinghies imaginable, while still being rigid and stable enough to allow for Ikey's 'gammy' leg. She had a fair turn of speed for rowing, sailing and towing and he smuggled a narrow wooden centreboard into her, plus removable midship thwart to allow her to fit over *Bloodhound*'s skylight. She carried a single jib-headed sail on a revolving mast with no shrouds or stays. On coming alongside, a string was pulled which revolved the mast and rolled up the sail; both stowing and reefing being carried out in the same manner. The spar was jointed to enable it to be taken apart and stowed inside the dinghy for voyages.

With *Bloodhound*'s dinghy safely out of the way, Uffa attempted to re-gather his thoughts and return to writing, his most profitable source of income; a difficult task as his concentration was becoming more easily shattered with the advancing years. He could forgive the major interruption like the unexpected arrival of an old friend or customer, even the joy of some strange new craft passing up river, but minor irritations caused him to rant and rave like the true British sailorman he was until some odd chance or quirk restored his basic good humour.

A necessary evil in Uffa's life was the telephone, and there were times when he cursed its malevolent ring. On one occasion, in the midst of a thunderstorm, he picked up the receiver after a buzz only to hear 'Number, please' followed by the operator's voice assuring him that the call did not originate from her. This occurred three times in rapid succession, with Uffa growing more frenzied at each ring. With the third jangle he threw in the sponge. Assuming a high-pitched, pious church voice he greeted the operator with, 'It must be the Lord calling. I expect he wants me for a sunbeam,' but the spell was broken and he did no more writing that day.

Procrastination was walking death to Uffa; and one of his major aggravations, when consumed with an idea and anxious to put wheels in motion, was to lift the receiver, hear the operator's click and no anticipated 'Number, please'. Over the years he devised several methods of handling the situation. One of his favourites was to say 'Your knickers are coming down', which more often than not brought the speedy and spontaneous response 'No they're not' from the telephone girl. 'Oh yes they are, otherwise you can bring that mink coat back,' Uffa would chuckle. 'And on the way perhaps you'd be kind enough to get me Cowes 555.'

Often Uffa would burst into a little ditty, sometimes slightly *risqué*, whilst awaiting the 'Number, please', and although in time he built up a considerable rapport with some of the girls at the exchange, one or two of whom sailed and knew him off duty, it never occurred to him that the delay could on occasion be governed by the operators' desire to perceive which gem of wisdom he would conjure up to gladden their day.

The perpetual comings and goings and lack of privacy at the floating bridge caused Uffa and Alma to long for a home they could escape to and call their own, and when the Padmore Estate at Whippingham was split up and sold, Uffa purchased twenty prime acres of land with frontage onto the east bank of the river between the Folly Inn and the Old East Medina Mill.

Uffa decided to undertake the ground clearance and house design himself. After several false starts it was eventually called 'Twenty Acres' and, as with any new scheme, it took priority over all other commitments. A case of all hands to the pump, skilled workmen being taken off other projects and drafted to clearing bush, felling trees and laying the drive. For the latter, in addition to the lorry loads of flints purchased, they removed shingle from the foreshore, and even secretary Charles was despatched to join the workmen with stiff brushes to sweep the beach every evening and cover up traces of Uffa's transgression. Then, impatient to be installed within the boundaries of his new estate, a small hut, which later became the dogs' hut, was erected amongst the trees to serve as a retreat during the planning stages.

On the not infrequent occasions when funds dried up, or when prospective owners who had paid deposits on boats clamoured for delivery, a temporary halt was called to work at Twenty Acres and the men returned to their lawful employment; not always eagerly as there was a lot of fun and larking around as well as hard work in the fresh air and sunshine of those early days at Folly.

The house was not large, but what it lacked in size it made up for in clean-cut nautical beauty, for the whole of the interior was in light waxed oak-panelled plywood; and the doors, staircase and floors were of matching solid oak. Solid oak large double bunks, with full-length drawers beneath, were strategically sited in each of the three bedrooms where all cupboards were camouflaged behind the panelling. Most of the woodwork was created by Uffa's boatbuilders, so all was dovetailed and perfection.

The front and only entrance was from the drive to the north; and, as one entered, the sole bathroom huddled to the right under the stairs opposite a smallish kitchen with a solid fuel-burning stove, which also fed the central heating. The water, as on the floating bridge, was rainwater collected and stored in tanks in the roof. When one of the bureaucratic departments sent a form demanding to know the source of his water, Uffa replied, 'The good Lord supplies my needs.' There was no gas or electricity.

Facing the front door, at the end of a passage, was the dining-room, the first of two large and airy rooms with picture windows giving breathtakingly beautiful panoramic views across the river to the west and up river to the south, which took up the greater part of the ground floor. Uffa's combined library and design office, approached through the dining-room, was perhaps the more magnificent of these two lovely rooms.

The dining-room itself was designed and built to the shape of a table Uffa had acquired from Queen Victoria's estate at Osborne. He had the natural instinct of a magpie when it came to possessions, but his paramount joy was to own artefacts which had previously belonged to the titled or famous. On divers occasions he boasted the use of Prince Henry of Battenburg's twelve-bore gun; ownership of a door from the Empress Eugenie's yacht, and the pillars from Handel's organ; the five-oared gig from the old *Britannia*, her gaff jaws, one of her bunks and a photograph of her framed in her mast hoop; the library doors from Lord Gort's old home, East Cowes Castle; plus Sir James Barrie's bible box in which Uffa housed his telephone, and Lord Byron's piano. Uffa had a knack of giving things away without quite managing to relinquish ownership, saying, perhaps, 'That's yours on permanent loan' so that the recipient of the gift was never truly sure of rightful title. On one occasion he presented his hostess with a pair of binoculars only to scratch his name on the leather case with a pair of scissors when he spotted them on a subsequent visit.

A large dining table was to become something of a prop in Uffa's life. Despite a handsome collection of desks and drawing tables in all shapes and sizes, wherever he was the dining table sooner or later took over as the centre of influence; and it was here that Uffa held sway and where those closest to him at any one given moment – members of the workforce or whoever happened to be in view when the teacups were paraded – sat around for afternoon tea or discussion. The current mail and plans which normally spreadeagled the table were pushed to one side for meals, or removed *en bloc* for more formal entertaining.

So proud was Uffa of his new creation, Twenty Acres, that on the one occasion when Alma found herself locked out without her keys and had to force an entry, Uffa flew into a towering rage, deducting the cost of the boatbuilder's time repairing the damage from her meagre housekeeping allowance.

One blot on Uffa's otherwise perfect horizon was a public towpath along the eastern bank of the Medina passing through his land near the water's edge. This became an obsession with him, particularly as a number of workers travelling on foot or bicycle made use of it as a short cut from the Newport area to the plywood factory north of the Folly Inn, cutting some two miles from their journey to and from work.

Finding himself helpless to prevent pedestrians using the path, as it was a public right of way, Uffa concentrated on the cyclists, getting up at seven-thirty in the morning to catch them and take them to task, letting them know in no uncertain terms that they were trespassing on his property, and reminding them that it was against the law to cycle along the towpath. In the main, as Uffa's abuse became more violent and his language more colourful with each passing day, the cyclists took the long route to work or dismounted when crossing his boundary; but one or two of the not so easily intimidated continued to cycle past, ignoring his shouting and screaming, and their presence was like a red rag to a bull.

Uffa, despite his somewhat precarious financial position, went to the trouble and expense of erecting, at strategic points, two stiles which straddled the towpath, forcing the cyclists to dismount and carry their machines over the stiles before continuing on their way. This ploy eventually eliminated all but Uffa's greatest foe, a man who could stand up to him and give as good as he got when it came to a slanging match.

Uffa became so haunted by this one man who dared to defy him that one day, under the guise of shooting rabbits, he lay in wait with his twelve-bore and shot the front wheel off the man's bicycle as he was cycling past. The badly shaken and bruised victim threatened to inform the police that Uffa had attempted to murder him, to which Uffa retorted that he would at the same time have to explain how he came to be cycling along the towpath against the by-laws. Then, crossing the path, Uffa picked up the rabbit which he had previously shot and planted on the seaward side, and marched off.

Although nothing further came of the incident, talk of murder had the effect of quietening Uffa, and he put the story about that he had accidentally potted the wheel of a bicycle while aiming at a rabbit on the other side of the towpath. Later, though, when things had settled down and nothing more seen or heard of the enemy, he boasted of his achievement. The story soon got around that there was a lunatic at large at Twenty Acres and, during the period of Uffa's occupancy, there were no cyclists and few walkers on the towpath. This darker side of Uffa's nature probably caused him to have as many enemies as friends within the local community.

With a real house set in a real road, the next stage was to learn to drive his first car, a second-hand Morris. There were no breathalysers in those days, so Uffa decided that he should learn to drive with the mainbrace well and truly spliced as that was the condition in which he anticipated he would be most likely to find himself. He all but went berserk with his new toy, and within a very short space of time was obliged to change to something bigger and better as his cars took considerable punishment.

Uffa got a kick out of shining the car's headlights into the rabbit-infested fields to dazzle and mesmerize the rabbits at night. On one occasion, after a particularly hairy drinking session and dinner, he and two friends decided it might be fun to have a rabbit shoot across the fields near Twenty Acres. His current car boasted a sliding sunshine roof, and with one man standing on the passenger seat next to Uffa, with head and waist out of the roof, clutching a twelve-bore, and the other marksman on the roof above Uffa, with his feet on the opening of the roof just behind the windscreen, they set off in the excitement of the chase. Uffa made for a ploughed field and, instead of remaining still as he doubtless would have done if sober, thus allowing the headlights to shine straight across, he drove up and down the furrows of the ploughed field with the two guns banging away, but no rabbits.

Uffa then had the notion that they might be more successful if, like Brer Rabbit, they penetrated the depths of an enormous bush some twenty feet in diameter and ten feet in height, being convinced that when he came out the other side they would be surrounded by rabbits. He plunged through the bush at thirty miles an hour and, to his surprise, lost the man from the sunshine roof before they were a quarter of their way through. The other unfortunate, who had been standing on the seat alongside Uffa, was flattened backwards onto the top of the car directly they entered the bush, with only his lower limbs remaining inside. The gun was torn from his grasp by the branches and brambles and landed beside the victim who had been swept from the car roof. The badly scratched and shaken passengers floundered back into their positions and the car set off again.

Next Uffa drove under the low branches of an oak tree, sweeping off the one man and flattening the other again. They had still not potted a rabbit, but there were plenty of bangs, empty cartridges and giggles. Finding his way blocked by a five-barred gate, Uffa drove through it at speed and was overjoyed to see it disintegrate into a thousand fragments. Finally the car gave up the ghost and settled into a little hollow.

In the light of day when the garage experts arrived to rescue the car from its muddy grave, they found it with broken half shafts and a burnt out clutch.

Fortunately there were few cars on the road in the late thirties when Uffa, also in his late thirties, learnt to drive for it naturally followed that, with his obsession for speed, Uffa would approach the narrow Isle of Wight lanes like the James Hunt of his day. Not only did he charge around with what the local Police Inspector referred to as 'joyous abandon', but he took grave exception to timid passengers who 'braked' on his behalf when Uffa failed to do so. Despite repeated warnings, one particular friend could not refrain from putting his foot down when he felt in danger; and, after the front passenger seat had been forced right back by this nervous friend, Uffa had it repaired with bolts only strong enough to support a person sitting normally. From then onwards, anyone who 'braked' out of turn with sufficient power to place undue pressure on the rear of the seat found themselves thrown back as the seat collapsed.

Uffa's partial success at taming apprehensive passengers did not end with throwing them practically arse over apex. He installed a harmonium pedal on the floor of the car in front of the passenger seat, connecting the pedal up to the brass dial of a spring balance altered to reflect tons instead of pounds. After the fascinated passengers had observed the spear shooting round the dial for some time they would almost invariably, to Uffa's huge delight, enquire what the dial registered, and receive the stock reply: 'It's all the energy you are wasting putting your foot on the brake.' Needless to say, there were one or two of Uffa's acquaintances who refused to set foot in a car with him.

When, out of the blue one horrendous morn, the Electricity Company's representatives called upon Uffa at Twenty Acres to inform him of their intent to erect high-powered cables and pylons across his land, the shocked Uffa invited them into the house and plied them with sherry in an endeavour to find out where exactly the monstrosities were to be sited for, although provisionally placed well away from the house itself, Uffa had no intention of allowing such an outrage to occur on his land without a struggle.

Promising to return in a month's time, the delegation assured Uffa that he could do nothing to prevent the construction work, there being Acts of Parliament to override objections from citizens such as he.

Uffa was not long in scheming a way out. Hurriedly drawing up plans for two smaller editions of Twenty Acres, so sited as to make it impossible for any cable to pass over his property, and calling them butler–cook's cottage and chauffeur–groom's cottage respectively, he sent the plans to Newport for approval. The wheels of local government ground a little faster in those days and, when the men from the Electricity Company returned a month later, Uffa electrified them by producing his trump card, the approved building plans signed and stamped by the Planning Office. The cottages were never built, of course, but presented with a *fait accompli* the Electricity Company backed down, and the cables eventually went not only underground but around Twenty Acres.

Old Bob Savage, who had taught the boy Uffa to box and perfect his swimming, was still licensee of the Folly Inn when Uffa purchased Twenty Acres, and before long he and Bob were to be observed, heads together, plotting the revival of the Folly Regatta which had lapsed many years before. Lennie Mew, the brewer, was enthusiastic, and George Barton the Harbour Master his usual cooperative self, and between them they mustered up various interested parties until, when the day of the inaugural meeting arrived, no less than twenty-three appeared on the doorstep of the Folly Inn at opening time for the first session.

Uffa was proposed as President, and he agreed to take charge provided they accepted his three proposals. Firstly, to form ten small committees to deal with the divers activities from sailing to shore sports; secondly, to each put a guinea in the kitty to start the ball rolling; thirdly, to each drink a pint of bitter beer, of which he would stand the first round. Uffa himself agreed to give all the advice necessary, but not be eligible to vote.

Uffa's method of choosing Committee Chairmen was simplicity itself, merely a question of YOU SUGGESTED IT, YOU DO IT. Whenever anyone recommended something new he would say, 'Right. You are now the Chairman. All you have to do is collect a Secretary and Treasurer to form your Committee, and proceed full speed ahead with your part of the Regatta.' This democratic method of election eliminated what Uffa described as 'idle chatter over frivolous or unworkable schemes'.

By closing time, when each of the twenty-three members had stood his round of pints, they were mellow to say the least, and so full of beer that Uffa was convinced it would run out of their ears if they tilted their heads sideways. Uffa and one or two other revellers felt the urge to continue, so they staggered to their cars and zigzagged their way to Lennie Mew's house in Newport where the party continued until five in the morning.

The Regatta posters when printed appeared in true Uffa style, announcing 'Fun and Frolic at the Folly' and 'Dancing on the Spacious Lawn', the lawn being a rough grass field, which had been scythed into reasonable shape, and had a decided slope. A brass band, playing from two farm wagons, fought valiantly to be heard above the jollification.

This first revived Folly Regatta was a resounding success, there being something for everybody, whether sea or land lubber; and the tradition has been handed down through the years, with the exception of the break enforced by Adolf Hitler, and shows every sign of being maintained now that the Folly Inn is run by Mahala's daughter, Lucy, and her husband, John McQueen-Mason. Additionally, the new Harbour Master of Cowes, Henry Wrigley, ably abetted by Alan Cundall at Folly, is if possible even more enthusiastic than was George Barton in his day to make it an event to cherish and remember for all the family.

[10]

Uffa jogged along happily enough at Twenty Acres, the peace and solitude enabling him to maintain the goal of writing a book a year, until the public tracked him to his new lair. Charles would cross from West to East Cowes and walk along the river bank to Folly, take dictation and notes for most of the day, sometimes transcribing them at home until ten o'clock at night; while surprised visitors felt thwarted when calling at Kingston to find no floating bridge, Uffa having towed her up river and moored her off the bottom of Twenty Acres.

The pub, Trinity Arms, a useful enough stop-gap, proved far from ideal for boatbuilding and Uffa, continually on the lookout for waterside premises in the Cowes area within his price range, finally, in the late summer of 1938, concluded the purchase of a boatyard next to Lallows currently trading as A. N. Compton Limited, with Cecil Donne and Arthur Lowein, father of Bobbie Lowein the well-known yachtsman, as directors.

The Medina Yard contract also encompassed Medina House, half of the old Birmingham Hall and birthplace of the famous Dr Arnold of Rugby School immortalized in *Tom Brown's Schooldays*, Dr Arnold's father having been Collector of Customs in those far-off days of sailing ships when Cowes was a thriving seaport. One of Uffa's first acts was to knock a hole in the wall at first-floor level to integrate house and yard.

Medina Yard was a draughty, rambling yard on several floors at various half levels, and included a small slipway which Uffa was permanently extending or repairing and which, like some ever open-mouthed monster, consumed innumerable tons of concrete and man-hours. The yard fronted onto Birmingham Road where Uffa had deep entrance doors fitted, the height of two floors, so that large timber lorries were able to drive right through for unloading, and the cement lorries could go straight down the yard to the slipway and disgorge their cargo at the low water mark.

In the days gone by, the old Trinity Wharf at East Cowes had a beautiful king-post roof built over its floating pontoon, and when removed at the turn of the century it was re-erected on top of Medina Yard in the form of a lookout from whence it afforded a bird's eye view for Uffa's Chief Draughtsman Bill Waight and his minions, who beavered away in the drawing office below.

The covered garden at the rear of Medina House formed part of the shipyard; and the front entrance, facing Birmingham Road, became a shop and store where, in the large windows, Uffa displayed his books and odds and ends of wire and fittings, planning one day to extend it into a bookshop and chandlery, a dream which never materialized. Two rooms, both sea-facing, were reached through the shop, one of which became Charles's office. The second room Uffa let to Captain Barton, the Harbour Master, a useful friend and ally.

There were three rooms and a kitchen on the first floor of Medina House, Uffa selecting for his office the road-facing room above the shop as it was nearest the works, and it was the wall of this room that he partially knocked down to thrust a direct entrance and door into the yard. The remaining two rooms faced the sea and, because one of them could only be reached through his office, Uffa turned it into a makeshift bedroom. These two habitable rooms were adequately furnished with odds and ends picked up in the sale rooms. Additionally there were three empty rooms and a bathroom on the second floor, and a small roof garden on top; whilst in the lower part of the building were cellars, one of which housed the fitting shop where Bob Dickerson, the former sea scout who had sailed with Uffa to France and Sweden, was in charge. Bob, though not a trained engineer, could also make himself useful with engines.

Uffa's small workforce and dinghies were dwarfed by Medina Yard's spaciousness after the cramped working conditions suffered at the Trinity Arms and, with the unsettled European situation, orders were not coming in nearly as quickly as had been hoped and expected. Looking ahead with more foresight than the majority of politicians of the day, Uffa set about applying for Government contracts, hopefully to run concurrently with the pleasure craft orders. His direct tenders were unsuccessful, but he did succeed in obtaining a sub-contract through another Island company for some Ministry of Supply pontoons.

All the chasing around for orders, plus time and mental energy expended on the Medina Yard planning and development, meant shorter periods, if any, devoted to writing. Announcing that he could no longer concentrate at Twenty Acres as there were too many interruptions occasioned by the constantly ringing telephone and unexpected visitors, Uffa rented a cottage near Quarr Abbey where, when there were no urgent or immediate problems, he and Charles would retreat to write; and while all this was happening another event had taken place which was to affect Uffa's life.

Lord Ruthven, Peter Davies's father-in-law, travelling from London to his Bembridge home, shared a first-class railway compartment with an attractive, well rounded lady in her late thirties, Mrs Laura Louisa Enoch (Cherry to her friends), and her teenage son, Bobbie Sach, who was home from boarding school. Charmed by his companions, Lord Ruthven soon discovered that they had several mutual acquaintances at Bembridge where Cherry, following the death of her second husband, à member of the diplomatic service, had opened a boarding house to supplement her small income. Promising to recommend her establishment to his friends, Lord Ruthven took his leave; and it was not long before Uffa found himself partaking of Mrs Enoch's hospitality.

Cherry said she discovered Uffa was different the first night he dined at her table. After the meal Uffa proposed a walk to settle the digestion and, as they strolled and chatted along the beach together in the moonlight, to Cherry's complete and utter astonishment, Uffa said 'Nice night for a swim,' threw off all of his clothes and dived naked into the water.

From then onwards Uffa and Charles frequently put their work behind them and drove from the Quarr cottage to Bembridge for a chicken lunch with Cherry, and afterwards Uffa would send Charles off for a couple of hours' stroll before they returned to pick up the threads of their respective lives.

Cherry's son Bobbie, who loved all things connected with boats and the water, and Uffa got along like a house on fire. Bobbie was full of hero worship, and was also of an age to appeal to Uffa who basically had neither the time nor the patience for young children, though he sometimes went through the motions to please clients or friends; so there was nothing more natural in the world than for Uffa to take a personal interest in improving Bobbie's sailing and showing him the workings of Medina Yard, nor that occasionally mother came too.

Alma knew there was another woman, as she had known of others in the past, in particular the wife of one of Uffa's friends who took a Machiavellian delight in leaving personal belongings behind in the bedroom for Alma to find when she returned from work, and she hoped and prayed that this affair would blow over also; but Uffa was beginning to find fault with all that she did no matter how hard she tried, and to have less and less time for her.

Uffa invited Cherry to Twenty Acres and allowed Alma to play hostess on New Year's Eve, 1938/39. His wife, unhappy with the arrangement but uncomplaining, still hoped against hope. When towards the end of the evening Uffa suggested he and Cherry walk the dogs, three wire-haired terriers and a Welsh springer spaniel, their progress as they disappeared into the semi-darkness was observed by the already suspicious Alma from an upstairs window. What she saw made her blood run cold.

With difficulty Alma managed to control herself as the lovers returned, though trembling within; but later on, when Uffa pointed out a heap where one of the dogs had messed on the floor, instead of cleaning it up as was expected, she answered back with 'What are you going to do about it then?'

Uffa's reply was to stride to the window, rip the curtain bodily from its fittings, wipe the excreta into its folds, and fling it to the floor for Alma to wash.

'Uffa needs to be understood,' murmured Cherry, with a sympathetic look in his direction.

'Alma's buggered off and left me with the dogs to look after!' cried the outraged Uffa to his father.

They were at the house in East Cowes, divided into two flats since the death of Mrs Fox, where old Mr Fox lived with Ellie and Mahala's eldest son, Peter Dixon, who was apprenticed to Uffa.

'Can you move out to Twenty Acres for a couple of weeks until she gets back? I thought it would make a nice change for you.'

Within a few hours they were installed at Folly, where it did not take the astute Ellie long to realize that Alma's personal belongings had gone too; and so began a routine, that was to last for many moons, of Mr Fox and Ellie travelling periodically to East Cowes to air out their home and collect further items of clothing for the various seasons as they came and went.

In the early days Uffa steadfastly returned to Twenty Acres each night; and on the first Sunday he brought Cherry to lunch, introduced her to his family, and instituted a Sunday pattern which continued, provided there were no other commitments, as long as they lived at Folly: that of piling into Uffa's car for a drive round the Island and afternoon tea with friends or in some out of the way tea shop. Uffa was justifiably proud of his Island, and derived enormous pleasure from showing Cherry its every nook and cranny.

Uffa was also making a great deal of fuss of his father, and it was not long before Mr Fox was crying 'You're not getting another penny out of me', but Uffa was persistent and his father a sitting duck. When Mr Fox became adamant that it was his duty as a father of two other children in addition to Uffa to consider his daughters, particularly Ellie who had suffered a lung complaint all her life and was not considered sufficiently strong ever to work and support herself, Uffa listened but did not give up.

A day or two later he returned to the attack with a new scheme. If Mr Fox put up his remaining capital, a limited company would be formed into which Uffa would place his business assets, and he would further guarantee his father and Ellie a home with him for as long as they lived, plus their share of the dividends.

Mr Fox slept on this latest proposal, and next day the terms were agreed. He assented to release his cash to Uffa, but wanted no part of the Company for himself – the shares and dividends must be Ellie's. He also extracted a solemn promise from his son that, when Mr Fox died, Uffa would take over personal responsibility for Ellie; and so on 3 April 1939, Uffa Fox Limited was born, with two directors, Uffa Fox and Miss Elfrida Fox.

When the time came Uffa kept the book royalties, his main source of income, for himself, and the Company never paid Ellie a dividend; but he honoured the promise to his father of holding out a guiding hand to Ellie for the remainder of his life, and in the long term that proved more important than financial consideration.

Meantime another season had come and gone and all was not well at the Bembridge boarding house. In retrospect, Charles could not recall meeting any guests at all on the occasions he lunched there. Uffa, by this time well versed in Cherry's affairs, offered her and Bobbie employment with the newly formed Uffa Fox Limited, free tenancy of the upstairs flat, plus use of the first floor sitting-room overlooking the sea and the kitchen where she would prepare his lunches and be on hand to make cups of tea or coffee throughout the day.

For her part, Cherry was able to furnish Medina House tastefully with quality carpets and antiques, Uffa being especially delighted with the large mahogany dining table which now held pride of place in his office.

I was nearly sixteen when, in the summer of 1939, I was invited to Twenty Acres for what turned out to be a busman's holiday. Uncle Uffa, upon gleaning the information that I had recently passed my exams in shorthand and typing, was dictating letters before we had even completed our first meal together.

Just as quickly he contacted my mother, Mahala, and almost before I realized what was happening I found myself a permanent member of the Twenty Acres family and employed by Uffa Fox Limited. I was filled with pride, convinced that Uffa was impressed with my work, but pride goeth before a fall. He informed me later that the overriding factor in my favour was an air of peace and serenity which soothed his troubled brow and enabled him to concentrate on his work. In the years that followed I could not help but observe that the persons who survived longest in his company were the quiet ones.

There is no doubt that Uffa was sorely in need of additional secretarial aid. Charles, who had been appointed Company Secretary, was fully occupied with wages, book-keeping and general office routine since Alma's departure; and, without Alma's help and encouragement there were no new books. The 1939 publication, *The Crest of the Wave*, was not so much a new book as a collection of some of the better material

90

from earlier works bound together into a smaller, popular-sized edition. Uffa was desperately anxious to get another book away to the publishers, and he and I completed the outline of several chapters, which were filed under 'book' or 'biography' before the first of two major crises struck.

The relationship between Uffa and his men was an especially close one. He knew personally their families and shared their joys and sorrows, helped out with interest-free loans for house purchase deposits when required, and was available generally with advice and help. They responded in turn beyond the call of duty when Uffa was behind with an order or otherwise in need of assistance, and thought nothing of coming in at midnight to launch a boat on the high water if she had come up for a scrub on the noonday tide. They also cheered him up with the latest blue jokes to add to his already extensive repertoire.

There were verbal battles of course, some more heated than others, when Uffa's effing and blinding could not only be heard from one end of the yard to the other, but oozed out onto the street or sped rudely across the water. Uffa seldom lost his cool if an employee showed him a mistake when made, as between them they could rectify the error. What really made him see red was a cover-up or botched job. There was one particular man, however, first class at his job, who had the misfortune to be blessed with a temper as fiery as Uffa's own. During the course of an especially virulent confrontation, the man in question was misguided enough to drag Uffa's current domestic arrangements and treatment of Alma into the fray.

Uffa stormed wild-eyed into the office, trembling from head to foot, nostrils quivering, white with shock and rage. Like many a person involved in a clandestine situation his head had been in the clouds, leaving him blissfully unaware that his *affaire de coeur* was an open secret, and moreover that sympathies lay with the injured party.

Uffa brooded the night away and by next day, Saturday, had reached a decision. The man must go. Uffa did not want to see his face in the yard ever again. The petty cash was raided to purchase insurance stamps (the men's cards were never stamped until the last possible moment), the man's wages due in lieu of notice carefully calculated and packeted; and on Sunday morning Uffa fetched me from Twenty Acres to type up a prepared and carefully worded accompanying letter. Everything was done according to the book. There must be no slip-up. We then drove to the man's home. Uffa posted the envelope through the letter box and drove sadly away, for the man had been a good and loyal worker and Uffa grieved that it should end this way.

At ten o'clock on Monday the discharged man entered the yard with an escort, the local union official, and an ultimatum. Uffa had committed the cardinal sin of sacking the man on a Sunday and, unless he were reinstated immediately, the union intended calling all their men out on strike.

Uffa's reply was in the form of a question: 'Who pays the men's wages?' He continued: 'The day you pay the wages you have the right to play the dictator and I will abide by your decision, but as long as I pay the wages I shall employ whoever I choose. Moreover nobody is going on strike. Any man who walks out now is sacked by me and need not bother to return.'

By midday there was a hush over the yard. Uffa had taken on the unions.

[11]

On the morning of Sunday, 3 September 1939 Uffa drove my grand-father and me to Cowes where, just before eleven o'clock, he switched on the wireless in Cherry's sitting-room to hear the dreaded news that England was at war with Nazi Germany. With the insouciance of youth my strongest recollections of the moment were the gravity of my elders, who had lived through and understood the horrors of war, and the body-tingling warmth from the sherry of which I had been allowed to partake for the first time.

Uffa telephoned Ellie to make sure that she had heard the news and not been overcome. Then, while Cherry made herself ready for lunch at Twenty Acres, we walked quietly up and down and along the floors of Medina Yard, pausing frequently by the silent workbenches, dust from the wood shavings softly powdering our shoes, the smell of varnish suspended in the balmy air. 'There are going to be some changes here,' remarked Uffa grimly.

The union's call to the boatbuilders, who were completely innocent and uninvolved in the dispute, to down tools, and Uffa's response, had been as traumatic and heartbreaking for the men and their families as for Uffa. None had wanted to leave, and Uffa certainly did not want to lose them. When they walked out Uffa wrote on his calendar, 'This is one of the saddest and unhappiest days of my life.'

The untimely departure of the main workforce left Uffa with a nucleus of boatbuilding apprentices, unusually silent and overawed at the responsibility thrust upon them, fitters and draughtsman; and these boys and men rallied valiantly to breach the gap as far as they were able.

Uffa meantime, when the yard had closed on the day of the walk-out, slowly mounted the stairs of Medina House and drew himself a hot, steaming bath. Only in the bath was he completely without interruption and able to let his thoughts run free. Lulled by the sensuous warmth of the water, the pain of the day submerged and a pattern began to form in his mind. There could be dozens of boatbuilders working on their own account, victims of the political situation, finding themselves suspended in limbo, unsure of the future and vacillating which way to turn. Another thought. To work on pontoons one did not necessarily have to be a boatbuilder. Carpenters and joiners, looking beyond to the possibility of being drafted into the forces, might well prefer the security of a reserved occupation.

Uffa spent the evening in meditation and list making. Next morning, with a column of names before him, he set about contacting by telephone the men on his roster, and more often than not if the person at the other end of the line was not available himself for work he could furnish information of a friend or acquaintance who might well be interested. When approach by telephone was not viable, Uffa jumped into his car and sped from one end of the Island to the other seeking out prospective employees. He devoted a week to tracking down and interviewing and, when Medina Yard opened its doors one week after being blacked by the union, Uffa had a new and efficient non-union workforce.

With typical Uffa over-enthusiasm, plus the need to prove he could not be beaten, he ended up with more men than the original team, and so had the additional task of creating further employment and finding more money for wages. He also decided that this was the moment to modernize, leaving behind the saw, hammer and chisel image by investing in more sophisticated equipment such as drill guns, paint sprays and machine saws.

The increase in the number of workmen necessitated improved amenities and enabled Uffa to indulge in one of his pet idiosyncrasies, the communal loo. One of the cellar rooms in Medina House was earmarked for conversion; and here Uffa installed an open-plan lavatory system comprising urinals and a two-seater loo, being of the opinion that the art of conversation was being lost through the selfish act of one man shutting himself away in the smallest room. Until the novelty wore off he would dash from wherever he was in the house or yard to sit down and hopefully converse when nature called.

The men humoured Uffa up to a point but were far from sold on the idea, and remained unconvinced even when Uffa entered into lengthy discourse on the subject. Uffa failed, he said, to understand why they joined one another happily at the urinals but objected to sitting down together. In an effort to boost worker participation he called early morning conferences from his seat on the throne; but although the various department heads summoned stood by, notebooks in hands, they steadfastly refused to enter wholeheartedly into the spirit of the thing. As one man remarked 'You can lead a man to the water . . .'

The plumbing revolution extended to the Medina House bathroom where Uffa's first bidet was installed. Not the common or garden simple oval basin type, beloved on the Continent and used for everything from bathing babies to bottoms, but the sophisticated model with pressurized douche.

The apprentices, acquiring via the bush telegraph news of some foreign contraption established in the upstairs bathroom, bided their time until one afternoon when, secure in the knowledge that Uffa was absent and the flat empty, they crept upstairs and into the bathroom. The mysterious object was hidden under a table, the table in turn being completely covered and obscured by a large tablecloth which extended to the floor on all sides. A vase of flowers rested on the tablecloth. Quickly removing the flowers, tablecloth and table, the naked and forbidden object was revealed to their fascinated gaze. Larking around, as apprentices will, they turned the taps on full, and leaped hurriedly backwards as a gush of water shot up like a rocket, spread itself over the ceiling into a corpulent mushroom, cascaded and showered not only themselves but the whole of the bathroom.

Hurriedly mopping-up and tidying the scene of the crime, the apprentices sped guiltily back to their workbenches and passed an anxious time fearful lest their misdeeds were discovered until, over-hearing Uffa comment later that the bathroom ceiling had sprung a leak, they realized joyfully that their transgression remained hidden. Many years after, when Uffa was more open and waxing forth on the subjects of bidets, and the apprentices were grown men, one of them related the story to Uffa who laughed loudly and long.

In the days to come Uffa was to mount a one-man campaign in support of the bidet. He believed the British to be hidebound on the subject and brainwashed into thinking of them as sex objects rather than useful all-purpose basins. So repressed and ignorant were some of his fellow countrymen before foreign travel was made available to the masses that he felt compelled, when first he exposed a bidet uncovered and in all its glory, to fill it with floating ducks to soften the impact.

When not working or being kicked up the backside by Uffa, his apprentices spent many fun-filled hours marvelling at his various antics, or joining in the latest craze. There was seldom a dull moment. Uffa tamed them with his Good Boy money system. Each week they received a Good Boy payment of from two to five shillings, depending on age, which was written on the bottom of the timesheet and paid auto-matically. If Uffa caught a boy misbehaving his Good Boy money was stopped, a gargantuan loss if the boy's total weekly wage was the princely sum of twelve or fifteen shillings. Only once, when in a parti-cularly foul temper, Uffa unexpectedly cut all of the apprentices' Good Boy money to punish the misdemeanour of one boy, did they show resentment of the system. They could also sometimes augment their pay with Mud Money for working on a particularly gruesome slipway job, or Dirty Money for mucky labouring work.

There were occasional unexpected treats and excitements, such as the first year of the war when the Workhouse Pond between Cowes and Newport was frozen over, a rare occurrence in itself as the Isle of

Wight is normally blessed with clement winters. Uffa bought, begged or borrowed sufficient pairs of skates to take the boys skating, and between them they invented a new version of ice hockey. One of Uffa's first tasks after the declaration of war had been to erect a builder's type gantry over his car to save time and expense carrying timber from Newport to his new sawyer and sawing machines; and the boys who could not pile into the car for the journey to the pond clung to the gantry, like firemen on call.

The youngsters, who for the most part had never seen an ice skate before, strapped their skates on, gave themselves a push off from the bank and covered several yards, pawing the air with their hands, before landing on their *derrières* in a series of resounding thuds. Uffa, still sitting on the bank tying his skates, was so overcome at the sight that he fell over backwards with laughter where he lay, giggling and helpless for several minutes before summoning the strength to resume tying his own skates and take to the ice himself.

Observing that I had difficulty in standing, Uffa made me cling to an apprentice who was better able to keep his feet.

'Grab hold of his guts!' Uffa screamed. 'Hold on to his guts!' he kept repeating.

I had already suffered the indignity of being forced into a pair of Cherry's long bloomers to cover my scanty underwear 'for decency's sake', having – unaware that it was to be sports day – come to work in a skirt; not to mention being squeezed in the back of the car with half a dozen apprentices.

'Which are his guts?' I finally cried, pink with embarrassment at my ignorance in not knowing which part of the male anatomy constituted the guts, and Uffa went into hysterics again.

Directly the boys had found their ice legs, Uffa and Bill Waight picked up sides, and the fast and furious fun commenced. Half of the players were flat on the ground at any one given moment, while the remainder floundered on. Periodically Uffa had to stop for air as so much laughter was taking all his wind. He said he never enjoyed a game so much in all his life, especially when his unsteady-footed niece who had been placed in goal dived out full length whenever the puck was sent in her direction, not only spreading herself over the maximum area of goal, but in the process distracting the opposing team with her un-intentional burlesque, causing them to lose balance and fall. Nobody remembered who won, or which side they were on, and it did not seem to matter.

Young Bobbie Sach, Cherry's kind-hearted and amiable son, was amongst the first of the apprentices to volunteer for military service; for life at Medina House where he was permanently at Uffa's beck and call, and a threesome in a two-person situation, had not been all fair weather sailing. Bobbie's dream was to be selected for the Air Sea Rescue Branch of the Royal Air Force where he could combine the pleasure of messing around in boats with the joy and satisfaction of saving the lives of aircrew who had ditched in the sea, and it was an exciting day at Medina House when his acceptance came through; and when he came home on his first leave in RAF uniform, looking considerably less than his nineteen years, Cherry's heart nearly burst with pride.

Uffa listened intently to Bobbie's tales of airmen snatched from a watery grave, and was saddened by the ones they could not reach, those beyond the range of the Air Sea Rescue launches. He heard of the helpless frustration of the Coastal Command pilots who so often pinpointed the ditched aircrews, knowing full well that they were at the mercy of the wind and sea and that unless rescue arrived soon they would drift away and die of exposure and starvation, the rescue service unable to reach or get help to them. Uffa and Bobbie talked for hours into the night puzzling a solution. If only there could be some way of getting a boat to those aircrews, and all in peril on the sea.

The new-found comradeship between Uffa and Bobbie was shattered one dreadful day early in 1941 when Cherry received a telegram regretting that her only son was missing in action. Witnesses later confirmed that Bobbie's rescue craft had inched too far into the French coast in an endeavour to wrench a pilot from the enemy's clutches, and been shot up and captured by a German patrol boat.

Uffa was a great comfort to Cherry in those heartbreaking days before the Red Cross received news that Bobbie was safe, though wounded. Bobbie spent many weeks in hospital, and was later transferred to a prisoner of war camp in Germany where he existed for the next four years. His internment was a constant and nagging reminder to Uffa of the horrors and loss of life at sea. The family had also the additional worry of Mahala's second son, Glan Dixon, who was training for air crew and lost his life soon after D-Day.

Those remaining behind did not escape the war. Air raid warnings were an almost daily occurrence on the Isle of Wight, not necessarily because the Island was bombed every day, although it did have more than its fair share of bombs, so much as that the planes passing overhead to bomb Portsmouth, Southampton, London and places north alerted the Island Observers as they flew over. Additionally, the planes frequently jettisoned bombs on the Island, particularly when intercepted by our fighters overhead, irrespective of their officially designated target. This meant that the workmen frequented the spare cellars beneath Medina House, which had been converted into air raid shelters, for long periods of time when there was no immediate danger.

Hundreds of manhours were lost unnecessarily until Uffa sent his men and apprentices on a plane spotters' course. The successful spotters took turns in the Medina House lookout, sounding the works' klaxon directly they identified a German plane; and only if the klaxon sounded, indicating enemy planes in sight, did the men down tools and dash for the shelter. The system was so efficient that local people within earshot paid more attention to Uffa's klaxon than to the official air raid warning. The men did have the natural right to take shelter all through the official alert, which frequently lasted for hours on end, but mostly they chose to continue working until the last moment, putting their trust in their workmates who were surprisingly accurate.

Fired with a new idea, plus an urgent need to do more for his country, Uffa was one of the first to put his name down for the Local Defence Volunteer, later the Home Guard, when the call came. In his enthusiasm he not only committed himself but his entire workforce, whether they wanted to participate or not; and in many cases this presented a personal problem of some magnitude for some of the men were already air raid wardens, firemen or Red Cross workers in their own town or village.

The day after breaking the news to the men that they were to be enrolled, Uffa was approached by one of the painters wanting to know if he would be expected to kill Germans should they arrive. When Uffa promised him a medal if he killed ten, the man replied that he couldn't possibly kill as he was a Christian.

'What the hell do you think I am?' exploded the indignant Uffa. 'A bloody heathen?'

Eliciting the information that the man was a conscientious objector, Uffa sacked him on the spot and said he never wanted to see his face in the yard again.

The following day another man reported to Uffa, pleading that he had other voluntary commitments and could not join. He too was sent packing, but he refused to go quietly and wrote to the House of Commons complaining. In due course Uffa found himself the recipient of a letter informing him that he was much too vigorous and drastic, and that he must reconsider his ways and reinstate the man. Much to Uffa's annoyance, a similar letter was sent to the local Home Guard Commander at Billingham Manor.

Uffa did not relish official pressure of any kind as he needed Government contracts to survive, his major worry at all times being to keep the workforce going and pay the wages. During the early days of the war he quoted for almost anything that would ensure him a place on the approved list of contractors for direct Government work, his first contract being for hundreds of pairs of oars – rather a waste of the skills at his disposal but an effective means to an end, for the oar contract was followed progressively by more rewarding and interesting contracts. Uffa did not bother to answer the House of Commons letter, and to his relief nothing further was heard on the subject, the workman in question meantime having obtained employment elsewhere.

Uffa was a great romancer. One of his tales was that, when recruiting for the Home Guard, he confronted the men with two piles of pay packets, one containing a week's pay and the other a fortnight's. A pile of enlistment forms was alongside.

'Sign this and pick up a week's pay. Refuse, and get double pay and the sack,' he claimed to have said.

But it was just one of his stories for nobody working in the office ever filled the pay packets twice, it being considered miracle enough in itself when there was sufficient money in the bank to fill them once.

Uffa named his unit the 'Uffashots', and their function was to protect Medina Yard. He also hedged his bets by volunteering to cover the Duke of York pub, the local grocer's shop and the police station. They seldom drilled, and had a rag, tag and bobtail appearance that made *Dad's Army* (the television series based on the Home Guard) look like a crack Guards' regiment; but, when other units were battling with spades and pitchforks, the Uffashots had guns and each man had fired five rounds on the practice range.

Uffa also, in the early days of the war, got his hands on the machine gun from a German plane and charged around with it mounted on the gantry over his car until apprehended by the police. Medina House and Yard were sited opposite the police station in Birmingham Road and the police, who derived as much enjoyment from Uffa as anyone else, closed their eyes to his almost daily infringements; but when, as on this occasion, complaints were received from members of the general public who feared for their safety, they were forced to take action.

At first Uffa was proud and delighted with his rank of lieutenant, particularly as he had been without a commission during the first war; but later, when certain local tradesmen who ran their units according to the book were promoted over him, he complained bitterly. He wrote long letters to a vast assortment of people including, rather inconsequently, one of the Sea Lords, laying out numerous irrelevant reasons why he should be promoted to Captain or Major.

The Uffashots were also official firewatchers, which came under another department. Technically, if a man belonged to one, he was excluded from the other; so Uffa's men were never in the wrong as, whichever duty they were accused of failing in, they claimed to belong to the other.

There was a different guard on duty at Medina Yard each night of the week and the general routine, except for one non-drinking night, was to spend two hours working overtime and then adjourn to the Duke of York public house across the road until throwing out time. Certain nights were especially notorious for their heavy drinking sessions. On one such night the siren sounded from the police station opposite for the guard to turn out, but the men were in a drunken stupor and heard nothing.

Next day the Firewatching Chief called and censured Uffa, claiming that he had attempted to enter the Yard during the raid to call out the firewatchers, but everything was locked and silent and he could make no entry; furthermore there could have been serious consequences had an incendiary bomb fallen on the building. Uffa's reply was, 'You could have broken a window, couldn't you?' From then onwards the authorities did not rely too heavily on firefighting support from the Uffashots, despite some nights' guards being more serious and efficient than others.

Uffa participated in almost all of the drinking sessions. He was at this period of time like a man who had lost his way, and only appeared completely happy when drinking heavily. The alcohol fattened him out, the once lithe figure of which he had been so proud turned to stomach, and the workmen learned to be wary of him until mid-morning when the hangover normally wore off.

Typical of Uffa's early morning condition was the day the conscientious Marian, who subsequently married Peter Dixon, arrived for work and stood outside the office waiting for Charles to open up.

'Why don't you go on in?' queried the bleary-eyed Uffa, suddenly appearing behind her.

'I am waiting for Charles to arrive with the key.'

'I'll bloody soon get you in,' growled Uffa, and with one mighty kick burst the door open.

Some of Uffa's orgies were wilder than others, and frequently after the pub closed they would continue drinking in Medina House until the early hours of the morning. On one occasion, when very much the worse for drink, a sword fight took place. By the grace of God there were no casualties, but next morning a sword was found impaled in the floor of Uffa's office with the point and several inches of blade protruding through the ceiling into the storeroom below.

One night, when falling up Medina House stairs, Uffa's false teeth dropped into Cherry's cat's sand tray as he vomited. He inserted them straight back into his mouth, which revolted even the hardiest of his drinking companions. What Uffa failed, or did not wish, to appreciate was that each guard did duty only once a week and had six days in which to recover, whereas he was participating almost every night.

Many German planes were shot down over the Isle of Wight, and of all the parts recovered from the planes the cannons and machine guns caused the biggest headache for, although they had armourers down from Woolwich, they failed to make them operational. Uffa persuaded the Brigadier in charge of the Home Guard to let him take one of the machine guns and some ammunition to his works for Bob Dickerson and his nephew Glan Dixon, who had a way with guns, to work on.

The plan was to simplify the gun and make it operate on the Lewis gun principle by eliminating the compressed air and electrical control used in the German planes which operated on a twenty-four-volt battery; so they stripped it down, put in a small clip of ammunition, and experienced no difficulty getting the gun to fire a short burst. According to Uffa the armourers from Woolwich, who had tried weakening springs and various other methods in an attempt to make the guns fire electrically as they had done on the German planes, were quite astonished at the success of his direct and simple approach to the problem.

On the strength of his victory with guns Uffa was allowed to be one of the first on the scene whenever a plane was shot down, a privilege he revelled in like a small boy. He also managed to talk the Brigadier into a system whereby all the cannons and machine guns salvaged on the Island were handed over to Uffa for conversion, and additionally that his Home Guard unit should keep half of the spoils. Before long he had in his possession some dozen cannons and machine guns and thousands of rounds of ammunition, with which he determined the Uffashots would defend Medina Yard to the last drop of blood.

From time to time there were combined Army and Home Guard manoeuvres, which mostly took the form of the Army attacking the Home Guard units. Before any manoeuvre took place Uffa would invite the umpire to meet him in Medina Yard and show off his armament; and, because of his superior fire power and the fact that the Uffashots' sole task was to defend the Yard complex so they never moved, they invariably defeated the Army units.

One day, fed up with Uffa's cock-a-hoop attitude, the umpire decided to bring in the Army for some infighting, but Uffa was prepared and mobilized his forces accordingly. His defences were thrown around the grocer's shop, the Duke of York (he had taken the precaution of making the licensee, Harry Wingham, a sergeant in the Uffashots and referred to the manœuvres as 'The Battle for the Duke') and the police station. Inside the police station were dozens of policemen, but they were only supposed to fight if attacked by the Germans.

Uffa's men stood on the roofs dropping offcuts and small blocks of wood to represent hand grenades and, while the Army dodged the grenades, the police unexpectedly swooped out of the station like a swarm of bees and pounced. Soon there was not an Army man left with a weapon on him, for the Army had marched and fought its way from Brading, some twelve miles distant, and was in no fit state to withstand Uffa's unorthodox secret weapons of wood blocks and policemen.

When it was all over, Uffa, hands behind his back, walked over to the

Brigadier, who was observing the mêlée from the road. He raised his eyes heavenwards and, as the Brigadier followed his upward gaze, Uffa whipped out a brace of pheasants from behind his back and presented them to the Brigadier.

'Shot them down during the fighting, sir,' he said with a wicked grin. 'So you can take them home with a clear conscience.'

Some time later, after the Uffashots had been issued with standard Home Guard rifles, the Top Brass withdrew all of the cannons and machine guns, except one which Uffa did not let on about, and with them a little of the spice from his life.

[12]

Uffa's personal life was becoming happier and more settled, for Alma had divorced him smoothly and cleanly without damage to Cherry or his pocket book, leaving him free to marry the woman he loved. A quiet Island wedding was arranged with his friend of many years' standing, Sir Peter Scott, performing the duties of best man.

There was no time for Uffa and Cherry to take a honeymoon. Uffa, in addition to his everyday task of running the yard, was experimenting with a notion that had tormented his brain since the capture of his newly acquired stepson, Bobbie Sach; that of rendering a navigable craft to those men unfortunate enough to find themselves drifting helplessly over the seas and oceans of the world in small round inflated rubber dinghies. His early war contracts had ranged from pontoons and folding canvas and plywood boats, to paddles and experimental protective covering and sails for rubber dinghies, and the machinations of his mind reflected the scene within which he worked.

Uffa's first idea was to build a folding boat that could be carried and dropped over the side of a low flying aircraft to the men below, but he abandoned this thought immediately as impracticable for the impact on hitting the water would smash it to a thousand pieces. His next vision was to drop a folding boat to the men by using a parachute, but how?

The concept of a self-opening folding boat, carried in the bomb bay of an aircraft, came to Uffa at one of his daily office tea parties round the big dining table at Medina House, and he made his first model with thick drawing paper and strawberry jam.

Directly Uffa had finished tea that day, he bounded up the stairs to the drawing office to talk his invention through with Bill Waight. His parachuted airborne lifeboat would be of plywood, folded into a small compass, and be unfolded by the parachutes themselves as they lowered it into the water. Hopefully, when it reached the sea it would be a complete boat which the airmen could row, sail or even motor until they reached help or a home port. The plywood bottom would shield them from the penetrating damp cold of the sea, and the airmen would not lose their legs as had happened in so many cases of exposure.

While Bill Waight set about preparing working drawings Uffa

alerted the boatbuilders and fitters to stand by to construct a mock-up wooden boat to scale. They also designed miniature parachutes and, after several experiments and by the time midnight approached, Uffa was ready to throw the final completed model from an upstairs window to the men waiting anxiously in the street below.

With bated breath they watched as the parachutes gradually unfolded the boat before allowing it to drop gently into the outstretched arms; while drinkers, who had been lately inbibing in the Duke of York, passed anxious hands over their eyes and momentarily contemplated signing the pledge. Little did they dream that from such a small beginning they might, some quarter of a century later, observe a non-sinkable capsule floating earthwards containing men returning from the moon.

'Can't think why you're buggering about with boats that fold,' called Bob Dickerson from the fitting shop. 'What you want to build is an ordinary lifeboat and carry it under the plane like a torpedo.'

Uffa was silent and thoughtful. Yes, he could see his folding boat becoming obsolete before even it had taken to the water.

Just before closing time Uffa had made his way to the Duke of York to wet his whistle. Young Ashley Wingham, who had been left temporarily in charge of the pub by his father, cast anxious eyes at Uffa's slate. Uffa rarely had cash to support the largesse he so frequently and generously scattered, and behind the bar door was a special board where his mounting debt was recorded daily. Uffa was far in excess of the limit normally imposed by Mr Wingham, and Ashley knew that his father was steeling himself to 'have a word with Uffa' directly he could pin him down alone.

After savouring a couple of quick drinks Uffa manœuvred Ashley to one side.

'You know that money-box your father keeps under his bed so that he can grab it quickly when the siren goes at night . . .' he began, and went on to extol the virtues of his new invention to the starry-eyed teenager before him.

By the time Uffa had triumphantly regaled him with the events of the evening, all by way of an overture leading up to a petition for ten pounds out of the box to go to London, Ashley was his slave and momentarily blinded to all thought of his father's impending wrath.

The two conspirators mounted the stairs to the master bedroom and stealthily withdrew the money-box from its hiding place beneath the wide expanse of the large double bed. Uffa's dark eyes glittered when they beheld the box's bulging contents.

'Better make it twenty,' he said, hastily stuffing the notes into his trouser pocket before Ashley could raise an objection.

Then, merrily chanting a little ditty he descended to the bar where, light-hearted and expansive of mood, he ordered another round of drinks 'on the slate' before returning to his brainchild.

They held several trial drops of the model and next morning, after only four hours' sleep, Uffa boarded the first steamer from the Isle of Wight *en route* to London where he hoped to find Lord Brabazon, then Colonel Brabazon, Minister of Aircraft Production. Lord Brabazon was a first-class pilot, sailing man and Cresta Run champion and, even more important, he and Uffa had known one another for nearly twenty years. When Uffa arrived at the Air Ministry he refused to be fobbed off by underlings, insisting that a message be sent all the way through to the great man himself; and, to the astonishment of the staff, Lord Brabazon instructed that Uffa Fox be shown up immediately.

Uffa brandished the model and recounted his thoughts to Lord Brabazon, who was already more than concerned at the shortage and daily toll of pilots, and the time and resources required to train them.

'Shall I throw it out of the window so you can see it work?' queried the zealous Uffa.

Lord Brabazon surveyed the busy London street below. 'No need to waste time,' he replied hastily. 'If it worked at Cowes it will work here. You have my approval and a completely free hand for, as you say, you may wish to change the whole conception of the boat itself.'

While in no way regretting his decision, for he was a man of action and would have practically sold his own soul to save the life of just one pilot, Lord Brabazon was soon to find himself on the carpet for allowing himself to be persuaded into a premature decision by Uffa's enthusiasm.

He was in trouble, not only with his advisers for not referring the plan for top level discussion, but also with the bureaucrats for authorizing work to be carried out before the issue of an official contract number. From all accounts the prompt arrival of a bill from Uffa Fox Limited against a non-existent contract completely threw the system.

Following his successful interview with Lord Brabazon, the agreed plan was to use the airborne lifeboat in conjunction with the American-designed Hudson aircraft already in use for air-sea rescue work; and Uffa returned to Cowes with, in addition to the verbal permission to proceed with the designing and building of a prototype, nominal authority to visit the Fleet Air Arm base at Thorney Island to measure up a Hudson.

On the morrow he and Bill Waight crossed to the mainland by the first steamer and, without a pass or written permission Uffa talked their way into the Thorney Island base only to find, on examination, that the jacks controlling the bomb doors of the Hudson took up so much space inside that all thought of a boat being stored in the bomb bay had to be abandoned.

Uffa recalled that before the war he had built an eighteen-foot jolly boat, *Wizard*, for an Air Commodore Burling, who was in charge of the flying boats at RAF Mountbatten, Plymouth. *Wizard* had been designed to fit under the wing of one of these large machines so that Air Commodore Burling could commute with her between RAF Mountbatten and his home in the Scilly Islands. Uffa, bearing in mind Bob Dickerson's suggestion, instructed Bill to take the lines from the outside of the fuselage.

He decided there and then that the boat should be designed to fit on the outside of the Hudson and streamlined so as not to interfere with the aeroplane's flying performance. Then home they dashed to commence the design and development of the first parachuted airborne lifeboat, to be suspended by one single bomb hook from the American Hudson, and attached to it like a torpedo.

Uffa went straight to work with his draughtsmen, borrowing extra ones as necessary from John Samuel White Limited (some of whom were on loan for three weeks and stayed for four years), and by midnight the same day he had designed the lines.

During his unsettled days after the 1914 war Uffa had been employed for short periods of time as a boatbuilder with two firms specializing in lifeboat construction, Groves and Gutteridge Limited and John Samuel White. The experience stood him in good stead, and enabled him with very little effort to design an unsinkable twenty-three-foot boat able to weather a gale at sea and to be driven easily through the water. The boat had to offer the minimum resistance to the aeroplane's flight, so he had also to calculate the weights and work out her displacement.

The lines were designed one and a half inches to the foot, or one-eighth of full size. During the night two of the draughtsmen faired them up, taking several prints from the plan so that, when other draughtsmen arrived for their day's work, they could continue on further constructional drawings. Meantime boatbuilders were rigging up their scrieve board ready to mark out the full-size sections so that they could make the moulds on the board.

In the early hours of the morning, when they had arrived at the final lines and displacement and the main constructional details of the hull, Uffa and one of the draughtsmen went down the flight of steps from the drawing office to the upper boatshop. The draughtsman called out the measurements of each offset and Uffa marked them out on the scrieve board which was already set in place with the waterlines, buttocks and diagonals marked in.

Next, battens were bent round and, immediately the full-size sections were drawn in on the scrieve board at the various stations on which the moulds were to be made, two boatbuilders started to make the full-size moulds; and, while all this was going on, other boatbuilders had set up the saddle alongside. After levelling fore and aft and sideways and planing true with a long trying plane, the centreline was drawn down with a chalk line, and the blocks screwed on to take the cross pole of each mould in its exact place; so that, as each mould was made and lifted off the scrieve board, it was set up in its true position.

The boatbuilders set them up level and plumb on the saddle so that, by noon on the day following their visit to Thorney Island, all the moulds were in place, horned off, plumbed, squared and levelled, and true in all directions. Uffa and his men had never before worked so fast, for all were conscious that the lives of precious and gallant airmen could rest in their hands. Theirs was the joyous weariness derived from expending oneself in the interest of others.

Down below the sawyers were cutting out the keel, bevelling and cutting in most of the rebates, and shaping the stem and stern post as far as they were able, so as to leave the minimum of hand work for the boatbuilders. After these three were fitted, set in place and fastened off, the ribbands were admitted into the moulds to take the timbers.

Uffa's version of a steam kiln was rigged up by the labourers; a long rectangular water tank with a row of gas burners beneath, for Uffa never steamed his timbers. He boiled them.

He divided his best men into days and nights for this momentous project, and the boat progressed. Timbers were bent, inner and outer diagonal planks fitted, fore and aft planking secured. Uffa moved a bed into his office, just through the door in Medina House and within easy distance of the boatbuilders working on the first floor. Day or night, whenever the workmen had a problem, he was on hand to iron it out; while a duty draughtsman slept on *Britannia*'s bunk in the drawing office on immediate call should he be required to draw up any difficult part for the tireless boatbuilders.

Uffa wrote that the three hectic weeks taken to complete the first airborne lifeboat were the most fruitful and exciting of his life.

Immediately the hull was completed they removed it from the moulds and spanned it so that it would not lose its shape. Then, after quickly cleaning it off and slapping a coat of varnish inside and two coats of grey paint outside, they secured it upside-down on the top of Uffa's car.

The following morning, accompanied by Bill Waight and a team of boatbuilders, Uffa set off with his car and the airborne lifeboat on the first steamer for Southampton *en route* to Cunliffe Owens at Eastleigh Airport. Cunliffe Owens were responsible for collecting the Hudson aircraft from Southampton Docks as they arrived in England from America, and briefed to assemble and put the completed aircraft through flying trials before handing them over for active service with the Royal Air Force.

At half past nine that morning they were offering the first airborne lifeboat up on the underside of a Hudson, and fitting it so snug that no air could penetrate and build up pressures between boat and plane which might force the boat off the fuselage. Quite a crowd gathered and Uffa was in his element. When all was ready, Uffa searched out the test pilot and asked his opinion.

'Not much,' was the terse reply after 'Bebs' had studied the Hudson and its appendage from all angles.

Uffa began to argue and explain, and when he had a valid point to put over few remained unconvinced. Uffa then took him to another Hudson alongside. They opened the bomb doors fully, and the test pilot checked them from all angles. Suddenly his eyes twinkled.

'I'll fly it if you have the courage of your convictions and come up with me on flight tests to make the notes and recordings that will be required.'

Uffa, brimful of confidence, was more than happy to accept.

Returning home to Cowes, Uffa made a full-scale wooden model of the lifeboat, loading it with the weight it would carry when fully laden. When complete, he flew with 'Bebs' in the Hudson with the wooden replica suspended below through all the various flying trials while, at Cowes, the original prototype was being completed.

By this time written authority to proceed had filtered through, and the Royal Aircraft Establishment at Farnborough alerted, so Uffa had all the technical help he needed at his disposal, plus the parachute problem taken out of his hands. Representatives of all the services converged excitedly at Cowes, and Medina Yard became a bustling and thriving centre of activity. Men worked day and night fitting in the watertight compartments, wooden daggerboards, watertight bulkheads and self-baling slots from the deck through the bottom, retractable rudder, self-righting air chambers, bomb hook, towing bar and sling-plates. Uffa never had more than three or four hours' sleep in any twenty-four, but the job satisfaction was infinite and made it all worth while.

The final flight tests with the wooden model and Hudson aircraft were the stalling trials. Uffa and the test pilot climbed to a great height before 'Bebs' cut the engine back and back until, at sixty knots, the aircraft stalled and started to spin down out of the sky. When the machine was back under control they flew level again, and then up to an even greater height. This time 'Bebs' put the flaps right down, cutting the engine back until finally, at forty-five knots, they stalled and started spinning earthwards. On this occasion they dropped for twice the time and distance, as forty-five knots is an extremely low stalling speed for an aeroplane.

Uffa nearly lost his all as the fields and trees rushed towards them, and he breathed a sigh of relief when 'Bebs' finally regained control and they levelled out. They were in their seventh heaven of delight that this final flying trial had proved as successful as all of the previous ones.

The next stage was to put the parachutes on the original prototype and drop her. The first trial was undertaken on land at RAF Netheravon near Salisbury. Uffa was overjoyed with the result, finding the parachute dropping flight particularly rewarding as the RAF photographers were operating from an identical Hudson that was obviously less heavily laden, and their craft was considerably slower than Uffa's machine with the airborne lifeboat suspended below, proving how little the streamlined boat affected the plane's flight.

They put the boat through every conceivable trial; sailing, rowing, capsizing, swamp tests, self-righting and, when all were successful, they cast around for a suitable engine. The choice of an engine was not easy, the main propulsion units eventually installed in all the early lifeboats delivered to the Services being the Britannia Middy engines, which consisted of twin cylinder power heads similar to those of the Britannia outboard motor. The conventional type of inboard motor was unsuitable for a number of reasons, and led to the suggestion that the engines be placed side by side, in view of their low power and compactness, in a forward position of the hull. This also helped the weight distribution during the drop.

The Middy was designed to operate as an inboard motor but with a vertical shaft drive, through bevel gears to the propeller, the complete drive unit being fitted immediately below the bottom of the boat. With this plant it was possible to install the power head under deck level, while the propeller gear housings, although protruding below the bottom of the boat, would still give ground clearance to the carrying aircraft. A loaded speed of six knots was stipulated, and a range of twelve hours required from a maximum of twelve gallons of fuel.

Unfortunately the Middy was no longer in production, but the manufacturers, the British Motor Boat Manufacturing Company, agreed to convert and recondition a pair of second-hand engines for tests. The combination of boat and engine proved so successful that, bearing in mind the urgency and the delay before new engines could be produced, the manufacturers were requested, by every means in their power, to secure second-hand units for reconditioning and converting.

Various municipalities, who had been operating fleets of small pleasure craft in their boating lakes, were approached, and a number of used Britannia engines obtained. These valiant little engines, cast aside by the exigencies of war and no longer responding to the peacetime call of 'Come in number twelve, your time is up', were destined to find themselves chugging gaily along, homeward bound, offering new hope to men whose time but for them might well also have been up.

The air borne lifeboat would be required at times to undertake quite long journeys; and to test the endurance of the engines and hull, as well as fuel consumption, a special endurance sea trial was arranged. The two engines were started at six-fifteen a.m. and run non-stop until early evening. By the end of the run it was estimated that when crossing the measured mile well over six knots were possible, even when loaded to the proposed full carrying capacity. Success was thus ensured.

After experiencing the Hudson's stalling trials, Uffa was less keen to take to the air and so, when it came to the first combined air and sea trials in the Solent, he chose to play his part in his natural habitat, the sea, sending Bill Waight up as an observer. There was an air raid in progress at the appointed time of the trials and, between watching for an aerial view of his house at East Cowes and the belief, on hearing a crackle, that they had been hit by gunfire from an enemy plane, the airborne lifeboat slipped away so effortlessly that she was half-way towards the awaiting Uffa and his men below, before Bill even realized that she had been released.

Uffa meantime was cast adrift in a round rubber dinghy in the middle of the Solent, tensed up and watching for the Hudson to appear. She was due to drop the airborne lifeboat from 600 feet at a flying speed of 110 miles per hour. He issued instructions that, should the lifeboat with its laden weight of nearly a ton show signs of hitting the dinghy, all were to dive overboard. The task of the airmen above was to aim the lifeboat directly at the dinghy and, as with any new invention, nobody could be sure exactly what would happen.

At the appointed hour the Hudson flew in overhead, dropping its smoke float frighteningly close. The function of the smoke float was to pinpoint the target position and indicate the true wind direction and speed to the pilot. He then circled and, flying into the wind, dropped his precious cargo.

The pilot parachute, attached to the fuselage of the plane, was wrenched open with sufficient force to lift the other parachutes off the deck of the airborne lifeboat, and these in turn opened up and lowered the boat at its planned thirty-degree nose-down angle towards the victims. To those waiting anxiously below her fall seemed slow at first, but as she drew near she gathered speed and, although she appeared to be heading straight for the dinghy, the men sat tight and held their breath until, with a mighty splash, she soaked them.

An explosion blew the parachutes away and two rockets fired out floating life lines. The excited men grabbed the nearest line, pulled themselves aboard, and hauled in the drogue and other life lines.

Within seconds they had the engines going, the mast up and the sails set and were enjoying a celebration cruise round Cowes harbour,

110

which had been denuded of sailing craft since the outbreak of war. Savouring the salt on his lips and the fresh tingle of wind on his face, Uffa's heart sang as he sailed the beloved Solent in his brainchild, the world's first parachuted airborne lifeboat.

[13]

The blitz of Cowes on the night of 4–5 May 1942 was one of the most vicious and highly concentrated attacks of the war. The first wave of German planes dropped incendiary and high explosive bombs and then, without giving the town time to mourn its dead, a second wave of bombers flew in spewing its lethal cargo of high explosives. The death toll was so great that the victims were buried in communal graves, and the number of injured was incalculable.

During the first of the raids an incendiary bomb landed on Medina House. The Home Guard and Firewatchers worked bravely to put out the flames and, through their gallant efforts, the fire was contained before it had time to spread and engulf the adjoining Medina Yard, although some damage was sustained.

In the mêlée Uffa suffered the misfortune of breathing in grains of sand and dust from a bomb that exploded near the water's edge, and retired choking to the police station. Thereafter, despite X-rays to the contrary, he was convinced that gravel had lacerated his bronchial tubes. The story grew like a fisherman's tale with the passage of time until, in his advancing years, he could be heard boasting of the large stones still embedded in his chest from the night he was bombed. He was in truth plagued with bronchitis as he grew older, a weakness he inherited from his mother. He also spent long periods drinking in smoke-filled bars, and the condition was aggravated by what he termed 'brewer's asthma'.

Medina House was temporarily uninhabitable, though not nearly the shambles it appeared at first glance. The indefatigable Uffa soon had the men sweeping up plaster and broken glass, and within days a canvas was placed over the roof and it was 'business as usual' on the lower floors. Uffa was later able to negotiate the purchase of the fire-damaged Westbourne Hotel, which adjoined Medina House, for a fairly nominal sum, erecting a corrugated iron roof over the bomb-scarred timbers. He proceeded to knock holes at strategic positions, as he had done between Medina House and the Yard, to link up once again the two halves of what had been Dr Arnold of Rugby's birthplace, Birmingham Hall.

1. Uffa with Mahala and Dorothea.

2. Uffa and Mahala during the First World War.

3. Uffa as a choirboy.

4. The Cowes Sea Scouts board *Typhoon* before her departure.

5. An old floating bridge at Cowes, similar to Uffa's.

6. Alma, late 1920s.

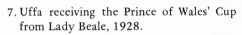
7. Uffa receiving the Prince of Wales' Cup from Lady Beale, 1928.

8. Uffa at the tiller of his schooner *Black Rose,* 1931.

Uffa winning the final race
for the International Canoe
Trophy, 1933.

10. Uffa and Bill Waight in
Brynhild, 20-foot, double-
handed, sliding-seat canoe,
1936.

11. Uffa enjoying himself in the land of schnapps, 1937.

12. Uffa outside Medina Yard, ready to ship the two Flying Fifteens to the mainland.

13. Uffa and Cherry's wedding (with Peter Scott).

14. Uffa commandeering the phone at Medina House.

15. *'Dad's Army'* Uffa during the last war, with Sergeant Joe Morey.

16. Uffa riding Frantic away from Puckaster (Jack the butler looking on).

17. One of Uffa's parachuted airborne lifeboats.

18. The 8-year-old Prince Charles receives sailing tuition aboard *Bluebottle* from Prince Philip and Uffa during a regatta at Cowes.

19. Uffa with Prince Phil
    Coweslip.

20. Uffa and Prince Philip
    submerged in *Coweslip.*

21. *Coweslip* being launched down the Solway slipway, Uffa aboard and Yvonne holding a bouquet.

22. Uffa and Prince Charles sailing.

23. Uffa hinting to Prince Charles that he was late arriving. (Josephine is on the left).

24. From the *Daily Express*, 1 February 1962.

"The Duke says will it be all right if he borrows it next Thursday?"

25.Uffa greeting visitors to the Commodore's House.

26. Uffa presiding at tea with family and friends. (His younger sister Elfrida is in front, facing the camera; his elder sister Mahala is immediately in front of the window.)

27. Uffa Fox trying out *Britannia*.

28. *Britannia* demonstratin[g] self-righting ability, b[ut] John Fairfax rowed her [across] the Atlantic.

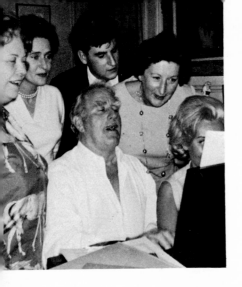

29. Uffa at the piano with Monique Barbier, a concert pianist. *Standing, left to right:* Yvonne, Christine (her daughter), Peter Terry and Josephine.

Uffa and friends playing cricket on the Brambles sandbank.

31. Uffa the artist, in the Commodore's House look-out.

32. Uffa on Tennyson Down.

Most of Uffa's clothes were destroyed in the fire and, at noon on the day following the blitz, he could be seen organizing his men still dressed in red slippers and odds and ends of clothing hastily thrown over his pyjamas, for he had to completely rearrange the men's work schedules.

Uffa thought of the raw materials arriving at the entrance door of his yard as the thin end of a wedge, and the finished product as the thick end. Fearing another raid, he decided to close temporarily the thin end of the wedge and, by concentrating on half completed and nearly completed work, get as many units as possible away from his yard and the danger area of Cowes. This thinking also gave a more immediate boost to his cash flow problem which was a never-ending worry, particularly since his book royalties had dried up and he was contemplating the purchase of yet another property, but this time in the relatively peaceful security of the back of the Wight.

By lunchtime on the day after the heinous raid the men were reorganized and working productively, and Uffa had for the first time a free moment to consider his own personal comfort. Mostly he was in need of a hot bath and, with local Cowes services destroyed and no gas or water, he made his way to Newport at the invitation of his friend, Joe Mew, who lived in an old house alongside his family's brewery where there was a constant supply of hot water from the brewery itself.

Uffa found the roads out of Cowes barred time and time again by bomb craters and unexploded bombs, and the streets were crowded with people trekking from Cowes in the direction of Newport and other parts of the Island in search of food, water or shelter. He collected so many people *en route* that he was like the Pied Piper, with refugees not only inside the car and outside clinging to the gantry, but draped over the bonnet as well. With so many people on the front of the car he could hardly see out, and his slow progress was guided by the many passengers.

Prior to joining Joe Mew at his house in Newport, Uffa visited one of his favourite pubs, the Wheatsheaf, still clad in pyjamas, slippers and other motley garments, where he was able to unwind over a few drinks and a hearty meal. Then on to the brewery for the promised bath, but he and Joe yarned for so long that there was no time for the eargerly awaited soaking before Uffa was forced to return to see what was happening at his works at Cowes, still in 'bombed out' gear but lighter of heart.

His arrival at Medina Yard was greeted with the news that Mahala and her family had been made homeless by the discovery of an unexploded bomb nearby. Quickly organizing a temporary billet for them with Bill Ablitt and his wife, he bundled them into the car and off to Calbourne, where the children were to sleep in rows on the floor with the Wingham children from the Duke of York, before finally driving back to Cowes and his own personal disaster.

At nightfall Uffa wearily retraced his steps to the Mews' house where, in addition to the long awaited bath, he was offered the hospitality of their home until he could find suitable alternative accommodation. Lennie, another member of the Mew family, kitted Uffa out with a suit of clothes, so they were really friends in need.

A few days later Uffa and Cherry moved into the Blackgang Hotel at the back of the Wight, and when hotel life proved too expensive Uffa had the brilliant idea of utilizing the dogs' hut from Twenty Acres. He had it taken down and re-erected on a clifftop site between Blackgang and Chale where, cleaned-up and slightly extended, it became their home. Sadly, with the gradual erosion of the cliffs at Chale the hut, along with several other cottages, has since been claimed by the sea and is no more.

Uffa frequently remarked that nothing would give him greater pain than to look down from heaven and behold an unspent five-pound note languishing in his bank, and he lived his life permanently guarding against such an eventuality. The local tradesmen ran a bush telegraph system whereby, should one of them receive wind of a new contract, a sizeable cheque or any other clue that Uffa might be in funds, he would immediately render a statement of account and alert his friends to do likewise. One such clue was if Uffa walked into the barber's shop and said 'I'll pay for everybody if I can have mine cut first.'

Uffa had an assortment of methods of dealing with those desperate enough to call in person demanding payment for goods or services rendered. By far his most successful ploy was to say, 'You're always kind and helpful so I'll tell you what we do. As soon as a cheque comes in we put some of the worthier names in the hat. The first half dozen to come out we pay if they're small, or give something on account if they're big; but if anyone's rude to me their name doesn't go into the hat at all. Now, as you're so kind, I can promise you that your name will definitely go into next month's hat.'

Should the creditor demur, Uffa would turn on him sharply and say, 'If you're not careful your name won't go anywhere near the bloody hat.'

Sometimes the creditors would leave laughing; and, still chuckling, go down and regale Charles with the story. 'But we'll have to have the money,' they would add.

On other occasions, when representatives called seeking orders and the cupboard was bare, Uffa would send out the message, 'Tell them we have no more vacancies on our list of creditors.'

Or should a representative, unfamiliar with the boss's appearance, call and buttonhole Uffa, who, with his shoes tied up with string instead of shoelaces often gave the appearance of being the untidiest and most impecunious of the workforce, demanding to see Mr Fox, Uffa would introduce the embarassed Charles as Mr Fox and disappear. When one such representative subsequently announced that Charles did in fact resemble Uffa, Charles began to wonder, with his impish sense of humour, if Uffa's employees, like dogs, grew to resemble their masters.

Thursday was the most traumatic day of the week for Uffa and the office staff as it was pay day, and one seldom knew from one week to the next where the wages would come from, or indeed if they could be generated at all. The indigenous Islander is the soul of honesty, so there was nothing unusual in the youngest junior being despatched optimistically with attaché case and cheque to collect the wages. Her only fear was not of mugging but of humiliation, for it was not uncommon, on presenting the cheque, for the bank manager to manifest himself, tut-tutting and nodding his head from side to side. He would then disappear into the nether regions and telephone Uffa to confirm that the cheque could not possibly be honoured, while the unfortunate girl, whose instruction was not to leave the bank under any circumstances, hung around in hopeful suspense. Uffa meantime inveigled the manager into increasing his already substantial overdraft, or raised the wind elsewhere. When Uffa's first bank could shoulder his finances no longer Uffa threatened to sell his overdraft to another bank, which offer was readily accepted.

The new bank manager bent over backwards to help Uffa, but there were limits even to his generosity. Uffa would write flowery screeds to the bank explaining in glowing terms the excellence of his financial situation and proving that, although he did appear on paper to owe the bank a great deal of money, they would be quite erroneous in believing this to be the true situation. Some of the letters had to be forwarded to Head Office, and the long-suffering bank manager would receive communications back couched in somewhat unflattering terms, such as 'We thought you would have more sense than to be taken in by all this.'

When, in desperation, the bank manager called in person the whole office trembled. Uffa, unabashed, would turn up the heating until his somewhat corpulent opponent was reduced to such a weak and sweating state that, mopping his brow, he would gasp, 'All right, just one more week.'

If Uffa had nine lives with his bank manager he had ten lives with the police who, bearing in mind the importance of his work during the war, turned a blind eye to minor infringements unless their attention were specifically drawn to his misconduct by an official body or member of the general public. One such occurrence involved petrol coupons. With the arrival of petrol rationing Uffa applied for a special allowance, listing War Department contracts, and claiming innumerable miles which must surely have put a big question mark in the mind of any recipient at the Ministry with the remotest knowledge of distances on the Isle of Wight. Uffa's theory was that the Ministry would undoubtedly cut him back, so it was necessary to at least quadruple his basic requirement to allow for the contingency. Uffa's accompanying letter however was so brilliant that there was no cut back at all, and even he gasped when the first wad of coupons fell from the envelope.

Consequently Uffa had unlimited mileage throughout the war, which he generally put to good use, picking up pedestrians whenever they were in need and seldom driving with an empty car. He would also go out of his way to perform small acts of kindness. Stopping his car, for example, at Whippingham school during air raids and calling down the shelter, 'Everyone all right down there?' Miss Moody, the headmistress, said afterwards that the children used to listen for and be heartened by his appearances.

Uffa also used the car for social purposes and this, not unnaturally, created jealousy amongst those car owners who were less fortunate, one of whom complained to the police that Uffa was using his special petrol for joyriding, thereby forcing the Inspector of Police to interrogate him on the subject. Smarting from his interview at the police station, Uffa, who had been running a works canteen in the basement of the Westbourne Hotel with staff he had inherited with the property, walked into the canteen and, observing two policemen who used the canteen by arrangement, eating their lunch, furiously announced the immediate shut-down of the canteen.

Uffa's workmen were incensed at the closure, as they travelled from all parts of the Island and could not possibly return home for their midday meal. Also the canteen helped to supplement their home rations. Even Uffa, who fed well all through the war, found that he had cut off his nose to spite his face when the Ministry of Food threatened to withdraw his catering licence.

Within a short space of time the canteen reopened under the management of his sister Mahala, who had returned to the Island and was obliged to undertake war work; so, as with so many of Uffa's actions, nobody completely understood the motive. Had he peremptorily closed the canteen out of spite and temper with the police for chastising him, or because he wanted to make a clean sweep of the catering department, or both?

During a visit to London to confer with Air Ministry experts and collect engines for the airborne lifeboats, Uffa fell foul of the London police. Some while previous, in the blackout during an air raid, he had been tearing along a country road without lights and collided with an army lorry. The crash had ripped off both doors on the driving side of his car, and even after repair neither door subsequently locked, in breach of the emergency regulation requiring vehicle owners to lock and immobilize their cars.

On this occasion Uffa parked his car outside the Hyde Park Hotel in Knightsbridge, and was enjoying coffee and port with the men from the Air Ministry, when a waiter broke the news that a policeman was outside and demanding to see him. The policeman gave Uffa a dressing down not only for leaving the car unlocked but for having no identity card (he had not replaced the one lost in the air raid), a road fund disc that was faded and unreadable, an expired licence, and for leaving secret plans and equipment in the unlocked car.

When Uffa, who had partaken well of the port, was asked to indentify himself he said jocularly, 'Actually it would be much easier for me to prove to you that I am somebody else for I am wearing the brewer's suit, it having been given to me by a friend after I was bombed out,' and he turned down the inside pocket of the jacket to reveal the name Leonard P. Mew, Esq.

The policeman finally elicited Uffa's name and address, and a report of the offences were sent to Cowes where the Island police decided against taking any formal action.

Another wartime escapade took place as Uffa, driving along a fast stretch of road between Cowes and Newport, failed to stop when signalled to do so by the soldier on traffic duty who was bringing his troop out onto the main road from Albany Barracks at Parkhurst. The Army reported the occurrence to the Cowes Police, strongly recommending that charges be brought as it was not the first time that Uffa had put the Army at risk.

Uffa accepted the inevitable and decided to fight his own case, not on the grounds that the soldiers were lying as their evidence was irrefutable, but on the theory that their khaki uniforms blended so well with the March countryside that they were rendered invisible. Such was his power of eloquent reasoning that the case was dismissed by the Magistrates.

The local press, wise to Uffa and with tongue in cheek, reported the incident under the heading 'The Invisible Man'; and one young wag at the Cowes police station remarked, 'Had you been travelling at your normal speed they wouldn't have read your number in the first place.'

[14]

Uffa maintained that during his lifetime he had visited many homes and gardens in all corners of the world but none more beautiful than Puckaster, and from the moment he and Cherry knew it was on the market it became their dream home.

Puckaster Cove is half a mile east of St Catherine's Lighthouse, and is the only spot at the back of the Wight where one can land in most weathers, as the wind is nearly always south-westerly. The cove itself shelters under the lee of St Catherine's Point and is situated on the Undercliff where the cliffs, five hundred feet or so above sea level, drop vertically for three hundred feet before levelling out. From this ledge the land slopes rapidly in the direction of the sea before reaching another cliff some eighty feet in height.

There were endless possibilities for the horticultural enthusiast, Uffa's and Cherry's never-ending joy being the grounds and gardens which had been planted by generations of loving hands. From the house itself the lawns spread downwards at an angle of forty-five degrees, so that the tennis court below required netting on three sides only, for the northern side was open and whenever the ball was lobbed towards the lawns it simply rolled back down again; while beyond lay the Elysian delights of the croquet lawn. Between the lawns and the sea was an enormous mound of rocks filled with spring bulbs, crocuses, snowdrops, narcissi and daffodils, forming two sides of the Big Nook which housed palm trees, King Solomon's seal, camellias, azaleas and almost every type of flowering shrub.

The outbuildings were mellowed and had been carefully thought out over the years. There was a stone potting shed with mullioned windows, heated glasshouses sporting three succulent vines which gave grapes in rotation for five months of the year; a peach house, walled garden, vegetable gardens and paddock. The estate also encompassed a farm and a farm cottage as old as Puckaster itself; while on the low cliff above the cove stood the fishermen's cottages, a relic of the days when the cove had supported three families. A boathouse with slipway, breakwaters and groynes helped complete the vision of beauty.

The puzzle surrounding Puckaster was that it had been on the market for many years, yet nobody had been able to purchase it. Undaunted, Uffa made up his mind to take the bull by the horns, travelling to London to confront the lord of the manor in person.

'So you want to buy Puckaster,' commented the owner, a timber merchant.

Uffa launched into a paean of praise, momentarily forgetting that he was speaking as a prospective purchaser, rapturing over every detail even down to the little rose-trellised shelter which housed the gardeners' wheelbarrows.

At the end of Uffa's outburst the owner said, quietly, 'Yes, you can buy it,' and slowly opened the top left-hand drawer of his desk from which he extracted a scrap of paper with an incredibly low purchase price written upon it.

Uffa placed a lump of sugar on the table to sweeten the deal and, hand trembling with emotion, wrote out a cheque for the ten per cent deposit.

After yarning and drinking a glass of sherry together, the owner suddenly said, 'Do you recall which drawer I took this paper from?'

Uffa pointed silently to the top left-hand drawer.

The owner indicated, and said, 'Now, go down two drawers.'

Uffa did so and gasped for, to his amazement, he found himself holding a piece of paper with the price of Puckaster shown at almost double the agreed price. The desk proved to have ten drawers, each one containing a slip of paper showing a higher purchase price. Uffa's face reflected his astonishment.

'It is quite simple,' smiled the owner. 'People coming to purchase Puckaster can utter ten words of complaint against it and still be permitted to buy it, but each word of complaint costs £1,000, for I will only sell this property to somebody who will love and cherish it. Even before you have ever lived in it you love it, and unlike the rest of the people who have come to buy Puckaster, you have spoken the truth from your heart whereas they, thinking to reduce the price by finding fault, only increased the price until finally, by uttering more than ten words of complaint, lost all chance of purchasing the property.'

The house itself was cosily beautiful in well mellowed local stone, blending harmoniously with the sheer rising cliffs; and the steeply pitched roof, once of thatch, was now covered with red-brown tiles and an overmantle of lichen. The house was on two floors and as one entered from the front or western side, the main rooms, comprising Uffa's study, the library and oak-panelled drawing and dining rooms, all led conveniently off a large entrance hall; while on the east was Cherry's favourite morning room with french windows leading out onto the terrace. Here she and Uffa ate breakfast in the early morning winter sunshine when it was too cold to eat out of doors, and often during the afternoon they held large tea parties with guests overflowing onto the terrace beyond.

Uffa turned the smoking room, which also led off the entrance hall, into a drawing office as he considered smoking to be a filthy and degrading habit, although he did once lend his name to a cigarette company when the financial reward was sufficiently high. A pantry adjoined the smoking room, and then came the servants' hall, large kitchens and workroom; while on the floor above were ten good-sized bedrooms and the bathrooms.

Adjoining the house, and shielded from all winds, was a large stable yard, harness room and loose boxes; and it was only a matter of time before Uffa was looking around for horses to fill them. He also kitted himself out rather smartly in riding gear, in keeping with his new country gentleman image, and took to wearing breeches and riding jacket all day and every day. When asked at Medina Yard why he wore riding breeches to work, the politer of his responses was, 'To keep the wind out and the wind in and increase internal combustion.'

Of the various horses Uffa rode and owned by far and away his favourite was the mare Frantic. She was bright chestnut with three white socks and stood at fifteen-two hands. She was a fun-loving, lively horse always eager to go, and was what her previous owner described as 'a daisy cutter', her feet hardly leaving the ground at a walk, trot, canter or gallop. She was full of zest and eagerness, and the name he bestowed upon her must surely have reflected some of Uffa's own restless soul.

In Uffa's youth, when he had spent many hours boxing, he found that if he could get his mind into the brain of his antagonist, life in the ring became that much easier, and he found the same tactics paid off with a horse or a dog. After purchasing Frantic, followed by a hair-raising ride home to Puckaster with his arm still strapped to his ribs from the latest of his many falls, Uffa settled Frantic down in her loose box. For the first week he hardly left her side, grooming, feeding and riding her so that they saw one another under all conditions and so adjusted quicker to the ways of one another. By the end of the week Uffa was in love with Frantic and knew that he would keep her until the end.

At three o'clock one morning, elevated after a good dinner and drinking session, Uffa staggered into the loose box to say 'good-night' to Frantic. In his mood of *bonhomie* he carelessly left her door ajar, and to his surprise the nimble-footed mare darted quickly past and disappeared into the blackness of the night. Uffa, resplendent in white tie and tails, found himself in solitary state. Suddenly overcome with fatigue he stretched himself out on a bed made of Frantic's hay, covered himself with the remainder, and was soon fast asleep.

When the indignant Frantic returned and found Uffa snoring in her loose box she soon nuzzled him awake. Uffa, tipsily shaking the hay from himself, made his way to his own bed. Half-way up the stairs it occurred to him that, although he had often seen Frantic tucked up in her loose box, she had never seen him in his bunk, and he resolved to remedy the situation.

The following day, at the end of a light-hearted gallop over the top of the downs, Uffa rode Frantic into the house. He had taken her indoors before, through the hall, drawing-room and library, ducking from side to side to avoid the chandeliers, but they had never taken the stairs together. The Puckaster staircase was wide and heavily carpeted, so there was no danger of slipping. They mounted the first five stairs to the lower landing, turned right, and at the end of the landing right again; and, climbing the final seven stairs, arrived in the main passage opposite Uffa's bedroom door. He bent down to open the door and Frantic stepped through.

The moment Frantic walked into the centre of the room Uffa felt the floor surge up and down under their combined weight. Quick as lightning he slid off the saddle to spread the load, having a sudden mental vision of Frantic's legs splintering through the floor boards to the dining-room below. Subdued, Uffa led the mare quietly from the bedroom, gently down the stairs and out of the house. The experience, coupled with the thought that, had he damaged Frantic's legs he would have been obliged to shoot her, had a sobering and profound effect upon him and he vowed never to take a horse into the house again.

Frantic had a streak of wildness that would sometimes take even Uffa by surprise. On one such occasion, on a beautiful spring morning, Uffa set off innocently enough for what he thought would be a reasonably normal and pleasant ride, only to find Frantic in one of her abandoned and uncontrollable moods. On the way through Niton village Frantic was capricious, and by the time they started to ascend St Catherine's Down she was definitely above herself. They fairly flew along and over the downs, taking five-barred gates in their stride, with she and Uffa all but parting company at the final hurdle.

On the return journey she had still not calmed down, and set off at a wild gallop through the village, with Uffa yelling 'Gang-way' at any pedestrian unfortunate enough to find himself on a converging path. A solitary policeman, standing with stopwatch in hand as they flashed by, dropped his other hand which had been held aloft, as they passed. Further along Uffa sped by another policeman, also with stop watch, and he too lowered his right arm as they thundered by. Frantic had been timed through the speed trap set for motor cars.

After lunch Uffa telephoned his friend the Chief Constable to clear the air.

The Chief Constable chuckled. 'We have timed you through a built-up area at thirty-seven miles an hour on a bright chestnut-coloured thoroughbred mare, and are contemplating preparing a charge against you for exceeding the thirty-mile-an-hour limit.'

'I am sure Frantic was doing no more than thirty-three,' murmured Uffa meekly.

'But that's still over thirty,' laughed the Chief Constable. 'However, don't worry unduly as we have problems this end. The fact is we do not know of a precedent and might have difficulty bringing this charge against you and the mare into Court on that account.' And sure enough, two weeks later Uffa found himself on the receiving end of a call from the Chief Constable saying, 'We are not proceeding with the case as there is no precedent.'

Uffa derived great satisfaction from the company of farmers and local landowners, frequently drinking and lunching with them at the Wheatsheaf Hotel in Newport, especially enjoying market day. Once, on the day of the Autumn Fair, after a good luncheon followed by liqueurs which made him feel well and truly cherished, Uffa bid for and bought a Shire colt and its mother in two separate lots for no other reason than that he could not bear to see them parted.

On various occasions during Uffa's infatuation with horses he suffered concussion, fractured jaw, broken right arm, broken arm at the elbow, torn shoulder muscles and a twice-smashed ankle. The ankle was so badly damaged the second time around that it warranted being welded together with screws, and locked solid. Uffa, when he received word that the type of surgery required involved screws, loudly demanded the services of 'the best screwer in the country' to perform his operation.

He completely disorganized the nursing home during his sojourn, even commanding that his own bed be brought in. Finally, with leg firmly encased in plaster, he left for Puckaster to the muffled cheers of the hospital staff. Years later one of them remarked that he was a patient one could enjoy 'in retrospect'.

Within hours of his discharge Uffa was arranging to be driven to Cowes. Once there he designed and had made a catafalque, two planks wide and some thirty inches high, on which he reclined resting one plaster-of-paris-encased leg on the plinth while the other swung dangerously in the breeze. He was carried round the yard, cussing and swearing, by two labourers who acted as bearers.

After work Uffa invited several of his employees to join him for a pint at the Duke of York. A fine drizzle was falling, something he would normally take in his stride for such a short outing; but today he despatched one of his underlings to fetch a large umbrella. Surrounded by his entourage, supported by his labourers, and holding the black umbrella open and aloft like an Indian potentate, he traversed the main road from Medina Yard the hundred yards or so to the pub. Once inside, the other customers were edged over to make room for Uffa and his retinue, but their amusement as he held court far outweighed the inconvenience.

Early in 1943 when Uffa put Twenty Acres up for sale, he invited his father and Ellie to make a home with him at Puckaster. Old Mr Fox delighted in the many quiet walks to be found within the confines of the estate, but after only a few months his tranquillity was shattered when a stray German bomb exploded nearby as he was walking alone. Flinging himself to the ground he escaped physical injury; but he was no longer a young man and the shock sustained had a profound effect upon him with the result that, towards early summer, he became unwell and took to his bed. When Mr Fox expressed a desire to be examined by the family doctor, Uffa bundled him and Ellie and their belongings into the car and drove them to the East Cowes flat where Ellie hurriedly attempted to air the bedding before getting her father back into bed. In the event the move did nothing to improve Mr Fox's health, and ten days later he was dead.

Ellie stayed on to live alone at East Cowes, and within a few days of her father's death received official notification that, as she no longer had an elderly dependent relative, she must register for war work. Uffa immediately incorporated her into his team, putting her to work running off prints for the draughtsmen, a job at which she excelled. Ellie also acted as general factotum to Uffa, who had been deprived of the services of a housekeeper at Cowes since he and Cherry moved to Puckaster, and this position Ellie continued to hold throughout Uffa's lifetime.

Uffa commuted between Puckaster and Cowes, working and playing hard at both locales. At Puckaster he employed three gardeners, mostly engaged on food production, making a particular killing on early tomatoes, taking advantage of the void left by the German occupation of the Channel Islands. He also found eager markets for his fruit, especially the wartime luxuries of grapes and peaches, although the peaches could only be sold locally as they did not keep too well.

Additionally at Puckaster there was a full-time draughtsman, so Uffa was never idle. Many of the workmen were imported from the yard to help out, priority being given to those who lived nearby. Some of the airborne lifeboats were kept there, and the men turned their hands to anything that came up; boatbuilding, house maintenance, fruit picking or whatever. Uffa had been granted permission by the Air Ministry, the Naval Authorities and the Royal National Lifeboat Institution to form his own lifeboat station at Puckaster so the men were also on stand-by for rescue operations.

From the cove Uffa took his airborne lifeboats into the steep breaking seas beyond, and carried out rough-water trials with drogues and storm sails. It was a period of deep personal satisfaction for, not only was he reasonably stable financially, but his heart was filled with a great joy emanating from the many letters of gratitude received from men whose lives had been saved by the airborne lifeboats.

Not that it was all work. There was swimming, fishing, archery, tennis and croquet, and just the fun of being in the almost perpetual summer and serenity of Puckaster. Another sport was cricket on the tennis court. Uffa, armed with cricket bat and a dozen or so old and stringy tennis balls, would, during the luncheon break, set himself up at a makeshift wicket, and while he batted the remainder of the gang would bowl and field as he thwacked the balls from one end of the grounds to the other, for he was a powerful slogger.

One evening, after a day's buffeting on rough-water trials, Uffa and his companion, Wing Commander Bill Thomas from the Air Ministry, had changed into dry clothes and were looking forward to a fireside chair and warming drink when, some five miles out to sea, they saw a Typhoon pilot bale out. The machine hit the water long before the pilot floated down on his parachute.

Nearby was a large American ship, and although Uffa knew she would make a lee and launch one of her boats to save the pilot, there was always the possibility, with the fierce gale that by now was blowing and the heavy sea running, that the ship's boat might be damaged in the launching or hauling up; so instead of one man in the sea there might be ten.

'Far better one too many to the rescue than one too few,' he said to Bill.

Weary as they were, they launched the boat, and were so quick off the mark that she was actually in the sea before the Typhoon pilot reached the water. Uffa had penned up Bruce, his black labrador, in the boat-house; but hearing the boat being launched he leapt at the window, which was over three feet from the ground, breaking the glass and tearing through the wire netting outside, and then swam after the boat until dragged on board, wet and dripping, by Uffa. They sailed out on a compass bearing for Uffa knew that the swiftly flowing waters round St Catherine's Point would take their craft and the pilot at the same speed, so their bearing would remain identical.

The wind was so strong that it was quicker to sail than motor, and although they could not have launched more rapidly or sailed faster to reach the pilot, by the time they were alongside he had already been scooped from the sea by the efficient crew of the American ship. They were also joined at the scene of the drama by two Royal Air Force Rescue Launches while an Air Sea Rescue Walrus flew overhead.

The would-be saviours separated and made their way back to their respective bases. The ebb had finished running and the flood was beginning to make, which meant that they would not fetch up at Puckaster Cove but two miles to leeward; then close in under the shore they would work their way to windward away from the strength of the flood tide.

Suddenly they were startled to find their course converging with that of a small landing craft some thirty feet in length, with a high towering prow that could be lowered like a drawbridge to enable vehicles to drive on or off, which loomed up out of the darkness of the night. They yelled across the high and choppy seas to one another, and discovered that she was from a different American ship that had rescued the crew of yet another ship which had sunk in the gale.

The crew of three was highly delighted to find someone with local knowledge for they were at their wits' end wondering how and where they could land on the south of the Isle of Wight without being blown to smithereens by mines. Struggling with the elements, Uffa transferred to the American craft and guided them into the cove, while Bill Thomas manoeuvred the lifeboat alone. Once closer inshore, out of the tide and where the water was smoother, the American vessel took the airborne lifeboat in tow with the aid of her powerful diesel.

They arrived home to Puckaster Cove, not with a Typhoon pilot but with three American seamen who had rescued the crew from a smaller ship that had been sunk, transferred them to the parent ship, and then found themselves unable to be hoisted back aboard in the teeth of the gale. Before long they had the lifeboat hauled out to safety, the American craft securely moored just below the high water mark, and were snug in the friendly warmth of Puckaster where they all wallowed in hot baths before being served with drinks and one of Cherry's scrumptious dinners.

After a good night's sleep the guests departed. Uffa was thrilled some three days later when the Americans returned with the tidings that they had been awarded gallantry medals for their part in the rescue operation. Uffa always rejoiced when he was able to entertain or aid American or Canadian servicemen, feeling that in some small measure he was returning the incomparable hospitality and kindness he had experienced in their respective countries.

Towards the end of the war an innovation occurred which placed the Isle of Wight under the Hampshire Constabulary and, with the change-over, policemen unknown to Uffa appeared on regular traffic duty at the busy cross road in the centre of Newport. One day, in his usual tearing hurry, Uffa shot past the line of cars waiting on the left-hand side of the road and was surprised to find his way barred by a strange policeman on point duty.

Uffa was not used to being pulled up, and felt humiliated when the representative of the law took him to task in front of the waiting motorists. In a fit of temper he parked his car diagonally across the road, causing an almost complete blockage.

Jumping out of the car, shouting, 'If you can do any better you can bloody well have it,' he locked the car and made off, leaving it straddled across the road for three-quarters of an hour while he conducted his business in Newport. By the time he reappeared the policeman and snarl of cars had been joined by an Inspector and, despite his defence that he did not cause the obstruction but merely prolonged it, Uffa was taken to court, found guilty, and fined two pounds.

Uffa smarted at the decision, and was of the opinion that he had been treated unjustly and unfairly: so when, a few days later, a little French fishing boat drove in over the rocks and onto the shore of Puckaster Cove, and the five German prisoners she had contained could not be found, he formulated a plan. He closed up the house at Puckaster, moved into Westborne House at Cowes, and made up his mind to quietly help the prisoners if he were able so that the police would have to waste many hours looking for them. He wrote that all the time the prisoners were at large they would be a thorn in the side of the police and a blow to their pride, which would punish them for the blow his pride had sustained.

The next day Uffa returned to Puckaster for a quiet look round. Strolling by the little farm cottage which was empty, the tenants being away on a month's holiday, he noted that the glass in the casement window was broken near the latch, and the pane replaced by a piece of cardboard on the inside.

Investigation at the big house itself revealed that they had also opened a window into the dining-room and taken ham, eggs and other food from the larder. Uffa replenished the food, and did so from time to time over a period of two weeks until the day that his Niton maid, Dorothy, had the terrifying experience of seeing the face of one of the prisoners at the cottage window. Uffa was informed, and he agreed that the police must be contacted immediately. He also insisted that he deal with the police himself to show them how to round up the prisoners for his inside knowledge of the terrain would be invaluable.

The prisoners proved peaceful enough, in fact almost relieved to be taken into custody, so the police experienced little difficulty in making the capture. When the mission had been successfully accomplished, and the Police Superintendent telephoned Uffa to thank him for his help, Uffa, before making his peace, told the Superintendent what he had done.

'Here in the Isle of Wight we reckon to pay our fines out of court and not in court,' he added.

126

[15]

The Allied advance into Germany brought the long and eagerly awaited release of our prisoners of war, amongst them Bobbie Sach. His joy to be home, and Cherry's and Uffa's happiness at seeing him again, were incalculable. After the years of imprisonment, the freedom and wide open spaces of Puckaster were like a balm to his soul, soothing away the pain and confinement of his lost youth.

Uffa rejoiced at having his stepson by his side, proudly taking him on a round of the pubs and showing him off to his friends, and for the first week or two they were almost inseparable. Bobbie was enthralled with Puckaster, spending many happy and contented hours pottering around, unwinding mentally and helping out on the estate. Cherry, who had been initially the prime mover in the purchase of Puckaster following a letter from Bobbie soon after his internment in which he had expressed a deep longing for room to stretch and breathe, was in her seventh heaven of delight.

With her son safely home, Cherry's one remaining dream was that her husband would settle down to family life, for Uffa had been conspicuous by his absence of late, often choosing to stay at Cowes rather than come home to Puckaster now that the risk of air raids had diminished. Cherry, who had no illusions about Uffa, suspected the presence of another woman. The migraine, which had plagued her for years, was exacerbated by her fears and drove her to the aspirin bottle, while Uffa, to whom drugs of any kind, including the humble aspirin, were pure anathema, searched out the bottles and flushed the offending tablets down the lavatory.

Cherry's recourse to aspirin might well be construed as a cry for help in these more enlightened days, but in Uffa's eyes even the taking of such a commonplace remedy amounted to addiction. He himself, even when in extreme pain after his numerous riding accidents, stoically refused the support of the mildest of pain killers.

While not above playing the field himself, Uffa was intensely jealous of Cherry. On one occasion, when enervated and in need of a change of scenery, Cherry was invited to spend a few days at an hotel owned by a mutual friend. Uffa was so incensed when she announced her intention of prolonging the visit that he despatched a telegram to his friend, deliberately sending it through the hotel's switchboard for maximum embarrassment, saying 'If you don't return my wife by the end of the week you can keep her.' Needless to say Cherry returned post-haste.

Another bone of contention was the housekeeping allowance. Although Uffa insisted on entertaining lavishly and was open-handed in public – and to an extent this was an essential part of his *modus operandi* as the majority of his orders were obtained through social connections – he could be the essence of parsimony within the home. Cherry complained bitterly and often to Mahala that before he led her to the altar she could have anything she wanted from Uffa, but once married he appeared to begrudge her every penny. In desperation she ran up bills with the local tradesmen, which led to violent scenes when Uffa was confronted with the accounts.

The dropping of atomic bombs on Hiroshima and Nagasaki, which brought about the abrupt cessation of hostilities with Japan instead of the anticipated and dreaded years of bloody carnage, was received by Uffa with mixed feelings. Naturally, he would have been inhuman not to have rejoiced that the killing was over; but, by the same token, he would have been a fool had he not taken a serious look around and said, 'Where do I go from here?' for the whole of his boatbuilding operation was geared to designing and producing bigger and better airborne lifeboats; and suddenly, with the dropping of two bombs, nobody needed to be rescued any more.

The war had generally been good to Uffa. To him was granted the inner knowledge and satisfaction that he had saved the lives of many of his fellow men. Their very existence on this earth was his testimonial. He had also coincidentally acquired a country estate, additional property at Cowes, a fleet of large cars and an elevated lifestyle.

Abruptly Uffa found himself at a major crossroad. Should he soldier on with a reduced workforce, attempting to survive in a war-torn and weary Britain whose limited supplies of timber and other resources were of necessity earmarked for more urgent priorities than the construction of luxury sailing yachts, or should he, while the accounts were still showing a profit-making situation, sell the Company and concentrate on writing and design?

Uffa decided to sell, and before long negotiations were opened with the Dowsett and McKay Company for a takeover. Accountants were brought in and the terms tentatively agreed. Uffa would remain on the board at a contracted salary, as would his key personnel, and the Company would continue to operate under the name of Uffa Fox Limited. Uffa would also be called upon to give an undertaking not to trade independently under his own name.

At the eleventh hour Uffa had misgivings. Walking in the grounds of Puckaster with his secretary, Charles Willis, Uffa sought his advice. Charles was of the opinion that it would not be a workable partnership, and his response was in the form of a question.

'Do you honestly believe that you will be able to sit back and allow sombeody else to give the orders?'

When Uffa remained silent, Charles continued, 'You'll never toe the line.'

There was also the question of Uffa's name. Neither of them believed that he should forfeit the right to his own name, and by the end of their stroll a decision was reached. For better or for worse, Uffa would hold on to the Company.

The airborne lifeboat commitment had not completely dried up with the ending of the war, but the final contract was reduced, and by October 1945 Uffa was obliged to cut his workforce by half. The majority of the men were in the fortunate position of being able to pick up the threads of their old employment in the building and allied industries, but nevertheless it was a sad time for them and for Uffa.

Informing a man that his services were no longer required was one of the few occasions over which Uffa admitted weakness. He could quite happily sack a man in temper; but when the act had to be committed in cold blood he suffered agonies and shied away from the deed as long as possible, quite often keeping the person in employment long after it was commercially viable while steeling himself to impart the bad news.

Sometimes Uffa would stalk his victim for days, hoping for some minor infringement or piece of shoddy workmanship which would further justify the dismissal and ease his peace of mind; and if he were particularly fond of the workman in question, he would jump into his car immediately he had broken the news and disappear for the remainder of the day, usually ending up in some remote pub far from the scene of the crime. On other occasions he would pick on a victim and make his life so uncomfortable that the man himself would seek employment elsewhere, thus saving Uffa the thankless task of dismissing him.

By the end of the war Uffa was run down both physically and mentally. Over and above the extra heavy workload he had carried, he had been burning the candle in the middle as well as at both ends and, after a race under the Ocean Racing Club's Rules in one of his airborne lifeboats, he caught a severe chill which developed into pneumonia. When he recovered he was for many months without his usual strength and vigour, and the stresses of post-war Britain bore heavily upon him.

The Government put an immediate clamp-down on boat building for the home market, and it was a question of export or die. Fortunately England had some good friends in Bermuda so that, when the Bermuda Sailboat Club opted to form an International fourteen-footer class, they were swayed by patriotism to order an initial ten boats from Uffa, against strong competition from the Americans who could offer dinghies constructed in the new moulded ply. With an export licence, Uffa experienced little or no difficulty obtaining the timber; but chasing the fittings, which had been out of production for six years, caused many a headache.

Another ray of hope was an approach from the Fairey Aviation Group to design moulded plywood boats for their new marine section. Although Uffa was not particularly impressed with the medium as he knew it, having produced a not too successful experimental moulded plywood airborne lifeboat for carrying under the Warwick aircraft, he was excited at the project as there was the possibility of a royalty for him on each of the boats constructed. He also felt the wind of change, and if there was to be a swing against traditional boatbuilding, he wanted to be in on the ground floor. Fairey Marine were investing in the best of equipment, and their boats would not be expected to stand up to a drop from an aircraft as had Uffa's plywood airborne lifeboat, so in time he became quite enthusiastic.

The first of Uffa's designs to come off the moulds was the twelve-foot RYA Firefly. When the Royal Yachting Association invited several designers to submit plans for a twelve-footer, Uffa, who had already previously designed dinghies in that range for both Oxford and Cambridge Universities, submitted the plans of his Cambridge University Twelve Foot One Design. The RYA judged Uffa's design the best and Fairey Marine, who had set up two autoclaves (large ovens) in which the moulded plywood boats would be glued together and baked, received official RYA blessing to go ahead and produce the Firefly by this method.

The Firefly was selected for the 1948 Olympics and, despite the timber shortage, permission was given for British helmsmen who intended participating in the eliminating trials to purchase them. Hundreds of helmsmen were filled with a sudden desire to sail for their country only to find, after they had purchased their Fireflies, that they had urgent commitments elsewhere.

Uffa's marriage meantime took a turn for the worse when Cherry received proof of some of his extra-marital activities, and threatened him with divorce. Uffa's reply was to insert a statement in the local paper stating that he was no longer responsible for his wife's debts. The next round was also conducted publicly when the local press carried the announcement of a paternity suit to be brought against Uffa; a charge which he steadfastly denied, insisting that he had been impotent since contracting a disease in his youth, and that he had been made the fall guy.

Cherry continued to live at Puckaster and Uffa bedded down at

Cowes; but the situation galled him to such an extent that, in an attempt to get his wife out of the house, he had the electricity cut off. When this tactic failed, Uffa sent one of his own workmen who had been in the building industry to cut off the water supply. Cherry found that she could not exist without water, and was forced to move out and accept the hospitality of friends. She was a popular figure locally, and Uffa's autocratic treatment caused him to be ostracized by large pockets of Island society.

When Cherry bid adieu to the home she loved for the last time, Uffa hovered in the background checking that she took nothing to which she was not entitled. He also rolled up and hid a particularly fine length of carpet that had come from Cherry's former home at Bembridge. This prompted one of the men, who was something of an artist, to sketch Cherry with a suitcase in either hand walking towards the front door of Puckaster, while Uffa, on hands and knees, rolled up the carpet behind her: for Uffa's lifestyle, even in tragedy, was a constant source of entertainment to his workmen.

Uffa engaged a cook and butler to take over Cherry's duties in the house, and went on a wild entertainment spree until pulled up sharply by the bank. He was concerned over the amount of alimony he might have to pay Cherry, and demanded that Charles sign an affidavit swearing Uffa's total income to be so low as to be laughable. When Charles's conscience restrained him from perjuring himself to such an extent, Uffa became so unbearable that he left and took up employment elsewhere.

When the time came Cherry had no difficulty in obtaining her divorce, and was awarded an alimony sum that was hotly disputed by Uffa. He held the bulk of the amount back each month so that Cherry had recourse to engage solicitors and apply to the courts, and it was many moons before Uffa's own solicitors could overcome his stubbornness and convince him that his actions were causing more cost and harassment to himself than he could possibly hope to inflict on Cherry.

From the days of Uffa's phenomenal success with the International fourteen-footer he had been conscious of the need for a planing keel boat, and his thoughts and research turned increasingly to keels. He found the challenge a greater one than when he had designed the planing centreboard boat for the increased strains upon the craft meant a stronger, so heavier, hull plus the weight of the keel itself; but to offset the enigma, he had by now twenty years' knowledge of planing hulls and their rigs and sails, and additionally had acquired the technique of sailing this type of craft.

Such a boat would enable those who were past the first flush of youth, yet still wanted the excitement and exhilaration of a planing craft, to be able to enjoy the same fun but without the risk of capsizing. He also felt that, if he could produce a planing keel boat for something like the equivalent cost of a similar sized dinghy, he might well attract youngsters as well as a new clientele of all ages to the joys of sailing.

With cost effectiveness very much in mind, Uffa's thoughts turned to the keel of the International Star Class of America, of which there were several at Cowes. The Star's fin keel is a very simple cast-iron fin with a flange for bolting onto the hull and the bulb at the bottom, all cast in one piece at the same time. The Stars also have a wedge-shaped fin or skeg from the after end of the fin keel down to the bottom of the rudder post.

Uffa frequently had his brainwaves in the bath, and it was while soaking and relaxing that he mentally formulated the lines of his first planing keel boat. The Royal Yachting Association was seeking a design for a National One-Design Keel Boat with a two-hundred-foot sail area, which would give nearly the thrill of dinghy racing and handle without an experienced crew such as is needed to attain even reasonable results in dinghy racing, and Uffa decided to submit an entry.

He called his prototype *Pensive Temptress*, and she later became known as the *Flying Twenty-five*. She had an overall length of 25 feet 10 inches and a waterline length of 20 feet, a 3 feet 8 inches draught, and was conceived with a crew of two or three persons in mind. She had a light displacement hull to which a cast-iron fin and bulb keel, cast in one piece, was attached by means of bolts secured by butterfly nuts, so the keel could be removed easily for transportation and storage. Her rudder was attached to an inner frame and slipped down through a slot at the after end of the waterline so that it could also be removed.

Uffa was late in getting his plans off to the RYA, a delay caused by yet another of his riding accidents, and even later in building the prototype, which may or may not have had a bearing on the rejection of his design in favour of Tom Thorneycroft's National 200 square foot O. D. Class.

Although disappointed, Uffa continued to sail and experiment with *Pensive Temptress*. He could get her up to plane, which was the object of the exercise, but she was so wet to windward that the crew returned from each race looking like drowned rats. Uffa knew that he must return to the drawing board, and he questioned whether he was doing the right thing in designing to the RYA requirement of a 200-square-foot sail area.

Uffa was in the throes of furnishing Medina House, which had been rebuilt under a War Damage claim with one or two alterations, such as the dividing wall between the two first-floor seaward rooms being knocked down to form one large drawing-room, when Alfred King contacted him from Great Yarmouth to enquire if *Pensive Temptress* was for sale.

'You can have her if you bring the money in cash,' was Uffa's cheerful response, 'because I want to buy a piano.'

A few days later Alfred's brother, Cyril, arrived with a wad of notes, and Uffa's first planing keel boat went for a piano, if not for a song.

The King brothers raced *Pensive Temptress* on the East Coast of England where she attracted immense interest, everyone wanting to sail and race in her. She was brutally handicapped against comparable sized craft, but still managed to win most of her races despite the heavy odds. In her element in a good hard blow, though perhaps not quite so happy in lighter airs, she gave her new owners untold happiness and delight.

Once the repairs and decorations had been completed at Medina House Uffa developed a heat fetish, switching on all radiators and building mountainous wood fires to dry out the walls quicker. He closed all the windows and ran from room to room gleefully recording each new and escalating height of temperature. One day David Hillmer, who was working upstairs in the drawing office of Medina Yard, became aware of smoke penetrating from next door, and hurried downstairs to investigate.

He discovered to his horror that the excessive heat and lack of ventilation had caused combustion, and Medina House at first-floor level was smouldering and burning. David quickly raised the alarm and, with all hands to the pump, the situation was soon under control; but the disaster involved additional repairs to Medina House and further redecoration of the blackened walls. When the house was finally restored to Uffa's satisfaction he sold the adjoining Westbourne House, for which he had no further use, to his sister Mahala and her family.

Uffa's next bathtime divination was the Flying Fifteen. The principles that determined its size were the inherent belief that the greatest of all the planing dinghies were the International fourteen-footers, and the opinion that the helmsmen who sailed them were the cream of the dinghy world.

Many were the friends throughout the years who had suggested that, if he could build a planing boat comparable to the fourteen-footer that would not capsize, he would be rendering a great service to the yachting fraternity. He had already designed and built a keel boat that would plane. Now he must set about designing one that would be popular enough to be commercially viable.

In a flash of inspiration, born of years of thought, he decided to build a planing keelboat with a twenty-foot overall hull, waterline length of fifteen feet, draught of two feet six inches; and the mast, mainsail and jib of the International fourteen-footer – the basic lines to be a development of *Martlet* in which Stewart Morris won the Prince of Wales' Cup in 1947.

Uffa stretched out of the bath, extracted a stub of pencil from his dressing gown pocket, and roughed out the hull and fin keel on a magazine that had been lying on the chair nearby; and, once dried and robed, drew out the lines, keel and sailplan in more detail on his sketch pad. Years later, after hundreds of these immensely popular Flying Fifteens had been constructed in all kinds of materials in many parts of the world, he claimed he had no desire to alter one single line or detail from his first sketches of the craft.

Uffa originally called his new class Dainty Ducks, and the prototype, *My Dainty Duck*, named after his current lady friend, was soon built and launched. He was over the moon with excitement at her performance for, although the fin keel had a weight of four hundred pounds and the hull itself a minimum of two hundred and seventy five pounds, her lines and fin keel were so easily drawn that, in light airs, one could see one's face reflected in the water; and in a breeze her performance was quite dazzling.

Uffa was so overwhelmed by his brainchild that he went on to design a whole Flying Family, in increasing lengths of five feet, up to the Flying Fifty, the boats over twenty-five-foot waterline being cruisers with cabin accommodation. Then, later on, he also designed a Flying Ten and a Flying Twelve.

He set to work with his usual enthusiasm to form a Flying Fifteen Class at Cowes, encouraging selected workmen and friends to build on his moulds with free use of Medina Yard and its facilities. Until there were sufficient boats to form a class he put *My Dainty Duck* through her paces in the handicap classes where she stood up extremely well against fierce competition. He also carried her on the gantry of his car to regattas up and down the country, arousing interest and generating orders; and in between found time to publicize her by writing articles for the various yachting publications.

Once Uffa realized the potential of the Flying Fifteen he had no time for the International fourteen-footer and, should a client arrive intent upon having a fourteen-footer built, Uffa would do his utmost to channel him into a Flying Fifteen instead.

On one occasion a prospective Flying Fifteen client was yarning casually with one of the young apprentices in the boatshop, and the lad mentioned that he personally preferred the fourteen-footer, considering it a better buy than the Flying Fifteen. Uffa's fury when the client related his conversation with the apprentice and announced that he would have a fourteen-footer instead had to be seen to be believed. He stormed down to the boatshop and sought out the offending youth.

'You're fired,' he yelled, 'and do you know the reason why?'

'Yes,' responded the apprentice, on the verge of tears, 'for pinching that spinnaker boom yesterday.'

Uffa was silent for one stunned second. Then, 'You're fired twice,' he said; and he was.

Of all his peacetime designs the Flying Fifteen was undoubtedly Uffa's favourite, and in his opinion the most successful. It also, through friendships forged, brought him the greatest happiness.

When Uffa had completed the design of the Flying Fifteen he was without a sail marking, not being completely happy with his original sketch of a duck in flight, until, towards the end of a musical evening at Medina House, two friends were playing a duet on the piano. They became more and more excited the longer they played, and finished with a tremendous burst of powerful music. In that resounding flash Uffa beheld a vision of the title and sail symbol of the Flying Fifteen, for the accent of the yacht's design was power. 'Fortissimo!' he cried, and so was born the symbol of the sail, the 'FF' sign *fortissimo* in music enclosed in the crescendo V.

$\begin{bmatrix} 16 \end{bmatrix}$

Uffa's sailing activities were in no way confined to the Flying Fifteen or his own multiplicity of other designs. Although past his half century he never missed an opportunity to be on the water, frequently taking part in local races on the Solent or joining friends for the Fastnet or Cross Channel Races; and he still loved a good hard blow.

On calm summer's days he would have a close, cold water shave before going afloat to race, asserting that the first awakening of his senses to a fresh puff of wind or change of direction often came through the abrasive tingling of his face. He needed and made use of all the tricks of the trade in light airs, for he was primarily a heavy weather man.

When the racing craft were so close together, and the air so still and hushed that one could hear the tense breathing of the crew in the next boat, Uffa would create a diversion, perhaps bursting into a lewd rendering of Abdul Abulbul Ameer, relating a wickedly filthy story or, in full view of everyone, peeing over the side of the boat; and he was never at a loss when it came to repartee. Once, when relieving himself, one of the competitors from another boat jokingly called, 'Wish I had one like that, Uffa,' to which Uffa responded immediately: 'You couldn't possibly afford it. It costs money to run one this size.'

Always enterprising and eager for another challenge, Uffa borrowed a Dragon and competed in her for a week in the summer of 1949. By a coincidence the young Prince Philip was also at Cowes sailing Dragons, and it was at a yacht club dinner following the racing that he and Uffa formally met for the first time. Both keen sailormen, they got along like a house on fire, Uffa extending an invitation to Prince Philip to visit his yard next day to see his latest pride and joy, the Flying Fifteen.

Prince Philip sailed with Uffa in *My Dainty Duck*, and found her liveliness quite exhilarating. He also found Uffa's breezy and down to earth character a refreshing change from the formality and protocol of Court life, with which he was becoming increasingly familiar since his marriage to Princess Elizabeth.

When, after their sail, Uffa suggested that Prince Philip and his party join him for a drink at the local pub, they found that a small crowd had gathered in the street outside. Amongst the spectators near the entrance to the Duke of York stood Mrs Wingham, the owner's wife, who had forsaken her customary position behind the bar hoping for a glimpse of the royal visitor. She was quite nonplussed as the little group headed in her direction, and Uffa's 'Get yourself back inside, Missus, we're coming in' sent her scurrying through the door in time to serve her distinguished visitors; while Harry Wingham, who spotted the happening just as he was driving off in his car, jumped out and left the vehicle where it was in the middle of the road, as he sped back to be in on the great event.

One thing that really angered Uffa were press reports that he had taught Prince Philip to sail. Prince Philip was a first-rate helmsman long before he ever met Uffa, and Uffa greatly admired his ability to handle a boat and his quick and active brain. Uffa was convinced that, had Prince Philip devoted more time to sailing, instead of being the all-round sportsman that he was, he could have become one of our finest helmsmen.

Uffa was once again leading a bachelor-like existence, freely admitting that, although he loved the company of women and the pleasures they brought to a home, he was not good husband material. His machismo attracted women and he was seldom short of female companionship, quite often having a friend to look after his creature comforts both at Cowes and Puckaster.

At Medina House Uffa was never off duty. If not already up and about when the workmen arrived at eight o'clock he was woken by an apprentice with a cup of tea. None of the boys relished this particular task, as Uffa's early morning mood was inclined to be dominated by a hangover; or, if already awake his mind would be buzzing with new ideas, and the unfortunate Ganymede would find himself despatched hither and thither with messages, or orders summoning one or other of the workforce to the bedchamber.

Human nature being what it is, the tea boy was more often than not the newest recruit; and so, on this particular occasion, it fell to the lot of a fourteen-year-old, as his initial chore on his first day at work, to beard the lion in his den with a cup of tea. Knocking carefully on the door as instructed, he entered and was completely taken aback to not only observe two heads on the pillow, but to see Uffa with great presence of mind pull the sheet swiftly up and over the second head.

The boy stood transfixed for the moment not knowing what to do. Recovering his senses he dumped the cup of tea clumsily on the bedside table and fled. His anxious query when he rejoined the workmen in the boatshop, as to whether he had done the right thing or if he should have fetched another cup, sent a peal of laughter echoing round the yard.

Tony Dixon, Mahala's youngest son, was now working in the drawing office. He found his apprenticeship with Uffa a never-to-be-forgotten experience, saying that Uffa could be an ogre one minute and a benevolent uncle the next, but always fair. Tony's view was that, when in his uncle's company, there was always an air of something exciting likely to happen.

During the works' lunch hour the apprentices and workmen devised a game which they loosely termed hockey. The yard was littered with wooden gunwale knees and other odds and ends of wood which had been left over from the airborne lifeboat contracts, and the boys and men nailed straight pieces of wood to the gunwale knees to form hockey sticks. A cube-shaped piece of rubber was cut from a strip of fendering to represent the ball, and a pitch was cleared in the lower boatshop, where alas there was little boatbuilding activity, and battle commenced. The game was turbulent to say the least, and during one particularly hectic game Murray Dixon, Mahala's number three son, lost a tooth in the mêlée.

A look-out was posted to give warning should Uffa appear on the scene, as sometimes in the excitement of the moment the game would continue beyond the allotted lunch break. One unfortunate day the look-out was so engrossed in the game himself that Uffa, who had been attracted by the hollering and shouting, was upon them before he had time to sound the alarm.

Tony said that he could truthfully say that he had never heard such a volley of swearing and blasphemy emanate from one man in such a short space of time. Uffa threatened to fire the whole workforce, and such was the well-known current financial position of the Company, that many men feared he might carry out his threat, and stood shaking in their shoes.

Having got it off his chest Uffa was ready to make amends, and enquired what game they were supposed to be playing. He then patiently explained the finer points of hockey, organized them into two teams, and had a try-out of ten minutes each way. The men were so relieved at Uffa's change of mood that they made certain his team won, and with a 'Now get on with your bloody work and if I catch any of you at it again during working hours I'll definitely fire the lot of you' he disappeared from the scene as quickly as he had materialized.

However, that was not the end of the story. Uffa was bitten with the hockey bug. He decided to train the men up during their lunch breaks and form a works' hockey team, called the 'Uffashots' after his old Home Guard unit. When he considered they were ready for the fray he launched them into the hockey league.

Most of the local teams refused to play them more than once, being far from amused at their unorthodox sticks, which had been augmented in the fitting shop by rather lethal looking strips of metal along the bottom, and their almost complete non-observance of the rules of the game; and one well-known girls' school found them too boisterous by half. The only exception were the stalwart Young Conservatives who re-challenged again and again until Uffa gradually lost interest and the team disbanded.

Uffa had many problems more important than hockey to occupy his mind at this time. The Company was not doing well, the six-metre *Noroda* he had been commissioned to design and build broached and was unmanageable, and he could no longer afford to run his estate at Puckaster.

Knowing only too well that he must eventually retrench, Uffa had gradually over the years converted Puckaster's little farm cottage into a cosy and comfortable home, surrounding it with an acre of walled garden filled with an assortment of fruit trees and a glasshouse with peaches. When the final day of reckoning came and Uffa was forced to sell the Puckaster house and estate, he retained the cottage and so was still free to enjoy its beauty albeit on a smaller scale, and he spent many happy years commuting between Cowes and the Puckaster cottage.

Relinquishing the reins of Puckaster was traumatic and well-nigh impossible for Uffa, and his decision to retain the cottage left him with a foot in the door which enabled him to watch over his former domain. His unwelcome and uncalled-for advice and interference eventually led to an acrimonious situation developing between himself and the new owners.

One of the final straws, almost a year after he had sold the property, involved the then monarch, King George VI, who was recovering from a serious operation. Without first consulting the owners, Uffa wrote to Clarence House, the current home of Princess Elizabeth and the Duke of Edinburgh, offering Puckaster to the King for his convalescence.

In those days Uffa corresponded in the main through Prince Philip's friend and Private Secretary, Lt Cdr Michael Parker, and not with His Royal Highness direct. Within the generous flow of the letter Uffa not only donated a house that was no longer his, and committed the new owner to putting down carpets and hanging curtains; but, in the final paragraph succeeded in talking himself out of what was to have been his own contribution.

1st October, 1951.

Lieutenant Michael Parker R.N.,
Clarence House,
London.

My dear Michael,

Possibly, because you are so closely connected with the Royal Family you do not realize how the King's illness means so much to us all and how deeply a great many people are touched by this.

Last Thursday, on my way home from a dinner at The Royal Thames Yacht Club (where I collected a cup I had won, and had to attend a dinner the night before to do so), my taxi drove by Buckingham Palace and there were all the people anxiously awaiting news. The taxi driver told me how people took their sandwiches for lunch and then spent their lunch-hour outside the Palace waiting for news. This letter is to do with the King's illness.

I should be delighted to help in any way, and the only way I know of that I can help is to inform you that Puckaster (the big house) is empty and that it is an ideal place for any man to live after a chest operation.

A doctor friend of mine, years ago, told me that while the London air did no harm to people, it also had no power to do any good – and the air at Puckaster, I can assure you, will make the King eat like a horse and sleep like a dog.

Some three miles away and to leeward is The Royal National Chest Hospital, which is (I believe) the most notable and best of its kind in the country and this is a useful thing. If you have a horse you want a Blacksmith's shop nearby and if you have a car you want a Garage and if you have a 'chest' it is just as well to have a Chest Hospital handy, for in it will be nurses and doctors all available for help of any kind.

Within a quarter of a mile is a pub called The Buddle Inn, and the landlord Bill Chandler used to live at Ryde and was an energetic and athletic chap. He collected a 'chest' through overdoing things and Mr Price Thomas, the man who operated on our King, took away one of Bill's lungs in the Brompton Hospital some eight years ago. Bill is now 100% fit and at the moment is away on a motoring holiday somewhere in Great Britain, which is, as you know, an ally of ours!

This sunlit ledge is the perfect place for 'chesty' people, and so I suggest the King comes here.

The entrance is at the north-east end so anyone coming into the hall is well away from any of the rooms (with the exception of the Dining Room) and this is a great advantage, for when we are in our homes we wish to be quiet and private, and defended from people who call by our servants. Also there are times when we wish people to come to dinner and go afterwards and this means they go straight into the Dining Room and straight out – without having a chance to settle down in the rest of the house.

I sold the house in December. I have not asked the new owner about this letter, for as you can well imagine he is sure to be delighted at being able to help the King in any way, as everyone in the land is.

I could take furniture out to furnish the rooms and my Steinway piano, and I am sure the owner would be delighted to put down carpets and hang curtains. I am sending him a copy of this letter and will ask him to ring you to confirm his delight at the prospect of helping the King to recover his former health.

I am also enclosing the following photographs, which I would like you to return:

1. Puckaster from the air.
2. The house from the grounds. The windows immediately above Bruce's tail are the west bedroom and study underneath it.
3. The lawn sloping down to the tennis courts, from the drawing room window, with the sundial on the rock.
4. The King can slide down this bank on air cushions and he will receive £5 if he can break the Puckaster record, which is a quarter way across the tennis court.
4a. Sometimes you only get halfway down before Bruce has you off your air cushion.
4b. You are then out of the competition and have to hold Bruce under the beech tree and let the others get on with it.
5. The King can use a bow and arrow from the veranda outside the Drawing Room window – I will give him half a crown for every rabbit he shoots!
6. When the King is fit enough he can ride over the most lovely downs as quickly or as slowly as he wishes. Just over my head is Jack my old butler. Above him is the bedroom and below the kitchen. The high part of the house was entirely given over to the servants.
7. The rocks and Channel seas in Puckaster Cove.
8. Even if the King does not play croquet, tennis, cricket, or have a go at archery, ride a horse, or explore the sea, he will be jolly hungry and look forward to sitting down and eating a jolly good dinner at night, and No. 8 shows the dining table.

The house is empty. It has open fires in all the rooms, but the hall fire will warm the whole house. So please put this proposal to His Majesty the King and let the owner and I know the answer as soon as possible, so that we can prepare the house and then, if he wishes, His Majesty can move in with his servants and staff.

The best train from London for the King would be the 12.30 p.m. Pullman from Waterloo, first stop Southampton, arriving at 2 p.m. and giving half an hour to catch the steamer. I can meet him with my 34 h.p. Packard which is quite comfortable, and he would be over and in Puckaster at 4. p.m. in time for tea – or of course, he could drive straight down from Buckingham Palace in his own car, or mine, and again catch the 2.30 p.m. steamer from Southampton.

But before putting this to the King, I think it would be a good scheme to talk it over with Her Highness Princess Elizabeth and the Duke of Edinburgh. I can assure you that if the King gets on this Island, he will live happy and for ever after. Queen Victoria, I am sure, owed a great deal of her health to the fact that the Island is easy to come to from the mainland and Princess Beatrice, our last Governor, lived to be a good age.

Whilst writing I have remembered that the Steinway tuner that comes down every three months from London also goes on to the Royal yacht to tune their piano, and so it might be much pleasanter for the King to have the piano from there over for this, and some more of his personal furniture from the Drawing Room. Then the Drawing Room will become a room of Royal furniture and, of course, would be much more delightful for the whole place if the King had his own furniture. The main thing is that the King should be content and happy and get well.

Best wishes,
Yours ever.

The new owners of Puckaster, whilst endorsing Uffa's good wishes for the King's recovery, wrote, 'Your proposals are absolutely fantastic and almost amount to farce. We do think it would be better for all of us if you would realize that Puckaster no longer belongs to you and that we are quite capable of deciding who should stay there and how the house should be arranged.'

Uffa was also planning a move at Cowes. He purchased the freehold of an old, rambling, disused and ancient warehouse, set back behind a grocer's shop and surrounded by water on three sides, and where, in the days gone by, brigs and other sailing vessels came alongside to load and unload their cargoes. The quay was in a poor state of repair and the building, if possible, even worse, the north wall bulging two feet out of plumb and the roof open to the elements. Additionally, the south-east corner had dropped some twelve inches during the many years it had stood in the sea.

Uffa made up his mind to convert the warehouse himself, mainly with the aid of one of his workmen who was a jack of all trades. Although the man gasped at the gargantuan building programme envisaged by Uffa, particularly when he announced his intention to build it without the aid of scaffolding, he listened carefully to the plans in detail and agreed that, under Uffa's guidance, it could possibly just be done. The townsfolk were more sceptical, expecting daily to see the whole construction fall down and disappear into the sea.

In the event Uffa built a beautiful, centrally heated home, later on installing a lift to all floors, and a look-out on top; the ground floor being reserved for his car, the storage of boats and their gear, fishing nets and lobster pots, in fact anything connected with boats and the sea. The quay was rebuilt with some difficulty, as it involved tidal work, and three pairs of davits were rigged in which to hoist up and hang various boats while, on the south-east corner, Uffa installed a scotch derrick for lifting out Flying Fifteens and other small craft.

From the windows and balconies Uffa could observe a never ceasing panorama of yacht racing, craft entering and leaving the harbour, and liners and major shipping making its way to and from Southampton and Portsmouth. The packet boat from Southampton came in so close to his window that Uffa could greet his friends as they arrived from the mainland, and when they took their leave he waved goodbye with a tea towel wrapped round a kitchen mop or broom.

The conversion had cost many thousands of pounds, and Uffa was indebted to his old friend Jimmy Damant, Commodore of the Island Sailing Club, for supplying mortages to keep the project going. Jimmy Damant at one time had such a big stake in the operation that Uffa referred to the property as the 'Commodore's House', and the name stuck. Shortly afterwards, when Uffa became Commodore of the East Cowes Sailing Club, it was generally assumed that the name derived from his own Commodoreship.

At the same time Uffa sold Medina House and Yard, deciding on the one hand to abandon the myriad headaches and problems associated with boatbuilding and on the other, by retaining a third interest in the new Company, Medina Yard Limited, and allowing himself to continue as Technical Adviser, to keep an eye on his old premises and retain use of the facilities. His one third interest in the new Company carried no directorship or shareholding, being in the form of promissory notes to cover the value he placed on plant, machinery and stock.

The association was not to prove a happy one. The Company, to augment the traditional boatbuilding, invested the bulk of its limited capital experimenting not too successfully with glass fibre, then in its infancy in this country.

There was also a clash of personality between Uffa, who continued to look upon the Yard and its employees as his own, and the working director. After a year Uffa demanded that his name be deleted from the Company's notepaper as Technical Adviser because he was never consulted, while the director claimed, 'I have felt all the way through that Uffa would have liked to both have his Yard and sell it.'

Unhappily the Company survived for less than two years before going into liquidation, and Uffa was saddened to see the plant and machinery he had accumulated over the years disappear under the auctioneer's hammer. He still had his own company, Uffa Fox Limited, which he had transferred to the Commodore's House, and he planned in future to concentrate on design, writing and any interesting challenge that might come his way.

Uffa's friendship with Prince Philip flourished, and when the town of Cowes presented His Royal Highness with his own Flying Fifteen, *Coweslip*, she was, after the trouble at Medina Yard, kept and maintained on Uffa's quay; an ideal arrangement as Prince Philip could land at the Commodore's House from the sea without having to run the gauntlet of the crowds in Cowes High Street.

In those early days of their association old Queen Mary was still very much alive, and kept a watching brief on the younger members of the family. After racing, Uffa and Prince Philip would sometimes return to the Commodore's House, where they would be joined by an equerry and Commander Michael Parker for an informal and relaxing belated lunch of steak or whatever. Sooner or later a telephone call would come through from Queen Mary to check that they had returned safely to the fold. On one occasion, after a particularly strenuous race and Prince Philip had gone upstairs to get his head down for a few minutes, Queen Mary was not pacified until Michael Parker went upstairs personally and peered into the bedroom to ascertain that Prince Philip was indeed there.

Before long Uffa was in financial difficulties. The amount of design work he received was insufficient to cover his outgoings, and he was forced to part with his remaining draughtsmen, relying henceforth on part-time labour only. At one point events seemed so insuperable that he even contemplated letting two floors of his home to help out with the expenses.

Uffa desperately needed to write another book, as his main source of income in the halcyon pre-war days had derived from his pen, but he appeared to have temporarily lost the vital ingredient. He also had secretarial trouble and got through girls at an alarming rate of knots. The ones he picked up at dances were seldom any good at typing, and the ones he procured through more orthodox channels were inclined to draw the line at taking dictation sitting on the lavatory seat while Uffa soaked in the bath.

Many chapters had been written up in fits and starts over the years, some on sailing, some autobiographical, and he was actively and constantly encouraged by his friend and publisher, Peter Davies, who came up with a plethora of ideas and suggestions; but they just could not get the book to the launching pad.

Alma, after serving in the ATS during the war, returned to the teaching profession and eventually to the Isle of Wight. Uffa made many attempts to patch up their differences; but when he called upon her, Alma, fearful of his silvery and persuasive tongue, would drown his speeches by reading from the Bible, mostly passages dealing with the 'Thou shalt not commit adultery' theme, and the perplexed and bewildered Uffa would depart with his tail between his legs convinced that his first wife had developed a religious mania.

Eventually of course Uffa wore Alma down, but she refused to leave her own little cottage and become one of his handmaidens. She did, however, much to the disgust of her family, join him at the Puckaster cottage from time to time where they went over and edited some of the already written chapters. Alma's interest was transitory though, for she had made a new life for herself and had no wish to be hurt again; and when it came time for Alma to leave Uffa had no taskmaster to prod him into further activity as she had done in the days gone by.

Uffa had two permanent and close companions, his mare Frantic and the black labrador, Bruce. Bruce came to Uffa as a small puppy, and throughout the years that Uffa lived alone they were well-nigh inseparable. Uffa's suits and reefer jackets were invariably dark navy, almost black in colour, with roomy poacher pockets inside; and when Bruce was a tiny pup he travelled around like a baby kangaroo in Uffa's pouch or pocket.

One of Uffa's favourite diversions was to go into a pub, order his drink and then casually allow his coat to fall open so that Bruce's little black head, accentuating the whites of his eyes, popped out and startled the fellow revellers. On one occasion the laugh was on Uffa for, when he lifted Bruce out to be admired by the astonished drinkers his hands made contact with more than he had bargained for as, in the excitement of the moment, Bruce had spent a penny in his pocket.

Bruce was an inveterate chewer. Not content with munching his way through the normal doggie diet of shoes, slippers and handbags, he dedicated himself to devouring almost anything within sight or smell. He particularly savoured the artefacts of the succession of well-heeled civil servants who arrived from the Ministries during the run of the airborne lifeboat contracts, a monumental disaster in an epoch of rationing and clothing coupons.

One of the most calamitous events occurred the day he chewed the lapels off the jacket of a senior official's suit; but the biggest crisis had Uffa rolling up with hysterical laughter. He burst into Dorothy Hounsell's office, quite out of control with mirth.

'Do take a look in the next office!' he gasped between giggles.

Peering through a crack in the door Dorothy spied a very serious and dedicated-looking administrator telephoning his headquarters while, seated at his feet beneath the table, Bruce happily tucked into the remains of what had once been a black bowler hat. Wartime Cowes proved far from the ideal locale in which to purchase a replacement bowler. Dorothy finally arranged for Morgans, the yachting tailors, to run one to earth, but not on the Island and not in time to prevent the

F

unfortunate victim from having to make his way bareheaded back to London.

By the time Bruce was fully grown Uffa had taught him a special trick, also useful in pubs, that of thrusting his cold wet nose up ladies' skirts. In addition to causing Uffa to double up with inward laughter as the women screamed or jumped in the air, it was a great ice-breaker, for by the time Uffa had rebuked his dog and apologized to the lady in question for his wicked hound's unseemly behaviour, an acquaintance-ship had quite often been forged and Uffa felt free to offer her a drink to compensate for the embarrassment.

Once, after Bruce had performed his trick with great success at the Buddle Inn at Niton, Uffa was approached as he was leaving by an old man who said, 'I am much older than you, but I have never had half the fun in life that you get, and incidentally the young woman that your dog startled and made jump is my daughter.'

When Uffa began to apologize, he said, 'Don't do that. Your face was a picture. I have never seen a countenance so alight with inward joy without breaking into laughter before.'

Uffa was a man who disliked his own company for any great length of time and occasionally, when the pubs had closed and he found himself at a loose end, he would round off the evening by dropping in at the local hop. After the last waltz at one such dance at Yarmouth, Uffa reeled towards his car only to find that it was non-functional. He and the gang with whom he had left the dance hall inspected the car, and by a process of elimination decided that the radiator was bone dry.

No water being readily to hand, and feeling the call of nature, Uffa opened his flies, climbed onto the bumper and peed into the radiator. He generously invited his newly found friends to join him and when some half dozen or so had happily, if not accurately, obliged, the car started up merrily and Uffa drove safely home. When relating the story later he referred to it as The Night of the Bumper Pee.

Uffa was not always the instigator of the mayhem, though his very presence often had an incendiary effect upon others. One year at Burnham-on-Crouch, when the Oxford, Cambridge and United Hospitals' three-cornered match had been followed by a boisterous dinner, drinking session and singsong, the young doctors and students manhandled Uffa, tied him to a chair, lashed some spars alongside the chair and, amid great hilarity, carried their captive back to his quarters. Uproariously they took the long way home, to Uffa's great constern-ation, as he had many friends at Burnham and had no desire to be accused of disturbing their sleep at such an unearthly hour of the morning.

Duly arriving at the Dormy House of the Royal Corinthian Yacht Club, with considerable difficulty they bore Uffa, still strapped to the chair, up to his little room. There was consternation however when they reached their destination for other forces had been at work. The room was still there but the bed was missing. Investigation revealed that some person or persons had managed to lift Uffa's bed out of the window and sling it down over the roof.

The discovery exhilarated and delighted the young men, some of whom had done rock climbing and mountaineering, and jolly as sandboys they climbed over the roof, eased away the ropes after untying them, and got the bed and Uffa, who had been all for sleeping on the bed where it was, back into the room.

The climbers' appetites were well and truly whetted by this new development, and as they had plenty of free ropes they took themselves back onto the roof and began lowering and sliding each other down over the roofs and in and out of the members' bedrooms. Their enterprise and high spirits were brought to an abrupt halt when one of the revellers climbed into an elderly gentleman's bedroom. He was outraged at being so rudely awakened, stuck a monocle in his eye, and demanded to know if the intruder was a member. Upon receiving a negative reply, he ordered the interloper to leave the premises immediately. The altercation had a sobering effect upon the trespassers who hastily bid Uffa adieu and disappeared into the night.

At breakfast next morning Uffa discovered that a retired Admiral was responsible for the idea of, and had organized, the slinging of Uffa's bed outside his room and tying it with ropes to the chimney pots and roofs. Uffa had been so late returning that the Admiral and his collaborators had wearied of waiting and missed the spectacle of his ignominious arrival at the Dormy House; but from their own rooms they had thoroughly enjoyed the sight of the young men clambering over the roofs, down the ropes and through the bedroom windows. Their glee was enhanced by listening to the conversations, from the loud and excited speech of the young climbers, to the sleepy growl of the members who were awakened from their slumbers.

There were one or two complaints after the night's escapade, but Uffa was able to convince the Commodore that he was, for once in his life, not the instigator of the frolic.

[17]

Prince Philip and Uffa were regular racing and sailing companions in
either *Coweslip* or the Royal Dragon *Bluebottle*, and they had a great
deal of fun together. Uffa wrote of Cowes week 1953 that Dick Free-
mantle was sailing past them in a Dragon and courteously raised his
hat in royal salute. That evening in the Club he turned to Uffa and
said, 'I'm damned if I ever take my hat off to you again, Uffa,' and
Uffa bet him three half crowns that he would.

Next morning, during the five minute gun when everyone was tense
and excited, Uffa related the incident to Prince Philip saying, 'What
about having Dick's hat off and three half crowns into the bargain?'

Prince Philip chuckled, and said, 'Right, I am all ready,' so Uffa
yelled out from *Bluebottle*, 'Good morning, Dick,' and off came Dick's
hat.

Another minute passed, and the atmosphere was even more tense as
they were only forty-five seconds from the starting gun, when Prince
Philip said, 'What about having Dick's hat off again?'

Uffa giggled, and called out once more, 'Good morning, Dick,' and
Dick raised his hat for the second time.

Apart from giving them a merry start to the day's racing it became
part of the sport, and during the course of the week they had the hat
off Dick at all sorts of exciting and unexpected moments.

Without turning this into a technical manual it would be impossible
to feature all of the many classes and individual yachts designed by
Uffa. His genius had earned him worldwide recognition, and yet there
was one thing he lacked. He had never qualified as a naval architect,
and it mattered to him. Not so much to put MINA after his name, nor
that the distinction would lead to more orders – for when a yachtsman
wanted an Uffa Fox design it was because it was an Uffa Fox design
and not because he was or was not a qualified naval architect – so much
as to belong.

There had been occasions when others who were more qualified
academically but less able from a practical point of view had succeeded
in making him feel inferior, almost as if he were wearing the wrong

school tie. Over the years Uffa made several attempts, directly and indirectly, to become a Member of the Institute of Naval Architects, but the answer was always the same. Pass the exams.

One of Uffa's all-time favourite and successful designs was the thirty-five-foot length overall cruiser *Stardust* which came off the drawing board for a Bombay yachtsman in 1939. Into her went Uffa's own thoughts and dreams of a round the world voyage, but as 1939 progressed it became increasingly apparent that it was not going to be the year that dreams were made of. She became his blueprint for a cruiser though, and whenever an enquiry arrived for a cruising yacht Uffa immediately dug out the plans of *Stardust* and took it from there.

Stardust was to pop up on the English yachting scene under a new name, *Mary Lunn*, and with a new owner, Viscount Runciman, and such was Lord Runciman's joy with her that when the time came for him to build a replacement he naturally turned to Uffa for a design, and so *Sandavore* was conceived and born.

Mid-way through the design of *Sandavore* Uffa became aware that Lord Runciman was the President of the Institute of Naval Architects, and was not slow in pressing home the advantage. He wrote a frank letter to Lord Runciman setting out his dilemma and his achievements. 'I have no desire to take an examination at my age, 54,' he concluded, 'and neither do I wish to become an Associate and be right down in amongst the new boys.'

Lord Runciman was quick to understand the predicament and promised to make some discreet enquiries, adding, 'You will appreciate this isn't the President's decision.' However, his influence obviously did no harm to Uffa's case, for within three months he was elected a Member of the Institute of Naval Architects, and another dream was realized.

Uffa was exhilarated to find himself emerging as something of a celebrity, with a correspondingly fuller and more varied life. He became a regular visitor to Buckingham Palace, and was a frequent guest aboard the Royal yacht *Britannia* while, during Cowes Week, the Royals would set aside one night for an informal dinner with Uffa at the Commodore's House, followed by a singsong round the piano.

When in 1954 the *Daily Express*, under the expert pilotage of Uffa's friend Sir Max Aitken, teamed up with the Ship and Boatbuilders' Federation to sponsor an Exhibition of Ship and Boatbuilding at Olympia – the first time for a great many years that there had been a purely Boat Show – Uffa was invited to join the experts on the *Daily Express* stand, where he referred to himself as the Chief Priest of the Technical Advisers. The Boat Show was to become an increasingly popular annual event which Uffa looked forward to immensely (even though it invariably left him exhausted with a sore throat and clogged-up bronchials brought about by too much talking and an overheated atmosphere), as he enjoyed meeting so many new and interesting people as well as renewing old acquaintanceships.

Uffa had been writing steadily for *The Sphere* over a period of time, and some of his articles were now being published in the *Sunday Express*, where his words reached out and caught the imagination of a wider and more comprehensive section of the public. There were also broadcasts and television appearances which, together with the not infrequent photographs of Uffa in the company of Prince Philip and other members of the royal family, made him an easily recognizable personality.

Uffa never lost his fascination for guns, and one of his favourites was Nelson's gun, the one used at Santa Cruz, which stood sentinel in the porchway of the Royal London Yacht Club at Cowes, of which Sir Max Aitken was Commodore. Late one night Uffa and Max eyed the gun and decided that, as it had not been fired for some hundred and fifty years, tradition demanded that they should see if it was still operational.

They assembled a bumper quantity of starting cartridges, and cut them open until they produced a good-sized mound of gunpowder. Uffa cradled the palm of his hand over the muzzle while Max blew down the touch hole, and by letting air escape they were confident that the gun was clear all the way through from touch hole to muzzle. Next they rammed the powder down the barrel and, in place of a cannon ball, followed it with large wads of damped down copies of the *Sunday Express*, and filled the touch hole with gunpowder. The muzzle was just outside the porch while the gun itself remained inside as, with a flaming newspaper for torch, they touched it off.

The gun did not respond with the crack of a modern weapon, but emitted a tremendous whirl and whaar. The recoil sent the gun clattering back inside the porch, to the discomfort of several members who had been observing progress from what they believed to be the safety of the rear. This was followed by a violent crash of shattering glass, the vacuum caused by the explosion having sucked the windows of the Yacht Club outside and into the road.

The dynamic experience did not deter the intrepid fusiliers from putting the weapon through its paces again at a later date, but when next they felt the urge they took the precaution of firing the gun from the safety of the Parade wall where the resultant blast had no adverse effect upon the Club's windows or members.

Provided it did not interfere with his designing and writing, Uffa planned the basic rhythm of his life to coincide with the seasons, devoting his summers to sailing, and the winters to lecture tours and other pursuits which forced him away from boats and the sea. He had numerous friends in all parts of the country and was a frequent guest in their homes, but he was no ordinary visitor who fitted quietly and unobtrusively into the ways of his hosts. No, within hours of his arrival the household would in all probability find itself revolving around Uffa. The telephone area would become almost his private domain, with calls arriving from assorted business contacts, publishers, the BBC, newspapers and just about everyone he knew within a radius of fifty miles. Sometimes it appeared that he had informed the whole world of his whereabouts.

Uffa also felt free to offer suggestions for improvements around the home. One of his first ports of call would be the kitchen to observe his hostess preparing dinner, which could prove nerveracking to say the least; but he would not be testing her culinary skill so much as checking on the saucepans. The reason was that shortly after the war Uffa was taken ill with a tummy upset, which he believed to have been brought about by overwork, a great deal of worry, too many late nights and a surfeit of drinking. The doctors in their wisdom decided to remove his gall bladder. At the ultimate hour Uffa received a telegram from two friends reading: 'Do away with your aluminium cooking utensils and you won't need an operation.'

Uffa doubted the possibility of such a simple cure, but he nevertheless experimented with his aluminium kettle and teapot, and after three days stopped feeling sick after tea as he had previously done. He resolved to carry out further trials, and within a remarkably short space of time felt so fit that he never did have the operation. His theory was that aluminium is a metal which wastes away rapidly in salt water, and as we add salt to most of the foods we cook we are continually filling our insides with aluminium which has a harmful effect upon our health and wellbeing.

He was quite obsessed with the aluminium cure and wherever he stayed, should he find aluminium utensils in the house, he would regale his hosts with the tale of his gall bladder and suggest that, in their own interests, they throw away their aluminium pots and pans without delay. When he was fortunate enough to be invited for a return visit, one of his first priorities would be to peer into the galley to see for himself if his instruction had been complied with.

He also developed a bee in his bonnet about emptying the bladder. Whenever poised to set forth on a car journey, even one of only a few miles, Uffa required everyone to go to the 'loo' and as he expressed it 'wring it out'. Quite often nobody wanted or needed to go; but it became such an issue with him that his passengers, particularly those who were accustomed to his ways, would go upstairs and pull the plug for no other reason than to keep the peace.

In between his sailings and his wanderings Uffa continued to design, and one of his favourites was the thirty-five-foot waterline cutter

Fresh Breeze, designed for Bill Morel of Porlock Weir in Somerset, and built by Harold Kimber. Uffa paid many visits to Harold Kimber's yard at Highbridge, observing the various stages of construction and helping solve any problems that might be encountered. He also spent wonderful days sailing, and riding over Exmoor, with Bill Morel, and it was a grievous day for Uffa when Bill Morel died before seeing the fulfilment of his dreams.

Uffa was disconsolate to see *Fresh Breeze* declining unfinished and unsailed in a mud berth, and with the blessing of Bill Morel's wife Wendy, to whom Uffa was a great comfort in the months following her husband's death, he purchased and completed her.

Finally, in April 1955 *Fresh Breeze* was ready for her maiden voyage, and they prepared to set sail for Cowes. For Uffa the designer, and Kim the builder, it was an exciting moment to observe the craft they had put so much work into, and seen lying idle for so long, come to life and adapt to their every wish.

Uffa had taken a leaf out of the book of the French fishermen on the Brittany coast, who have a rowlock in the stern of quite large vessels and can scull their boats with one oar when needing to move berth in the harbour, and had fitted such a one to *Fresh Breeze*. He also fitted her with a long sweep, and when they took on diesel and filled the tanks with fresh water, they sculled her with the sweep over the stern from berth to berth. This also gave them a jury rudder, should it ever be needed; and the rowlock itself had the elongated horns that close at the top, egg shaped, so that the oar would never jump out.

They had a quiet, uneventful sail down the Bristol Channel, and gently made their way southwards, sailing between the Scilly Isles and Land's End in perfect weather. Then, putting into Brixham as planned, Bill Morel's daughter Chloe, who had accompanied them on the first leg of the voyage, was put ashore as she had to dash up to the Midlands to play her cello in a concert. Her place was taken by Wendy, who would complete the journey to Cowes and stay over at the Commodore's House. The entry in the log read 'Changed Chloe for Mum'.

At Cowes Uffa attained a goal that had been with him since sailing aboard *Landfall* in the Transatlantic Race in 1932; he fitted his own yacht with a piano. The small upright piano was in the main saloon in gimbals, and when swung over, the keys downwards and the back of the piano upwards, it formed the cabin table.

Another innovation, which Uffa had previously tried out on *Flying Fox* and the Flying Thirty-five, was a saddle complete with stirrups, immediately abaft the wheel and with a clear view over the coach roof and dinghy, He claimed it to be more comfortable than a wooden seat, especially when *Fresh Breeze* heeled over; and that, because the saddle swivels, the helmsman is always plumb over the wheel in the most comfortable and effective position for his work.

Uffa sailed and raced *Fresh Breeze* at Cowes, and across the Channel, and found her a delight to handle. Sometimes he packed as many as twenty aboard her, the sound of the piano and voices raised in singing carrying joyfully across the water; and when Prince Philip sailed her Uffa insisted that any womenfolk aboard, Uffa's friends or crew members' wives, keep themselves below and out of sight.

From his earliest schooldays, long before he was introduced to the delights of sailing, Uffa had been a keen cricketer, and even in his late sixties he managed to fit in one or two games a year for his Club at Northwood, Cowes. He was a powerful slogger, hitting out at every ball coming his way, and as he never did anything by halves would normally either be out in the first over or go on to save the side, thinking nothing of hitting the ball out of the ground for six.

He also from time to time added a touch of light relief to the game, picking up the bat at the end of each stroke, tucking it under his arm and strumming it like a banjo, all the while singing little ditties to entertain the batsman at the other end and nearby fielders. On one occasion a member of the opposing team remarked that he had never before seen anyone play such terrible cricket and make so many runs so fast.

From his window each year, at the time of the September equinox, Uffa witnessed the uncovering of the Brambles Sandbank in the middle of the Solent, which only dries out during the autumnal equinox; and he thought what fun it would be to combine two of his favourite sports, sailing and cricket, by organizing a cricket match on the Brambles. The first game was rather a scratch affair; but over the years it developed, weather permitting, into an almost annual event between Uffa's crew and a team from Parkhurst prison. Dr Brian Pollock organized the Parkhurst team and all the gear, and Uffa and his band of merry men collected and manned the boats.

One year Uffa loaded *Fresh Breeze* up with about thirty cricketers and, with an escort of the Harbour Master's launch and three dinghies, set sail for the Brambles. They approached the bank from the south-east so that the last of the ebb took them onto the sand and, when the time came to depart, the young flood would be running strongly enough to drive their loaded boats towards *Fresh Breeze*, and they would be spared having to fight the tide to get ashore or aboard.

Directly they had landed they ran out a kedge to ensure that if by chance the tide rose before they rejoined her, *Fresh Breeze* would not float away, and then rowed in the dinghies towards the Brambles. One little island of sand, just three feet in diameter, was uncovered so they landed there. By the time the stumps had been set up on this tract another patch was revealed some twenty-two yards away, where they positioned the second set of stumps. The sand itself was wavy, and there were frequent pools of water left by the receding tide.

Uffa won the toss from the Prison Governor and batted first. This gave him a distinct advantage as the falling tide was exposing more and more of the sand, and one of the rules of the game was that if one hit the ball into the water it was a six. They played with a baseball, which is lighter and softer than a cricket ball and ideal for playing on sand, and carried a plentiful supply of spares so that the game was not held up while lost balls were retrieved by swimmers or by dinghy.

The game had to be fast for the play could not last more than an hour, so there was a law that the batsman must run every time he hit the ball wherever it went. Should the rising tide demand that the game be speeded up even further, the batsman was required to run whether he hit the ball or not.

Uffa's team won by two wickets. Then there was a rush to gather up the stumps, plus the Red Ensign and Uffa's racing flag, the Skull and Crossbones, which had been planted on the Brambles to stake their claim. The tide was rising quickly and the stream running fast, which meant a mad scramble to get aboard the dinghies and to *Fresh Breeze* before the tide covered the sandbank for another year. Uffa never ceased to marvel at the wonder of nature which enabled them to enjoy themselves so much, in such a short space of time, on a tiny island of sand that was to disappear so rapidly leaving no trace of their erstwhile presence.

Whenever free to do so, Wendy and Chloe Morel sailed with Uffa in *Fresh Breeze*, and on one particular occasion they joined him for the race from Hamble to Poole. After the day's racing and a pleasant overnight stop at Poole, next morning they set off to race *Fresh Breeze* back through the Needles Channel and up the Solent to Hamble.

There was a strong south-west wind blowing, and with their great reaching sail set they fairly roared along until they entered the Needles Channel. Facing a dead run up the Solent to Hamble they set *Fresh Breeze*'s spinnaker to keep her flying ahead at maximum speed. At the narrows of Hurst it was necessary to alter course as the Channel changed direction, and they prepared to gybe.

The more experienced crew members went forward to handle the spinnaker, as it was the largest and most difficult sail on the ship. Suddenly, as they gybed, there was the dreaded cry of 'Man overboard'. Uffa quickly put the wheel hard across and gybed all standing, keeping it hard over so that the yacht turned in the smallest possible circle, until she came up head to wind.

The enormous spinnaker was twisting and turning, and entangling

154

itself round all the rigging, preventing the boat shooting ahead to wind, with the result that they stopped some ten yards short of the man overboard. Harry Spencer, who had worked for Uffa during the war, and was in Uffa's opinion one of the ablest men with whom he had ever put to sea, immediately switched on the engine, and they motored up to the victim. He had been knocked unconscious by the mainsheet that had pitched him overboard, and although unconscious was beating the water with his hands as he floated.

No sooner was the man aboard than they stowed the spinnaker and, as they had used the engine, abandoned the race and headed for Cowes with a wind out on the starboard quarter. *Fresh Breeze* had quite a list on as she reached along, and they laid the unconscious man out in the self-baling cockpit, head downwards, so that the water would run out of him as well as being pumped. By the time they moored up at Cowes he was showing signs of life, but they took the precaution nevertheless of putting him carefully into a car and driving him to hospital for a check-up, where thankfully all proved well.

On joining *Fresh Breeze* the man in question had declared that he had done a considerable amount of sailing, and it was not until after the accident that he admitted it was the first time he had been in a sailing boat. The incident made Uffa emphasize the importance, when joining any yacht, of always truthfully stating one's knowledge and experience in order that the skipper may allocate tasks within one's capabilities and, as one progresses, assign more difficult duties which, as happened in this case, could prove dangerous for a beginner. Life is after all a learning process, and there is nothing to be ashamed of in beginning at the beginning whatever one tackles.

Uffa had great fun with *Fresh Breeze*, incorporating many of his dreams into her; but from the very beginning, in his heart of hearts, he knew that his steadily worsening financial situation would not allow him to keep her. Apart from his natural extravagance and keeping up with the Joneses, a major drain on his resources was the Commodore's House, which cost a small fortune to heat in the winter, and was continually springing leaks and in need of repair in one place or another. The paintwork was wearing and looking shabby, and when the BBC approached Uffa for permission to televise his house for their series depicting the homes of famous personages, the paintwork was patched up only in the rooms that were to be shown. In the drawing-room, when Uffa detected that the fourth wall would not be within camera range, he had just three walls painted.

Early in 1956 Uffa authorized a Warsash broker to find a buyer for *Fresh Breeze*. Meantime he continued to sail her, and by the time she was finally sold an event had taken place which was to completely revolutionize Uffa's lifestyle.

[18]

Uffa was introduced to Madame Yvonne Bernard, widow of the French industrialist, in France at the 1953 La Baule Regatta. Yvonne, fleeing Paris for the unfashionable month of August, had opened up her waterfront residence, and was a prominent guest at the social functions organized for the visiting yachtsmen. She could speak no English, and Uffa spoke no French, but with the aid of an amusing sign language and interpreters, they struck up a light-hearted relationship.

Yvonne, Uffa's junior by two years, was attractive, chic, and, surpassing all else in Uffa's eyes, pleasantly rounded. Distance, the language barrier and other interests inhibited their romance until the spring of 1956 when Uffa revisited Paris, igniting a spark that was to become a flame. Once Uffa had made up his mind, the inability to communicate verbally did not deter him, although it did necessitate, when he proposed marriage, going down on one knee to clarify his intent.

His feelings were summed up in a letter to Buckingham Palace shortly before the wedding. 'For some eleven years I have been sad and lonely inside me, but this has all changed now and it is impossible for me to express the joy I feel at the prospects ahead. I have written to Yvonne once or twice every day and telephoned her every day, because her speaking voice to me is the loveliest music on earth. On Friday and Saturday night I had a quiet dinner at the Royal Corinthian Yacht Club, and although I enjoyed the dinner I disliked being away from my home, even though it was only 200 yards, because at home, with the telephone, I feel linked and connected with Yvonne in Paris. If an angel had come to tell me that this wonderful thing of Yvonne and I being so much in love with each other was going to have happened I would not have believed it, and I cannot tell you how happy I am about it all, although, at the same time, I also feel rather humble and frightened.'

Yvonne flew in from Paris in time for Cowes Week, and the nuptials, proposed for a week later, were not allowed to interfere with the sailing.

Britannia had arrived, Prince Philip and the late King Faisal of Iraq joining her on the second day. There was not a breath of wind, and as the royals would reach Cowes too late for the racing, it was planned that Commander Michael Parker, Prince Philip's secretary, Squadron Leader Henry Chinnery, his Equerry, General Sir Frederick (Boy) Browning, his Treasurer and husband of Daphne du Maurier the novelist, and Uffa would sail Prince Philip's twenty-four-foot *Fairey Fox*, one of Uffa's designs for Fairey Marine, down to Newtown. Then, as soon as he could make his getaway, Prince Philip would pilot the King of Iraq down in the little *Albatross*, a fourteen-foot speedboat.

Without even a wag of wind, *Fairey Fox* drifted quietly on the first of the ebb towards Gurnard, until given a tow by a friendly launch for half a mile, by which time a slight breeze had made in from the west, as frequently happens at about one to one-thirty in the early afternoon on windless days, and, with a fair tide, they soon covered the miles to the mouth of the Newtown River where the floods were still running in.

Newtown, with its oyster beds and flats, attracting rare wild birds from far and wide, has managed to retain its solitary peace and charm, and very few yachts put in there. The wind was westerly as they luffed in on to the western point, the entrance to Newtown, where they beached, then swam and sunbathed until spotting a plume of white water heralding the arrival of Prince Philip and the King of Iraq. Far from the madding crowd they were able to enjoy the delights of water skiing in this quiet little haven before settling down to a leisurely picnic on the beach, unseen and unmolested.

In keeping with most other normal families, the royal family derive considerable pleasure from informal picnics, but the occasions when they have uninhibited freedom to enjoy them are few and far between. On one occasion, when Uffa had been invited to sail as a guest aboard *Britannia* with the Queen, Prince Philip, the royal children and some of Prince Philip's relatives from Germany, *Britannia* anchored off an uninhabited island, and with the British and German children brimming over with pent-up excitement after their days aboard ship, they were all ferried ashore for a picnic lunch.

Relaxed after an agreeable meal, the grown-ups were sitting around idly chatting of this and that, leaving the children to play and let off steam, when the then very young Prince Charles began teasing his mother by aiming small, hard, round pellets in her direction. The Queen responded in kind, and within seconds a friendly battle was raging as the various members of the royal family pelted one another enthusiastically with rabbit droppings.

With the Cowes Week sailing and frenetic social whirl safely over for another year, Uffa and Yvonne were married quietly at the Newport Register Office, leaving soon afterwards for Paris, followed by a honeymoon in La Baule. They had made up their minds to winter in Paris and spend their summers in England, and in order to avoid currency problems it was settled that Yvonne would pay for everything in France and Uffa in England.

Uffa adjusted surprisingly well to Parisian life. The apartment was large and luxurious, tastefully decorated with antique furniture, tapestries and Aubusson carpets, and Yvonne converted one of the spare bedrooms into a study where he could work away undisturbed. His creature comforts were taken care of by Adele, who had been Yvonne's maid for too many years to remember, and there were cars and a chauffeur at his disposal. On high days and holidays, until her marriage a year or so later, they were joined by Yvonne's daughter, Christine, who was studying in England.

Yvonne's business affairs had become somewhat complicated following the death of her late husband, and during their early months together Uffa devoted considerable time and energy to delving, unravelling and eliminating non-profit-making sections. They also each attempted to learn something of the other's language, Uffa succeeding in finding Yvonne an English teacher who came from the Isle of Wight; thus ensuring, as he expressed it, that she would learn English with the right accent.

Uffa invested in a first-rate dictaphone, and finding the words flowing comfortably and easily, worked steadily at his articles and the book, posting the completed tapes to Cowes for typing. The tapes were a potpourri of outline thoughts for Joe Porter, a retired expert in power boat design who had helped Uffa with a power boat for Lord Beaverbrook the previous year and who worked at the Commodore's House in his spare time; day to day instructions for Ellie; messages for Dorothy Hounsell, who had joined the team during the war and was another of his faithful band of part-time helpers; plus jokes, anecdotes or mouthwatering details of some delicacy Yvonne might be preparing for his lunch. He also made constant use of the telephone, thinking nothing of ringing Ellie at one o'clock in the morning, upon his return from dinner or a night club, should some new scheme have niggled his mind during the course of the evening's entertainment.

After eight months in France Uffa returned to Cowes mentally stimulated. His lack of even a rudimentary knowledge of the French language had caused him to switch off from his surroundings when in crowded places, visiting the theatre, attending speechmaking dinners, or if the Paris apartment was buzzing with womanly chat, and disappear into his own thoughts; and being Uffa his daydreams, as likely as not, would be creative.

Uffa was brimming over with new design ideas, and his part-time staff was augmented by his nephew, Tony Dixon, newly returned from completing his National Service, and who was to remain with him until the end. Not that Tony had been idle whilst on duty, for Uffa had on occasion sent him back to camp armed with sets of plans to be drawn up, Tony somehow managing to complete them using the bed in his billet as a drawing board.

There were weekly articles to be written for the *Sunday Express* all through the summer, and the follow-up correspondence to be dealt with. The article to attract the greatest response from readers was one devoted to do-it-yourself kits produced by the Bell Woodworking Company of Leicester, and Uffa was subsequently recruited by them to design for home production.

Until this time boats aimed at the amateur constructor had been designed with a chine or a corner on them as on a box, making them stand out like a sore thumb against the rounded, smooth look of the professionally built boat. The chine is great for high planing speeds, as it throws the water out and makes a sharp edge for the water to leave, which is why all high speed motor boats are built with chines; but it is a severe handicap for the lower speeds of sailing craft, increasing the wetted surface; and this corner, or the lee bilge, continually pushing in and out of the water sets up strong resistance.

When Bell Woodworking came up with a plywood that could be bent both ways, Uffa was commissioned to design a round-bilged fourteen-footer for the home builder. The project excited him, as it would enable the man in the street to compete on equal terms with those fortunate enough to be able to afford a professionally built craft; and in that moment *Pegasus* was born. Deep-chested, she had an easy, firm, round bilge, long clean run and planing lines. Her completed shape was indistinguishable from that of a professionally built boat, and the prototype was completed in seventy-two hours as against a normal building time of two hundred and ten hours for fourteen-footers.

Pegasus was the first craft to be built to the Bell Round Bilge Method, heralding a great advancement in design suitable for the amateur builder. Another feature of the package was that the boat could be built on the crate in which the kit of parts arrived. An advantage to building on packing cases, apart from the saving on expensive moulds or stocks, being that one can move the whole operation from one site to another when space is at a premium.

Uffa also designed the catamaran *Bell Cat* for Bell Woodworking, but in this instance he decided against the round bilge as he considered it would prove too difficult for the average amateur builder.

In the main Uffa's theories and designs were currently in the embryo rather than the moneymaking stage, and when he next set off to winter in France, after a busy and socially successful season in England, he carried with him a warning from his bank manager that he was perilously close to the ceiling on his overdraft facility; and he left behind an assortment of unpaid bills.

Uffa's *modus operandi* with accounts was to pay the smaller ones first, thus for a fairly reasonable outlay cutting down on the actual number of people dunning him for settlement; the larger creditors, with luck, receiving something on account to keep them quiet until the next month's statement was due.

A major casualty of the current cash shortfall was the telephone which, after repeated requests for payment were ignored, was finally cut off. Uffa was so enraged at the Telephone Company's high-handed attitude that he vowed never to have a telephone installed in his home again; and for many years anyone wanting to contact him by telephone was obliged to do so via the grocer next door, and to hold the line while an assistant searched Uffa out in the Commodore's House. Despite the inconvenience Uffa grew to value life without the peremptory shrill of the telephone shattering his concentration at all hours of the day and night; but Yvonne felt cheated that in Paris Uffa was free to make his numerous calls to England while she, in a foreign country, lacked the facility to make even a local call.

Telegrams, speeding urgent messages from foiled callers unable to make personal contact with Uffa, became the order of the day. Uffa also had recourse to the telegraphic system, and when wiring his birthday greetings to Prince Philip, he additionally aired his newly acquired knowledge of the French language, thus:

'Many many beaucoup many happy returns. Uffa and Yvonne.'

And received a telegram in reply:

'Thanks thanks merci thanks. Philip.'

For Cowes Week, a portable radio link was established between the Royal yacht *Britannia* and the Commodore's House to avoid having to trouble the local grocer.

Uffa was a great lover of music and art, provided the music was traditional and the painting bore a reasonable resemblance to the subject it was intended to represent. He described himself as a worry painter. On days when life's problems appeared insurmountable he would disappear with his artist's materials, and ere long the task of producing a wave that looked like a wave assumed such gargantuan proportions in his mind that the original conflict appeared minute by comparison; and as his equilibrium had a habit of restoring itself before he was half-way through a painting, the look-out, which became his studio when in Cowes, was strewn with unfinished works of art.

Some of Uffa's happiest hours were spent dining aboard *Britannia* where there is not only a printed menu of the repast in store for the hungry diner, but also a programme setting out the accompanying musical feast. Seated at dinner one night he posed a question to Prince Philip.

160

'What happens if someone at this table wishes to hear a piece of music not on the programme?'

His Royal Highness found the question an interesting one, and replied, 'People who dine on board *Britannia* never ever think of asking for music not on the programme, and as far as I know it has never happened. It will be fun to see what will happen. Write the music you would like to hear on the back of your card, and I will have it sent to the orchestra and shall be most interested in the result.'

Uffa was particularly fond of the violin solo 'Meditation' by Massenet from 'Thaïs', which he wrote carefully on his card. By way of an encore he added another piece, the final movement from the 'Water Music' by Handel. Some time later Uffa was aware of someone breathing down the back of his neck.

'They will play the "Meditation" now,' whispered a voice from behind.

The violinist was inspired, rendering a brilliant interpretation, while his audience beamed its delight throughout.

Before long the same disembodied voice came from behind Uffa. 'We have no copies of Handel's 'Water Music' aboard, so would like to play the "Meditation" again.'

Prince Philip smiled at Uffa, and said, 'I now know many more things about this orchestra. It is helpful and happy to do anything for anyone. It can suddenly play something not on the programme which has not been rehearsed, and it is composed of wonderful musicians who cannot be taken out of their stride. Thank you very much for opening up a new era for the diners aboard *Britannia*.'

Uffa numbered many musicians and composers amongst his friends, one of the dearest and most sadly missed being Dr Hubert Clifford, composer of the 'Cowes Suite'. The 'Cowes Suite' is in four movements. The first one describes bustling Cowes Roads and the myriad small yachts that dance across the water, the majestic ocean-going liners and stately men-of-war, submarines, oil tankers, merchantmen and the hundred and one miscellaneous craft that wend their way up and down the Solent.

The second movement is 'The Buccaneer', a hornpipe or rock and roll in which the composer attempts to put Uffa to music, and introduces the melody of 'We be Three Poor Mariners', one of Uffa's favourite songs. Had Dr Clifford lived longer, and written his 'Cowes Suite' two or three years later, he might well also have incorporated 'Spanish Ladies', a song Uffa was to successfully record and which became closely associated with his name.

The third movement, 'Carnival and Fireworks', depicts the social face of Cowes Week, with the plethora of cocktail parties ashore and afloat, banquets and balls, culminating in the Friday night firework display excitedly watched not only by the yachtsmen but by holidaymakers and Islanders who flock into Cowes for the event until the town appears to almost burst at the seams.

The final movement, 'Royal Visitor', moulds together the trumpet fanfares and grandiose melodies of a regal occasion as *Britannia* steams proudly into Cowes with the royal family aboard.

When the 'Cowes Suite', with Dr Clifford himself conducting, was performed at the Royal Festival Hall in London, Uffa was called upon to make a speech and introduce each movement. They, with their respective wives, were entertained beforehand by Vivian Cox the film producer, on a diet of smoked salmon and champagne cocktails, which caused them to arrive in gleeful high spirits and for Dr Clifford and Uffa to turn in sparkling performances.

Several months later Uffa was invited by Lieutenant Colonel Vivian Dunn, the Royal Marines Head of Music, to introduce a performance of the 'Cowes Suite' at their Deal Headquarters. Included in the Band of the Royal Marines that night were several musicians who had formed part of *Britannia*'s orchestra when Uffa had made his unprecedented requests; this inspired him, as part of his introduction, to relate the story of music aboard *Britannia*.

At the conclusion of the 'Cowes Suite', Vivian Dunn beckoned to one of the Marines, and following a whispered consultation the Marine disappeared.

After the interval Vivian Dunn, while introducing a piece of music, announced: 'And now we have a surprise for Uffa Fox. A Marine on a bicycle has ridden to the cinema to collect the man who holds the keys and controls all the music, and he has sorted out the 'Water Music', which will be played in this the second part of the concert,' and, entirely without rehearsal, the Band of the Royal Marines rose to the challenge with an inspired performance.

Uffa's brainchild, the Flying Fifteen, was to remain his all-time favourite, and he raced the Duke of Edinburgh's *Coweslip* in regattas up and down the country projecting and encouraging the class. He toured with *Coweslip* upside-down on the top of his car, plus mast and boom, resting on a special superstructure of stainless steel tubing consisting of a goal post on each bumper bar, joined by fore and aft lengths of tube on each side, with two cross-members going over the car at the front and rear of the body where the curvature of the roof is double and extremely strong. The four-hundred-pound fin keel perambulated in the back of the car.

Although Uffa himself travelled thousands of miles with *Coweslip* aloft he conceded that, as this method of transportation involved having to bolt the keel on, in addition to rigging the mast and launching the boat at the end of each journey, those owners equipped with dual-purpose trailers had found the simplest and best answer to the transit problem.

Typical of Uffa's travels with *Coweslip* was the summer of 1958 when, with Yvonne alongside him, he set forth on an early morning steamer from Cowes bound for regattas in East Anglia and Scotland. After an overnight stop to admire and enjoy the beauties of Cambridge, they continued their journey to Lowestoft where, in the early afternoon, Uffa unloaded *Coweslip* in the grounds of the Royal Norfolk and Suffolk Yacht Club, bolted on her keel, and fitted rudder, mast and rigging, so that all would be ready for launching on the morrow.

Uffa was an enthusiastic participant in all of the races. The first day passed off without incident; but on the second day, after leading at the end of the first round, he decided to chance his luck and go close inshore. Safely manœuvring the pier, he sailed inside the ends of the break-waters, misjudged, and to his horror crashed into the end of one, bursting a hole through *Coweslip*'s bow on the portside and causing an immediate rush of water into the boat.

Luckily he had a first-rate crew, a lawyer from Norwich, who, quick as a flash, dived forward and deflated the buoyancy bags, enabling him to reach the damaged area, and rammed his handkerchief in amongst the planking, tapping it down as hard as he was able. Uffa meantime was driving away to windward, handling the bailer as well as the jib, mainsheet and tiller, for there was no thought of abandoning the race.

They set to work with a will, both bailers working overtime, to rid themselves of the water before setting the spinnaker. The inevitable delay enabled the following boat, with her spinnaker already set, to go through and take the lead, while Uffa, despite the catastrophe, finished a gallant second.

Immediately the race was over they sailed *Coweslip* under the crane on the Royal Norfolk and Suffolk Quay and hoisted her out to inspect the damage. Still dripping wet, Uffa, who had planned how to save the situation long before the termination of the race, telephoned his friend Leo Robinson of Oulton Broad, who hastily sent down a boatbuilder; and by nightfall the wound was healed, made watertight, and the repair painted over.

On the third day *Coweslip*'s starboard crosstree carried away before the starting gun: so, whereas on the port tack Uffa could drive the boat to her limits, on the starboard tack he was obliged to ease her through the squalls in order to nurse the mast, and once again he had to content himself with second place.

Before setting off for Scotland they made a detour to Leicester, where the Bell Woodworking Company fitted *Coweslip* with a new stainless steel crosstree. Next stop Dumfries, and then across Scotland to Gourock where, to the excited interest of their fellow passengers who were mostly holidaymakers, they drove the car with the royal *Coweslip* perched above onto the ferry for Dunoon, on the other side of the Firth of Clyde, and the Royal Marine Hotel, home of the Royal Clyde Yacht Club at Hunter's Quay.

With Yvonne and the luggage safely unloaded, Uffa drove along the shore of the Holy Loch to Robertson's Yard at Sandbank, and once again went through the routine of unloading *Coweslip*, bolting on her keel and so on in readiness for the next day's racing.

All the Clyde Yacht Clubs combined to make it a memorable week both afloat and ashore, and Uffa was reluctant to depart; but his schedule demanded that he re-load his precious cargo, board the ferry back to the mainland shore, and drive the hundred miles or so to the Solway Yacht Club.

The Solway members, inspired by their Commodore, Joe Girotti, had purchased the lease of an old tumbledown quay, and with their own hands made a concrete launching slipway and protecting pier. *Coweslip*, with Uffa aboard, was to be launched down the new slipway for the grand opening. Yvonne performed the honours by cutting the ribbon, and *Coweslip* was ceremoniously launched, Uffa quickly hoisting her sail and starting down against the tide for the regatta itself. He led the fleet home, but only just, winning the Kippford Quaich, before driving up, next day, for the regatta at Largs which the Queen and the Duke of Edinburgh would be attending.

On the first day at Largs Uffa was up at six o'clock to put *Coweslip* over on the early morning tide, returning as hungry as a hunter to the hotel where he consumed an enormous breakfast. There was hardly a puff of wind as the day progressed, the classes starting ahead of the Flying Fifteens being still only fifty yards or so across the Firth of Clyde on their way to the first mark. Uffa made up his mind, under these conditions, that the wind would pull south-west up through Firth, and though it was so quiet that they could see their faces reflected in the water, the Flying Fifteens moved gently out towards the Firth. Uffa kept to the south of the fleet near the Cumbrae, taking the first of the airs out of the south-west, and pulled ahead.

Once clear of the island they found a spanking breeze out on the Firth of the Clyde, and sailed along at a steadily increasing pace straight across the Firth. There were some four or five boats sailing at a reasonable speed while the remainder of the fleet, all classes, were becalmed frustratingly in the channel between Cumbrae and Largs. *Coweslip* was the first of the Flying Fifteens home, and second of the whole fleet, most of which had started first and had the misfortune to end up hours behind. As Uffa said, it was that sort of day.

After Largs, *Coweslip* was hauled up, dismasted and de-keeled for the last time, and put to bed on her cradle over Uffa's car ready for the journey south. Travelling from regatta to regatta, on this voyage alone, Uffa claimed that *Coweslip* had her keel bolts in and out no less than ten times.

Life was not all regattas and musical evenings. Uffa was seldom out of touch with his staff, mostly telephoning them at their homes at night, and there was always some new design in the pipeline.

One of his commissions was from George O'Day of Boston, builder of the Day boats of America, to produce an all-purpose sailing, racing, picnicking and generally having fun boat. Uffa's design, the famous Day Sailor, was an outstanding success, with fleets springing up all over the States and Canada. Later on, as the class expanded and the royalty cheques began rolling in, it became one of his most lucrative sources of income.

[19]

Despite being in regular contact with Peter Davies in the quest for a mutually profitable manuscript from Uffa's pen, nearly two decades were to run their course since the publication of *The Crest of the Wave*.

In his post-war wine, women and song era Uffa had been inconstant and unequal to the task of sustaining his writing and interest in any one subject for a sufficiently durable period to complete a full-length book, and with every advancing year there became less and less room in his literary parade, for whereas when he penned his early tomes sailing authors were few and far between, now every Tom, Dick and Harry who ever set foot in a boat was inspired to commit himself to print, and the bookshops were flooded with works on sailing in all its varying aspects. Additionally, escalating costs rendered the glossy, expensive Uffa-type book increasingly less viable.

Uffa, with his usual verve, had a plethora of ideas and wrote pilot chapters for several books ranging from a guide to life on the Isle of Wight to a technical work on the conception and building of a sailing boat, using *Fresh Breeze* as his inspiration, but for one reason or another they all floundered in mid-stream. The principal manuscript, on which he had been working steadily over the years and finally completed in Paris, his autobiography, was returned with so many suggested improvements that he was at a loss to know where to begin, and temporarily shelved the project. Adding to the dilemma, Peter Davies was a sick man with only a short span of life left, and changes were taking place within the publishing company itself.

At this betwixt and between stage Uffa found himself in contact with another publishing house, George Newnes Limited, who expressed interest in a book on sailing from the stable of a household-name author. Not one of Uffa's former lavish productions so much as a standard-sized book that would appeal to the vast new sailing community, an entirely different genus from the privileged few of the days gone by. Uffa jumped at Newnes' offer and, after a week spent at Cowes closeted with their expert, a format and contract were settled.

Overjoyed at the news, Yvonne, whose assets included a seven-storey car park with garaging for 1,000 cars in Montmartre, had constructed for Uffa a penthouse office suite on the roof of the edifice, which enabled him to be free of the comings and goings at the apartment and have all the time and peace in the world to cogitate and immerse himself in the necessary research and writing. At eighth-floor level it was so tranquil that Uffa once heard the song of a nightingale from the trees in the Boulevard de Clichy below.

Yvonne also engaged a bilingual secretary, Jacqueline, to help and guide his footsteps; and in the summer of 1959, twenty years after the publication of his last work, a new volume called *Sailing Boats* was launched. The book far exceeded expectations, and to the delight of both author and publisher was reprinted within four months of publication. A year later, *According to Uffa*, a manual on the handling and sailing of boats, made its appearance on the bookstalls with equal success.

Uffa was at Yvonne's house in La Baule, working on the second of these manuscripts, when he received word of the untimely death of Dr Hubert Clifford. The blow was a double one for, added to the great personal loss, Uffa and his friend had been collaborating with George Martin, Artists and Repertoire Manager of EMI Records, to produce a long-playing record of Uffa singing, and Dr Clifford conducting, a collection of sea shanties and Jack ashore songs.

The notion of a gramophone record had been conceived one stormy night aboard Sir Max Aitken's schooner *Lumberjack*. They were returning from France, with all but Uffa and Sir Max asleep below: and though *Lumberjack* was sailing fast, with a gale of wind blowing, she was well snugged down and no heavy water came aboard. It was such an exhilarating sail that they let the others sleep and took turns at the wheel through the enchantment of the night.

As Uffa steered he began to sing and, with a happy heart, he sang sea songs and shanties that he had learnt as a boy from his father and from captains of old sailing ships who had retired to live out their days at Cowes.

Listening to Uffa's seemingly endless repertoire, Sir Max said to him, 'You should record these songs, because although many are known, some are not, and none have been sung in that way before. Unless you put them down they will be lost in the years to come.'

The question now arose, if the record was to proceed, of finding a substitute for Dr Clifford. It has been said that after the darkest hour comes the dawn, and so it was in this instance, for the famous composer, conductor and arranger, Ron Goodwin, agreed to fill the breach. Not knowing Ron Goodwin personally, Uffa received the news with less than his usual enthusiasm, fearing that their relationship would lack the affinity which had existed between himself and Dr Clifford, to the possible detriment of the recording. He need not have worried, for in Ron Goodwin he was to find a kindred soul, as full of fun and the joys of life as Uffa himself, and with a delightful sense of humour all his own.

The first meeting between Uffa and Ron was scheduled to take place at Cowes, where the composer duly arrived after a pleasant crossing accompanied by George Martin who, despite his many other achievements, will doubtless pass into history as the man who had the foresight to anchor The Beatles and guide their footsteps up the slippery ascent of the recording ladder. Their steamer from Southampton was all set to pass within fifty yards of the Commodore's House at seven-twenty p.m. and Uffa, to surprise his guests and mark the occasion, determined to fire a grand salute from his muzzle-loading cannon in their honour.

Eager to make a thundering impression, Uffa rammed in a mass of extra powder much too tight, and when he put the match to the touch hole, a mere eighteen inches from his head, there was an almighty bang as the cannon exploded back through the touch hole and into his face. He snapped his eyes shut instinctively, but could not draw back in time to avoid his face and eyelids becoming peppered with a black powder which pitted the whole of his face and left him bleeding profusely.

Although in shock he remembered his assignation with the visiting musicians; so, quickly grabbing a towel and looking, as he described it later, like a 'spotted dick', he dashed to the car and drove the hundred and fifty yards to the pontoon, mopping up blood with the towel as he went. Ron Goodwin said that he would never forget being greeted by a dishevelled, bloody, pock-marked figure, swabbing its face with a bloodstained towel, as he stepped ashore on that eventful first visit to Cowes.

After settling the guests, Uffa cleaned up his face and doused it with TCP before joining them at the piano, where they worked away until dinner was served. Some of the songs they proposed to use were unknown without written music, in which case Uffa sang them line by line with Ron dotting the notes down as they went along.

Returning to the piano after a boisterous meal, they carried on singing and playing until the early hours of the morning, by which time Uffa had sung fourteen songs and Ron had scored the simple melody in Uffa's key. Their work was their pleasure and all were up and about again in time for Ron and George to catch the seven-fifteen steamer and be in London by ten o'clock in readiness for a new day's work.

Stage two of Uffa's musical adventure occurred a few days later when he visited George Martin's office in London, and sang the complete set of songs into a recording machine, to provide Ron Goodwin with a basic disc from which he could build up and arrange the music, at the same time retaining Uffa's individual lilt which Ron was anxious not to lose.

Next came a visit to the recording studio with George Martin, where they found Ron Goodwin standing by with twenty musicians and the superb Mike Sammes singers who were to give the record its muscle. When all were settled they went straight into action with a trial run of one verse and chorus, in order to test the arrangement of the microphone and various recording units, and directly the technical problems were ironed out they were ready to record.

Uffa's voice, due to his tendency to become even more bronchial with the advancing years, was inclined to lose strength when he sang too loudly or for too long, so it was suggested he confine himself to the verse only and leave the chorus to the Mike Sammes singers.

After the first song they were summoned by George Martin to the control room, which was set twelve feet or so above and well back, to listen to the playback. Uffa was truly startled at what he heard. The effect was beyond his wildest dreams. For years he had sung this particular song without piano or any musical accompaniment, booming in the bath, muted in his thickly carpeted rooms, or snatched from his mouth and rendered virtually inaudible in a gale of wind; but now, thanks to Ron Goodwin's genius at arrangement and the wonderful team of musicians and singers, it had been transformed into a pleasingly rhythmic melody that embraced his own voice with magic.

During the three half-day sessions they recorded the fourteen songs, Uffa relishing every moment, for he enjoyed being the centre of attraction and was completely without awe when surrounded by a captive audience to whom he was known. The only time he had suffered a tremor of fear of his fellow men had been in his younger days when confronted by a sea of faces on entering a crowded room alone. He had then taken a deep breath and dived in. The problem ceased to arise after he became a household name for there was invariably someone to call out 'Hello, Uffa' as he entered, and he soon found himself completely in the swim and in command of the situation.

This early apprehension taught him compassion, and in later years, when he spotted a youngster alone and ill at ease at a party he would thrust a plate of food or a tray of drinks in his or her direction with instructions to pass them around, knowing that, by occupying one's hands and self usefully in this manner, one quickly loses self-awareness in the interest of others.

Uffa also had a habit, more especially after he had made his name, of repaying help or hospitality by inviting those to whom he felt in debt to be his guest at other people's parties, clearing it with the host or hostess beforehand, of course; and almost always arrived surrounded by his satellites. A typical example of this was secreting the name of his bank manager, or others to whom he felt under obligation, in the depths of proposed guest lists for VIP cocktail parties when his advice and recommendations were sought.

The record, 'Uffa Sings', was greeted favourably by the press and proved successful within its specialized field; one particular number, 'Spanish Ladies', becoming a firm favourite with disc jockeys on request programmes; and it also, for some inexplicable reason, had a spellbinding effect upon children.

The older generation was equally enchanted, and Uffa was invited to sing the songs in person at Cherkley, the home of Lord Beaverbrook, to celebrate his eighty-second birthday, when the guest of honour was Sir Winston Churchill. He was accompanied by the Ron Goodwin Orchestra and Mike Sammes Singers, who enjoyed themselves so much that they said afterwards they would have happily played and sung without a fee just for the honour and pleasure of the evening.

Aware that Sir Winston would be present, Yvonne's cousin, Pierre Deleplanque, supplied Uffa with a specially made cigar, one metre in length, to present to the great man. Before commencing to sing Uffa made a little speech laughingly saying that the cigar was for a good boy, not that Sir Winston had ever been one. Then in more serious vein he quickly made amends by declaring that it was the greatest cigar in the world for the greatest man in the world. Sir Winston was highly delighted with his gift, and throughout the evening he conducted, beating time with the gargantuan cigar, for from his schooldays at Harrow and onwards he had revelled in a good old singsong.

Later on, when they were almost alone and the room was still, Uffa sang the 23rd psalm (Crimond) for the pleasure of Lord Beaverbrook who was well pleased to have had such a memorable birthday party.

The friendship between Uffa and Ron Goodwin, born one bloodstained night at Cowes and forged in London and Cherkley, was to prove an enduring one. Ever after, Ron was an always-welcome guest at the Commodore's House, and one of the highlights of Uffa's year was the annual jamboree in London when he was a member of Ron's party at the charity dinner in aid of The Stars' Organization for Spastics.

Uffa made frequent broadcasts and television appearances publicizing the record and his books, and was also invited to appear in the television panel game, *What's My Line?*. Almost without exception he happily and gratefully accepted any work or paid sponsorship that came his way. One offer he did decline, however, was to appear in cabaret at a top London hotel as a sea shanty singing comedian. In addition to not visualizing himself as a stand-up comic, he had recently been on the receiving end of some bad publicity following a scene when several women got up and staged a walk-out at one of his talks, protesting at the blueness of the content. He also from this time cut down on lectures, one of his less lucrative jobs of work in any case; for, wherever he lectured he invariably stayed at the top hotel and treated himself to the best of everything, so his out-of-pocket expenses had a nasty habit of soaring higher than the fee.

Uffa's ambitious imagination took flight with the record, and he began gathering together titles of well-loved and traditional songs to form into a song book, hoping to record many of the numbers himself. Alas, there was no demand for such a song book in a world where people no longer amuse themselves and each other, but worship, red-eyed and cramped, before the flickering rectangular box. Neither did EMI pursue the subject when he suggested further recordings.

Later on, Uffa was to compère a series of concerts entitled 'Music of the Sea' for the British Concert Orchestra under the baton of a friend of many years' standing, composer and musical director Victor Fleming, who also had his home on the Isle of Wight.

Their first concert, held at the Guildhall, Portsmouth, set the pattern for the remainder, which were to take place at assorted venues in southern England. They opened in fine style with the overture to the 'Flying Dutchman', music filled with the wildness of the sea in a gale; then, by way of contrast, 'Senta's Melody'. Next came contralto Noreen Berry singing 'Sea Slumber' and 'Where Corals Lie' from Sir Edward Elgar's 'Sea Pictures', first sung by Clara Butt at a Norwich Festival in 1899 followed by a Command Performance for Queen Victoria at Balmoral. 'Where Corals Lie' was a particular favourite of Uffa's.

The mixture of orchestral pieces and vocal numbers, and including the 'Cowes Suite', continued throughout the programme; and Uffa, a little lost without the backing of the Mike Sammes singers, rendered 'A Life on the Ocean Wave' before introducing Owen Brannigan to sing 'Hearts of Oak', 'The Bay of Biscay', 'A-Roving' and 'The Mermaid'.

The programme concluded with Sir Henry Wood's 'Fantasia on British Sea Songs' followed by Sir Malcolm Sargent's inimitable arrangement of 'Rule Britannia'. Although the attendances were not nearly as favourable as had been hoped and expected, Uffa revelled in the experience and was able to chalk up yet another 'thing done'.

By now the time of life had come for reaping laurels through past endeavours. Uffa's first award, The Diploma of Royal Designer of Industry at the Royal Society of Arts, had been made in 1955 and gave him untold joy and happiness, more especially as it was formally presented by His Royal Highness The Duke of Edinburgh, who said at the time, 'There is a tendency nowadays to imagine that everything new must be scientific or rational. Uffa Fox as a helmsman in his day was a world beater, and as a designer of boats he is also a world beater. I can state categorically that there is practically nothing scientific or rational about Mr Fox. Like all great designers his genius is entirely human.'

Uffa, spruced-up and penguin-like in his morning suit, was accompanied by Yvonne and myself when he attended Buckingham Palace to

171

receive the CBE. The Queen found time to chat with him personally during his part of the ceremony, and when his moment of glory was spent he joined us to view the presentation of the remaining honours. Displaying more than a passing interest in the number of what he termed 'worthy' women gathered there to collect awards for services rendered in their various communities up and down the country, he could not refrain from commenting rather loudly that one of them was even 'bedworthy'.

The neat and tidy morning-suited Uffa was in complete contrast to his mien on one of the previous occasions when I had accompanied him to Buckingham Palace. Rendezvous-ing at Waterloo, and anticipating a meeting with his publisher followed by lunch at Rules in Maiden Lane, I was greeted with 'We've got to go to Buckingham Palace first to deliver some plans to Prince Philip.'

Uffa bore the appearance of having suffered a rough crossing from Cowes to Southampton. His hair and bushy eyebrows stood raggedly awry, almost at attention. His navy blue suit, jacket buttoned on the wrong button, boasted an overmantle of dogs' hairs and fluff; while his black shoes, their uppers displaying a white saltwater tide-mark, trailed knotted and dangling laces. In his hand he clutched a bulging, old and crumpled brown paper and string carrier bag advertising the wares of the local butcher.

'Buckingham Palace,' said Uffa to the taxi driver.

The man looked him up and down and surveyed him from all angles, 'I often go there for a cuppa with the Queen myself', he remarked sarcastically.

Uffa, frozen in the act of opening the cab door, stood stock still. Unaware until that moment of any possible irregularity in his appearance, and shocked that the driver considered him other than Buckingham Palace material, he was momentarily bereft of speech.

'Take me there anyway,' he commanded, after a stunned silence.

'My name's Uffa Fox', he said to the policeman on palace duty, and was waved through immediately. He paid off the driver without a word, his ego for once deflated.

'Funny man, that taxi driver,' was his only comment as he entered the palace, straightening his jacket and brushing his shoes up and down on the backs of his trouser legs as he went. The friendly reception he was accorded as he breezed into the private apartments, like a breath of fresh air and with the tang of the briny still upon him, quickly restored his equilibrium.

Uffa's honours were not confined to his native land, for in 1961 the French Society for the Encouragement of Research and Invention made him a Commander of the Order of Merit, an award he particularly cherished as he was the only Englishman to be so exalted.

Uffa's designs were as many and diverse as they were fun for him to create, and all were tackled with the same spirit of positive enthusiasm. When commissioned to design model yachts for children he put as much of himself into the project as if he had been designing a world-beating ocean racing yacht.

He accepted the appointment of Consultant Naval Architect to Rover Gas Turbines, a subsidiary of the Rover Car Company, with high hopes. The thought of designing boats suited to the Rover Gas Turbine Engine appealed to the pioneer in him. The Company was equally confident, a spokesman saying, 'With Mr Fox to advise on marine applications we should see a revolution in power-weight ratios, and subsequently in speed and comfort in small craft.'

Much good work was put into the project, unfortunately to little or no avail for Rovers were taken over later by the Leyland conglomerate and the experiments doomed to take a back seat.

Uffa was proud and delighted when he was allowed to teach the royal children to sail. Prince Philip was himself a sailor prince, with a natural affinity towards the sea and those who sailed the ocean deep; and in taking Prince Charles, and as they grew up the younger royal children, with him aboard *Britannia* and to the Commodore's House, he fostered within them a similar love and understanding of the wind and the waves.

The untidy mixture of lobster pots, rolls of plans and drawings, antique furniture and junk, fishing nets, rare nautical books, silver trophies and the odd Eskimo canoe were a source of fascination for the young Prince Charles; but the sight of a kitchen was perhaps the greatest novelty. The kitchen is on the left at the top of the stairs as one mounts from the boatshop, and Prince Philip never went by without first popping his head round the door for a word with the helpers. While the grown-ups chatted over their pre-lunch beer or aperitifs, Prince Charles would amuse himself in the kitchen helping Ellie or whoever else was on duty. His eyes nearly popped out of his head when he saw a tin of peas being opened for the first time, and his sense of achievement when he was allowed to take the tin opener and open his first tin of fruit successfully was akin to scaling Everest.

Wherever possible on these informal jaunts Prince Philip introduced an element of down-to-earth reality into the lives of his children, so that they would develop a greater understanding and knowledge of the everyday world around them, and from someone like Uffa they could learn more of the facts of life in an afternoon than during a year spent in the classroom. They were also taught the practicalities of life. On one occasion, for example, returning to the Commodore's House for an impromptu lunch after a morning's sailing, the young prince remarked that he would like potatoes with his meal.

'If Charles wants potatoes then Charles must peel them,' ordered his father, whereupon Prince Charles made his way happily to the kitchen and applied himself diligently to the task of scraping his way through a large bowl of potatoes, doubtless savouring them all the more later for having been involved in the preparation and cooking.

Prince Philip's foresight in acquainting the heir to the throne from an early age with lifestyles other than those of palace and protocol must surely have contributed greatly to Prince Charles's ability, in later life, to mix naturally and converse on equal terms with people from all countries and from all walks of life.

The pattern of the Cowes Week dinner party changed radically with Uffa's marriage to Yvonne. Hitherto the dinner itself had been an all-male affair, with Uffa's assorted helpers and girlfriends who had been involved in the preparation and serving of the meal being admitted later for the singsong only. Yvonne, naturally, was not prepared to be confined to the kitchen, and in the course of time brought her own chef from Paris for Cowes Week and to supervise the banquet. When Uffa first broke the news that Yvonne would be present at the traditionally stag dinner he suggested that the royal party should also include members of the opposite sex, but for that year at least there were none to bring.

Money was no object at the Commodore's House when it came to entertaining. One summer, just before the Cowes Week dinner party, Uffa was approached by Ted Legg, the local fisherman, with a twenty-five-pound salmon that he had caught off Hill Head. Uffa measured the fish, and despite its length of forty-two inches and width of ten inches being much too big for any of his assorted fish kettles, had to have it. He contacted Joe Bowen of Atkeys, the ships' chandlers, with the measurements and commissioned him to construct a large tinned copper fish kettle within the day.

When the completed utensil arrived it was so huge that it had to be placed diagonally across the gas stove with all burners lighted to cook King Salmon. Fortunately Uffa had a belt and braces attitude towards the preparation and cooking of his food, duplicating most items of kitchen-ware, and surpassing himself with cookers of which the roomy kitchen of the Commodore's House boasted no less than five – two electric, one gas, one Aga, and, should all else fail, a reserve cooker for use with a bottle of butane or Calor gas.

In addition to the custom-made fish kettle, Uffa asked Harry Spencer, the pattern maker and rigger, to fashion a long wooden platter to suit the fish, and this also arrived in time for the evening's festivities. There were over twenty guests for dinner that night, including Prince Philip, Prince Charles and Princess Anne, and the *pièce de résistance* had the honour of being carved by Prince Philip himself.

Uffa was frequently asked if Prince Philip was a good skipper of a boat, and his reply was: 'If Prince Philip sailed and raced as much as ordinary sailing mortals he would be top flight. As it is, racing as he does only three or four days a year, he is seldom out of the picture and generally within the first three boats home. In all of the many years we have been sailing together, I have never known another helmsman take a boat so accurately across the tide when off the wind, when a straight line is the shortest and quickest distance between two buoys. He has the ability to swiftly assess the strength of the tide and keep his sailing craft on a steady course so that we never have to alter the trim of the spinnaker or other sails unless it is due to a shift or flaw in the wind.'

Asked to compare Prince Philip's sailing ability with that of Prime Minister Edward Heath, Uffa responded: 'Ted is a marvellous steersman; but Philip is better at the game because he has been at it longer.'

Uffa was none too happy with the way fellow yachtsman Edward Heath was running the country. Proud of his English heritage he felt that, by default or deceit, the steady influx of immigrants into Britain under successive Governments of both parties was robbing the grass roots Englishman of his identity, and was accomplishing by infiltration what Hitler had failed to achieve by force.

So enraged was Uffa by what he called the foreign invasion of his country that he sat down and wrote a strongly worded letter to the Prime Minister pinpointing the manifold disasters that would befall Britain if he steamrollered the country into the Common Market.

Mr Heath's reply was short and to the point. 'On this issue we must agree to differ.'

It was not all fair weather sailing for Prince Philip and Uffa. The intrepid mariners had their mishaps, as all sailormen do, like the day Prince Philip came within inches of losing his life when the wooden boom of Uffa's crane, which was about to lift *Coweslip* out of the water, collapsed.

Coweslip, with Prince Philip at the helm and Uffa crewing, had keeled over five minutes or so after the start of the Flying Fifteen race. She was one of the first of the starters to cross the line and had been going well on the starboard tack in a choppy sea when another yacht came in too close, one of the frequent extra hazards Prince Philip had to contend with as the price of fame. In the stiff breeze Prince Philip quickly took avoiding action, nearly touching another boat but averting a collision.

Almost immediately *Coweslip* was caught in a high gust of wind and went over. Her hull all but disappeared from view as she went down, her sails spreading soggily across the angry sea. They succeeded in righting the boat, and with difficulty got the sail down. Keith Beken, the yachting photographer, got a line across from his launch and towed them back to the Commodore's House.

Prince Philip stayed with the craft to fix the slings lowered from the crane to raise *Coweslip* onto the quay, and was the last to climb up onto the jetty from the landing stage as lifting operations commenced.

The waterlogged Flying Fifteen was about to be hauled up when the combined weight of boat and water ripped the back stays of the crane from the wall. It half collapsed, and as it did so the twenty-five-foot main boom crashed down missing Prince Philip by a terrifyingly small margin as he jumped smartly out of the way.

Prince Philip was in no way put out and was quite cheerful about his adventure, which was watched by half the population of Cowes and provided a field day for cameramen and reporters.

[20]

Life was traumatic at times, especially at Cowes where, by virtue of doubling as office, drawing office, workshop and general assembly point for visiting yachtsmen, clients and business associates as well as a home, the Commodore's House was lacking in one vital ingredient: privacy.

On the more hectic days of high summer when Uffa was battling with a deadline for an article or whatever, in addition to sailing, socializing and the day-to-day problems of running a Company, and Yvonne needed desperately to know the answers to such vital questions as to whether it was formal or cocktail dress for the evening's festivities, there was on occasion sufficient static generated within the four walls to power a lightship.

Out of season Cowes had little to offer a true Parisienne like Yvonne. She would champ at the bit with the frustration of not being able to pick up the telephone and iron out her own business problems as they arose. Consequently her visits to Cowes became shorter, and were in the main confined eventually to Cowes Week and other highspots.

There was also the language problem. They had got along marvellously when neither could speak a word of the other's language; but now they were able to communicate sufficiently to wrangle, and quite often problems arose out of a situation only partly understood.

A typical example of this occurred while they were staying with my mother and me at Rustington. Yvonne enjoyed antiques and was something of an expert on the subject. One morning, while Uffa remained at home writing and telephoning, she and Mahala ambled down to see Frank and Gladys Ellery at the local antique shop. Whilst there Yvonne fell in love with a charming little Regency footstool, and not understanding Frank when he said that the item was already earmarked for a dealer in Chichester, in the afternoon she persuaded Uffa to return with her to purchase it.

Frank was always more than generous with the gin and tonic, and they passed an enjoyable afternoon sitting around his cottage happily drinking, and discussing the footstool and the state of the world in general. The longer they lingered the more determined Uffa and

Yvonne became to secure the footstool; and Frank, who had also partaken well of the flowing bowl and was in no way a match for an Uffa in pursuit of something he had set his mind upon, allowed them to walk out of the cottage with the stool.

When the dealer from Chichester arrived to collect his property – he had not actually paid for the stool but he and Frank had a nodding arrangement – there was hell to pay. He was not the sort of man to settle for another item, allow the matter to drop, or see humour in the situation; and, despite his many years' friendship with Frank, expressed determination to not only have his pound of flesh but to put Uffa Fox in his place.

He sent a strongly worded letter to Cowes demanding the immediate return of his property. Uffa, not used to receiving letters couched in such terms, was completely taken aback by the ramifications of the whole affair. If he had given as much as a passing thought to Frank Ellery's assertion that the stool had been promised to another dealer, it had been dismissed in his mind as sales talk. However, rather than be involved in any unnecessary aggravation, he ordered that the stool be wrapped post-haste and despatched to Chichester. Yvonne, who was resting her feet upon it at the time, was not amused; and, despite Uffa's attempts to acquaint her with the finer points of the situation, which he barely appreciated himself, she was convinced that the stool had been reclaimed because of Uffa's failure to pay the bill.

Uffa never mastered the French language sufficiently to hold a meaningful conversation with Yvonne, the basic grammar being forever double Dutch as far as he was concerned. During their courtship he had roughed out a list of common usage words, with additional code letters to indicate certain vital messages, and he and Yvonne had great fun in the early days communicating via their respective lists. Later on when Yvonne was able to grasp the essence of some of his expressions and the songs he performed in mixed company she was quite horrified.

Uffa spoke the few stock phrases he acquired during his winters in France with a thick Isle of Wight accent and, if he had the misfortune to observe the written French word before hearing it spoken, invariably pronounced it as written. *Dans*, for example, as in *dans le salon*, rhymed with 'cans' for the first two or three years of his marriage.

His inability to utter more than the basic words in French gave rise to a general assumption that his understanding was limited also, whereas over the years his ear became quite attuned to the language: so much so that on more than one occasion when in France, while sitting writing quietly or immersed in his own thoughts, he would awake from a reverie to find that he was himself the subject of conversation. Sometimes he enjoyed what he heard, other times not. In the event he kept his counsel for there was a certain one-upmanship to be obtained from knowing other people's true evaluation of one's character and circumstances.

Undeterred by his linguistic shortcomings, or perhaps unaware of them, Uffa decided to produce an English/French dictionary, and Jacqueline was put to work typing never-ending lists of words from an assortment of dictionaries in her spare time. Uffa had been caught out on more than one occasion by words that are similar in English and French but which possess entirely different meanings within the two languages, and he requested Jacqueline to extract these, planning to list them separately as an appendix.

When Uffa discussed the project with me during one of his visits to my London flat, where he mostly stayed when in London on non-expenses-paid trips, I thought it rather a waste of time as the market was already flooded with works compiled by people who were far more qualified to tackle such an assignment. I did feel, however, that his list of identical words with varying meanings had possibilities, and suggested a slim volume devoted solely to these pitfalls. In time Uffa came around to the idea and approached several publishers; but this time luck was against him for, when he finally stumbled upon one who accepted the concept and was prepared to publish, the Company itself ran into difficulties and the dictionary failed to see the light of day. Many years later an American publisher came up with a similar idea.

Uffa's lengthy sojourns in France, where he travelled extensively visiting, amongst other places of interest, many well-known and lesser-known vineyards, vastly increased his knowledge of the wines of the country. He became something of a wine snob, and upon returning home was inclined to embarrass local restauranteurs by demanding to know why their wine list did not include some quite obscure French wine to which he had recently been introduced or, in the event that they could satisfy him on the wine, often suggested that they would have done better had they settled for another year.

Also during his travels Uffa collected pepper mills in all shapes, sizes and colours. From earliest childhood, when his mother had insisted on mill-ground pepper at all times and sent him off to school equipped with his own little pepper mill to sprinkle over his school dinner, the use of a pepper mill developed into something of a fetish. He referred to the mill-ground pepper as 'mouse turds', and when dining out, if he spied common or garden pepper on the table he would summon the head waiter, make twisting signs with his hands and call 'mouse turds'. His performance was invariable, and in certain French restaurants at which he ate regularly the waiters were under the impression that 'mouse turds' was the official translation of pepper mill. So, should you be travelling in France and, in response to your hand-twisting request for a pepper mill, the waiter responds 'mais oui, les mouse turds' you will know that Uffa Fox was here.

Added bonuses were the occasions when Uffa was able to combine business with his love of Continental travel. One such opportunity occurred when Baron Giannio Parisi, who had admired Lord Beaverbrook's Uffa Fox designed power boat as she sparkled her way across the blue waters of the Mediterranean from her Côte d'Azur base, invited Uffa to design a forty-three-foot motor cruiser for him.

Uffa made many trips to Venice, where the Parisi yacht *Anirus* was being constructed, and became a familiar sight amongst the gondoliers who were content to sit back at their ease and allow themselves to be propelled by the spirited Uffa. The climax of one of these visits was a charming ceremony, at the Gritti Palace where he was staying, when the gondoliers of Venice honoured him with the presentation of one of their traditional be-ribboned straw hats.

Now and then during the winter months Uffa and Yvonne would forsake Paris and spend sunny days with my mother and me in Mallorca, sometimes touring by car and combining the visit with sightseeing on the Spanish peninsula, other times travelling by air. One memorable Christmas the villa houseparty was augmented by my sister Lucy and her family who drove overland, via Barcelona, from Germany, and it was during this holiday that the family first became aware of a slight mellowing within Uffa.

It was the same old Uffa, of course, who dripping wet made a dramatic appearance in bathing trunks in the middle of the noonday terrace party, having braved the sea for a Christmas Day swim in the Mediterranean: and perhaps it was the balmy air and tranquillity still to be found in out of season Mallorca, or even the spirit of mañana. Whatever the reason, Uffa appeared less urgent and imbued with both time and a degree of new-found patience.

During these days Uffa seemed perfectly content to allow the hours to drift by, sitting on the terrace with his notes and jottings, dreaming a little, writing a little; and, when he was interrupted by Lucy's daughter Jane, instead of shooing her away as he might well have done in his younger days, he seated her at the table by his side, showed her the way to make the letters of the alphabet, and then how to link them together to form her first written words.

On a side trip to Ibiza from Mallorca the following year Uffa was very much into painting, palette and paints accompanying him wherever he went. Setting forth from Ibiza harbour one dazzling blue and white morning, we embarked aboard the local tourist boat to sample the joys of the beach at nearby Talamanca. Uffa swam and larked around and, after a gentle run up and down the beach to dry off and while everyone else was contentedly paying homage to Great God Sun, he unpacked his gear and settled down to the serious business of being an artist.

Uffa was progressing reasonably well and had filled in a goodish area of sea and sky, when an excited group of small children sped by, scattering sand in every direction. He gingerly removed the larger particles from his canvas with a palette knife and continued. Plop! A king-sized multicoloured ball materialized from outer space and landed smack in the centre of the painting. Wordlessly Uffa picked up the canvas and blew on it, but nothing moved. A blurred circle of mottled sand adhered to the tacky paint and, short of scraping the whole thing down and beginning again, there was nothing to be done.

'Time for lunch,' said Uffa, preparing to leave.

The Ibiza harbour boat had yet to arrive when we reached the embarkation point, and Uffa carefully rested the painting against a nearby post for safety and to dry. Nobody was quite sure how it happened, but one moment it was standing upright in all its glory and the next moment it was flat on its face. By this time we were convulsed with silent laughter, not daring to look from one to the other, for Uffa himself was completely without expression, his mien betraying no trace of emotion whatsoever.

At that moment the boat pulled alongside and, in the midst of watching the boatmen as they tied her up, came an enormous cry of 'Bloody hound!' from Uffa. He lunged forward, unfortunately not in time to prevent a mangy-looking stray dog from lifting its back leg against the masterpiece, though he did manage to cut it off in mid stream.

Poker-faced, Uffa lifted the painting with some delicacy and shook it dry. With both hands he held his work of art aloft, arms outstretched before him, picture-side upwards, in a sacrificial gesture. He raised his eyes heavenwards and searched the sky.

'Send over a brace of bloody seagulls,' he prayed, 'and I'll present it to the Tate.'

The gentle warmth and serenity of Mallorquian winters appealed to Uffa and Yvonne; and they were over the moon when, following the appearance of a feature article on Uffa in the local English language newspaper, he was contacted by Gay Niblett, a young English business-man whose Company was engaged in housing development on the Island, with a proposition.

Gay's latest project, an elevated Ibiza-type hillside complex, with the houses or flats set one above the other, the terrace of the one forming the roof of the house below, was already under construction at the delightful fishing port of Andraitx. Andraitx, then virtually unknown to the tourist population, is a popular anchorage for yachts-men, especially those desiring to escape the excessive summer heat and bustle of Palma.

The proposition which excited Uffa and Yvonne so much was an offer to assign one of these little houses to Uffa in return for the use of his name as a promotional aid for the scheme. Next day we all trooped out to inspect the site, and Uffa was thrilled to discover that the new properties were within a stone's throw of the villa owned by his old friend Bobbie Somerset with whom he had sailed the Atlantic so many years before.

By now Uffa had his feet well and truly off the ground, announcing that he would purchase an additional unit so that he could invite friends to stay. His two houses would be alongside one another and moulded into one at the constructional stage. There was just one fly in the ointment. He had no money with which to pay for the second house. This did not deter him, however, and he soon came up with a typically Uffa-like solution. He would pay for the extension in Flying Fifteens!

The bewildered Gay Niblett, who was not a sailing man, was somewhat out of his depth, and by the end of the day Uffa had convinced him, as well as himself, that the Flying Fifteens would sell like hot cakes in Palma where Uffa would preside over a new and expanding fleet.

Overflowing with enthusiasm, Uffa returned to Cowes and fished out the design of a chined version of the Flying Fifteen which he had drawn up some years previously. He set up a saddle in the area below the Commodore's House, and with the help of part-time labour building commenced. Upon completion, the first Chined Flying Fifteen was trailed to Paris and stored in Yvonne's garage until the moment was ripe for her chauffeur to tow it the rest of the way to Palma.

It was when the first boat crossed into Spain that the trouble began. The Spanish authorities demanded, as was their right in occordance with the law of the land, payment of certain taxes before the craft could be placed in the water. Neither Gay Niblett, who had kept his part of the bargain and had been dubious of the Flying Fifteen scheme in the first place, nor Uffa was prepared to face the additional and unexpected burden of the tax.

Meantime at Cowes Uffa continued merrily with the construction of Chined Flying Fifteen number two, and ere long she too was speeding her way across Europe to Palma. Soon the two Flying Fifteens were sitting in their respective cradles opening up and generally deteriorating under the merciless sun on Palma Quay. While all this was taking place, completely unaware that there was a problem, Yvonne busied herself with curtains and bits and pieces for the house.

The situation remained in limbo over a period of years until, in a last-ditch effort to resolve the deadlock, Gay Niblett offered Uffa a sum of money equivalent to the cash value of the original house at the time of their first meeting. Uffa, desperate for money as always, accepted the deal and relinquished his right to the properties.

182

Yvonne was completely and utterly shattered when she was finally put in the picture, and offered to refund the money Uffa had received rather than lose their dream home. A cable was despatched to Palma in an effort to redeem the situation, but so much time had elapsed since Uffa had accepted the cash that the property was already sold.

Uffa and Yvonne had great fun in France planning routes and touring the Continent, though one winter even Uffa had his fill, jesting that he had travelled so much that he felt like a pigeon. Mostly they were content to journey alone, but once or twice Uffa was able to persuade his new friends, Norman and Josephine Terry, to accompany them. Originally brought together through a mutual love of sailing and above all of Flying Fifteens, a bond that was to prove durable soon sprang up between them, Norman and Josephine becoming very dear to Uffa as time progressed; and the first boat he designed for them, the cruiser *Tenerife*, accorded many happy hours not only to Norman and Josephine and their teenage sons John and Peter, but to Uffa himself.

When Uffa set about designing the Terrys' next craft, a fast runabout, he produced the stepped power boat *Springer*, one of his less successful ventures. She did not steer well and, possibly due to the beam being too narrow for her length, had a marked tendency to broach (veer and swing broadsides to the sea) and become generally unstable.

Much to Joe Porter's astonishment and consternation Uffa decided to take Prince Philip for a run in *Springer*. Joe had been involved with Uffa in the design of the craft and was not at all happy with the end product. He pleaded with Uffa not to risk the life of the consort in her, being convinced that the boat was downright dangerous. In a moment of desperation, when Uffa remained adamant, he begged Norman Terry as the owner to intervene. Norman, the kindest and most easy-going of men, was in no way inclined to spoil the holiday by going against Uffa. However, after weighing up the pros and cons his sense of duty prevailed, and reluctantly he put his foot down to stop the excursion.

Later on he was to tackle Uffa on the subject of *Springer*'s performance. 'Look here, Uffa,' he complained, 'you've designed me a boat that I am unable to take to sea because it is too dangerous. What do you intend to do about it?'

Had Norman expected recompense he was in for a big surprise for Uffa's riposte was: 'You know in the olden days rich benefactors would come along and set themselves up as patrons of the art by sponsoring men with talent and genius. Well, what you have to do is to try to look upon yourself as one of my patrons.'

Uffa's propulsion through life was one of trial and error. A disaster was a step forward through experience gained, setting the antennae of his creative brain stretching out in each and every direction to discover the reason why. Researching and reading, he was never too old nor too proud to seek advice and learn. More often than not the persons with whom he spoke were less versed in design and seamanship than Uffa himself. Nevertheless, once a subject was reached that interested him he would listen intently and probe, his alert brain grasping and retaining the one solitary new thought or scrap of information to emerge from the conversation; and the *Springer* experience caused him to delve even more deeply into the whole question of broaching which had plagued him from the days of his first Atlantic crossing when he had nearly forfeited his life aboard *Typhoon*.

Uffa was very much into power boat design throughout the sixties, and it was another friend and patron, Sir Max Aitken, who, with his usual spirit of adventure, ordered a hydroplane for the 1963 open sea race of 190 miles from Cowes to Torquay. This was a great day for Joe Porter, former chief designer with the legendary S. E. Saunders, the man who half a century before had designed and built the hydrofoil *Maple Leaf IV*, the first boat in the world to achieve fifty knots. For Uffa, the eager young disciple who had served part of his apprenticeship to S. E. Saunders working on the famous vessel, the wheel had turned full cycle.

Black Maria, the single stepped hydroplane, was designed in the hope and belief that she would prove to be good in open sea conditions, and Uffa's first question to Sir Max Aitken when he returned from Torquay was 'Did she show any tendency to broaching?' The reply, 'No', was music to his ears.

The difference between the normal planing hull and the hydroplane is that the planing hull lifts her stem to give the hull an angle of attack which causes her to lift slightly, thus lessening her displacement and enabling her to run along in the groove she has cut. The hydroplane has two angles of attack designed into her hull and lifts out of the water aft as well as forward, running along level on two distinct planes. This economizes greatly on engine power and fuel, for the ordinary planing hull demands approximately double the power and so burns double the fuel to attain the same speed.

With an overall length of forty-three feet six inches, waterline length of thirty-eight feet and an eight-foot-six-inch beam, *Black Maria* was designed to accommodate a Ford 800 h.p. engine, and building commenced on this premise. Half-way through construction Sir Max had second thoughts. After serious reflection he believed that his boat should be an all-British affair, so the original specification was changed to two Rolls-Royce 240 h.p. petrol engines, which Uffa described as 'dreams of perfection in engineering but powerless to allow the boat to achieve her potential'.

When Uffa wrote from France to break the news of the power switch to Joe Porter he said, 'You have often heard me say "life is one disappointment after another". We have had one this weekend as during it we have lost three hundred horse power. You know, Joe, we are like the old painters. They had to paint whatever their patrons wished, and we, having put all the facts before the patrons, must then follow their wishes or be without boats to design.'

Black Maria, as so often happens with new boats, overran her completion date, leaving time for only the briefest of trials before the races were due to begin. The Cowes–Torquay race started off in calm, and the first leg round the Isle of Wight was in smooth water; but as *Black Maria* shot through Cowes Roads for the second time Uffa, an anxious observer, discerned too much spray flying off the starboard propeller, indicating that the stern unit was not hard down into its notch. Nevertheless she continued the journey to Torquay and finished tenth out of forty-five starters. Next day, in the race round the testing course in Torbay, she succeeded in taking the prize for the first British boat, so Uffa was well pleased.

21

The international airports of Paris and London were to become almost as familiar to Uffa as his beloved Isle of Wight as, during the months of winter, he winged his way back to England for an assortment of engagements ranging from his annual stint as Technical Adviser at the Boat Show to personal appearances on television and meeting with publishers or to check progress on boats being constructed to one or other of his designs.

One of these journeys in January 1963 was for the express purpose of joining in a recording at the BBC's studio at Bristol. The complexities of the mid-winter journey from Cowes to Bristol, with the ever-present threat of boat cancellations or delays, made Uffa accept with open arms Norman and Josephine's invitation to spend a few days at their Alvechurch, Worcestershire home and make the less hazardous journey to the studio from there.

Uffa had become a regular visitor to Alvechurch, and he and the Terrys such close friends that they could be completely open with one another. If Uffa overstayed his welcome and became too stroppy Norman had only to say, 'Uffa, you know your famous saying about fish and guests stinking after three days . . .' for Uffa to disappear with his tail between his legs until the next time.

On the night of the recording they set out by car with what they believed to be plenty of time in hand, even allowing for the adverse weather report, but Mother Nature was not on their side. There was snow and ice, and with every mile the visibility decreased, the roads becoming more and more treacherous; and it was only by a superhuman effort that they pulled up outside the studio with seconds to spare before the programme was due to commence.

All three entered the reception together, Norman and Josephine backing away as Uffa, catching sight of an old friend, advanced, hand outstretched in greeting, saying, 'Hello Eamonn, so nice to see you again.'

Eamonn Andrews, never knowing what Uffa would come out with next, hastily responded: 'Good evening, AND BEFORE YOU SAY ANYTHING, let me tell you that the moment you stepped through these doors, you stepped right into your own programme. For tonight, Uffa Fox, CBE, This is Your Life.'

For the next half hour or so, under the glare of spotlight and television cameras, Uffa was brought face to face with friends and acquaintances who had shared varying moments of his life, including the surprise appearance of his wife, Yvonne, who had been flown over from Paris especially for the occasion. The grand finale, and the moment to bring a lump to Uffa's throat, was the presentation of a certificate on behalf of the Goldfish Club, whose exclusive membership is restricted to aircrew ditched and rescued from the sea, in recognition of the many lives saved by his airborne lifeboats.

Uffa's subsequent and final word on the programme was 'It is quite painless. You just sit there like a stuffed turd while everyone comes on and says nice things about you. Then, when it's all over they hand you a cheque for £100.'

Not one to make concessions to age, Uffa continued to reach out eagerly and savour the fruits of life with the unbridled enthusiasm of youth. Even the mellowing process was not absolute. The low flashpoint of his temper, though no longer physically violent, could still be sparked if things did not go entirely his way, as happened in Paris one day.

Yvonne was an extremely good and generous hostess, happily entertaining Uffa's many friends who showed up in Paris from all corners of the world, for like Uffa she enjoyed the social life. At Uffa's request she organized a special luncheon party to include some of Uffa's friends from the French yacht clubs and a mutual friend, Ernestine, from San Francisco. Timing was of the essence for the first course was to be a soufflé of seafood, and Yvonne begged Uffa not to be late as was his custom; but her plea fell upon deaf ears.

The host eventually put in an appearance well over an hour late, by which time the soufflé had fallen to the point of no return. Yvonne, attempting to entertain their guests and at the same time resuscitate the meal, was at the end of her tether and, in the manner of a true Frenchwoman, excitedly censured her spouse in a mixture of French and broken English for his lack of consideration.

Uffa made no reply. Cutting his wife off in mid-stream, and completely ignoring his friends, he strode angrily through to the study where he flung some papers into an overnight briefcase. Still without a word of greeting, he stalked back through the dining-room, past the embarrassed guests and out of the apartment, picked up a taxi to the airport, and boarded the next plane for London.

Christmas in Paris was one of the highlights of Uffa's year, and 1965 was no exception. He dived into a round of eating, drinking and merrymaking with his usual reckless abandon, and with far too many late nights was easy prey to his old enemy, bronchitis.

Without giving himself time to recover, he flew to England for the Boat Show and to spend the New Year with Norman and Josephine. Uffa was inclined to treat his bronchial attacks lightly as they were something that had been a part of his life for so many years, and which in his youth he had thrown off reasonably quickly. This time it was different. After visits to the Shakespeare Theatre at Stratford-upon-Avon, and on to New Year parties, followed by more late nights, even Uffa's robust frame cried for help. He was so ill, and his life at such a low ebb, that for once he was content to remain in bed and be nursed by Josephine, who possessed the same aura of caring that had emanated from his own mother.

The days extended into weeks, and the planned brief visit swelled to well over a month before Uffa had regained strength sufficiently to leave the sanctuary of Norman and Josephine and resume normal life. During the convalescent period he put the finishing touches to the anecdotes he had been compiling, and the first volume, *Joys of Life*, appeared later in the year. The second volume, *More Joys of Living*, he was to dedicate to Norman and Josephine in recognition of the love and kindness they showed throughout his illness.

Also thanks to Norman and Josephine, Uffa discovered the fascination of the inland waterways, the Birmingham–Worcester canal running close by their home. The summer succeeding his illness found him with Norman and Josephine and their four shared labradors (Uffa's Bess was the mother and grandmother of the Terrys' exuberant pack, and more often than not Bess stayed at Alvechurch when Uffa was in Paris as the British fight against the dreaded rabies precluded the shuttling of Bess from France to England), chugging peacefully along the canal in Norman's steamboat *Charlie Allnut*, named after the hero of the film *African Queen*. *Charlie Allnut*'s boiler was fired by a paraffin burner not unlike a huge primus stove and pre-heated by calor gas, the pressure tank holding about four gallons and running at twenty-five pounds pressure.

The happy voyagers were approaching the six-hundred-yard-long Shortwood Tunnel when helmsman Uffa was startled to see dense smoke bellowing from the funnel, and raised the alarm. Hastily grabbing a fire extinguisher, Norman went into action, and the flames were to all intents and purposes soon under control. The outbreak gave every indication of having settled down completely, and they were just beginning to relax vigil when without warning *Charlie Allnut* not only burst into flames but the fire spread at an alarming rate.

With only a few yards to the tunnel entrance there was no alternative but to abandon ship, the three humans and four dogs leaping into the water and scrambling onto the canal bank. They were just in time to see *Charlie Allnut*, ablaze from stem to stern, Red Ensign still flying, sink ignominiously to the bottom of the canal.

At his best in moments of crisis, and as they huddled dejectedly on the canal bank, Uffa conjured up an old envelope and pencil and began sketching away furiously at the design of a new boat for Norman. Even the name, *Phoenix*, rising from the ashes of *Charlie Allnut*, was decided in those moments.

Returning to Cowes, Uffa bounded triumphantly into the drawing office where Tony was hard at work. 'Stop whatever you're doing', he cried. 'We've got a Mississippi steamboat to build.'

Tony played it cool. Years of close proximity to his uncle had taught him to evince surprise at nothing. Over a period of time it had become something of a battle between the two, Uffa on the one hand attempting to shock Tony into betraying surprise at his deeds and derring-do. Tony on the other acting out a role of quiet nonchalance. Removing the plan to which he had been applying himself from the board and replacing it with a virgin sheet of drawing paper, and with pencil poised at the ready, Tony raised his eyes enquiringly in the direction of his uncle.

Uffa excitedly handed over the crumpled envelope, by now a mass of rough sketches and barely decipherable scrawl. 'Here are the design details. Get right on with it because we've got to catch the post.'

Uffa's life was geared to the last post at seven forty-five. Countless times he would dash around all day designing, writing, telephoning, seeking advice here, helping others there, constantly interrupted by callers, with some of whom he would drop everything and disappear to the pub or one of the yacht clubs for hours on end. Then, when everyone was packing up to go home, he would charge in like a devil possessed demanding that nobody leave as there were vitally important letters to be done that must on no account miss the last post.

Once Tony had grasped the basics of the idea Uffa ambled through to the sitting-room, returning a few moments later with two glasses of sherry with which to toast the new design. Every ten minutes or so Tony was aware of a presence breathing down the back of his neck until, with a nudge here and a jog there, a rough lines plan emerged that was in complete harmony with Uffa's thoughts.

Tony's next task was to rush the drawing to the print room and do battle with the antiquated print machine, a Heath Robinson affair that had completed gallant war service and should have been pensioned off immediately afterwards. The machine took upwards of five minutes to produce one copy, and was tackled only by the bravest – less hardy mortals fearing for life and limb. Uffa was at stand-by with a stamped addressed envelope, and the instant Tony succeeded in running off a print that was half-way decent, it was hurriedly inserted into the envelope; and with the instruction 'Run like a stag', Tony bore it to the post office in the nick of time.

With the panic over for the day, and the design speeding its way to Norman, Uffa and Tony sat down quietly over a drink to resolve a plan of campaign for the drawings, and completion dates. Uffa pulled a totally unrealistic completion date out of the hat, and when Tony queried the feasibility of the timing he was told, 'I know it's impossible, but it looks good when I send the list to the owner.'

The thirty-foot waterline *Phoenix*, which Norman dubbed a 'Mississippi narrow boat', was designed with a flat bottom and a conical projection of the bow sections of the chine enabling plywood to be bent round the shape with comparative ease. Her engines were designed and built by David King, who was responsible for *Charlie Allnut*, to a concept familiar some hundred and fifty years ago in America.

Two cylinders, three-inch bore and eighteen-inch stroke, are placed one on either side, driving cranks on each end of the paddle shaft by means of wooden pitmans eight feet long. The paddle wheel itself is five feet in diameter with eight teak blades, while the steam was supplied by a vertical fire tube boiler (now replaced by a horizontal loco type) which enables the paddle wheel to turn at thirty-five revolutions a minute on a pressure of seventy-five pounds per square inch. After the experience of *Charlie Allnut*, Norman decided against a paraffin-fired boiler in favour of a coal-fired unit.

Colourfully painted, *Phoenix* arouses comment and interest wherever she goes, and has become something of a celebrity on the canals since she and Norman completed the Avon Ring and their adventures were featured on radio and television.

Another of Uffa's 'designs with a difference' came about when John Fairfax, after months of trailing all over London introducing himself to dozens of people in an abortive attempt to obtain sponsorship for a proposed venture to row the Atlantic single-handed, was advised eventually to obtain the backing of someone with prestige in the maritime and sailing world. His quest led him to Uffa, who was currently holding court at the *Daily Express* Boat Show at Earls Court.

The Dean of Sacred Cowes, as he was sometimes known, was seated behind a desk dispensing advice, his fine head of tousled grey hair shading the bushy eyebrows which by now also boasted more than a hint of grey. For a number of years Uffa had been obliged to wear glasses for reading, though his distance sight remained virtually unimpaired. Refusing to consider spectacles *per se*, he solved the problem by sporting a pair of gold-rimmed half spectacles for close work, which were normally harnessed midway down his nose. When he looked up from his work, his discerning brown eyes peering over the top of the lenses, he could appear to the uninitiated quite fierce and intimidating, especially when thinking deeply.

Biding his time until the crowd surrounding Uffa had dispersed, John advanced and introduced himself by declaring that he intended being the first man to row single-handed across the Atlantic, adding for good measure the news that he had no money, no boat, and was in need of Uffa's help.

'Row the Atlantic single-handed, eh? And what on earth makes you think you can do it, my boy?'

John Fairfax gripped the edge of the table and leaned forward tensely. He had been asked the question so many times, and there was no answer.

'Mr Fox, I don't need the earth to tell me what I can do, I know.'

Uffa frowned for a second or two, as deep in thought he stared formidably over the top of his spectacles while sizing up the man. After a few moments' contemplation his eyes lightened with a mischievous twinkle, and a wide grin cracked the weatherbeaten face.

'Right,' he said. 'I know exactly the kind of boat you need, and I will design her for you.'

Uffa proved as good as his word, and two months later John found himself the excited recipient of a lengthy epistle from Paris setting out Uffa's thoughts, and enclosing the Arrangement Plan.

Uffa wrote that he had given the Atlantic Row Boat a twenty-four-foot waterline and four-foot-nine-inch beam with a displacement of 1,860 pounds, made up of hull and gear: 860 pounds, and food, stores and clothing: 1,000 pounds; the overall concept based on his airborne lifeboat design which had brought so many gallant airmen home safely to Britain from as far afield as the Bay of Biscay and Heligoland. She could, he continued, be shortened to twenty feet, but he believed John would be glad of the extra footage when chasing away down the face of the great Atlantic Grey Beards. When the time came to hammer out the final details, however, they agreed to more or less split the difference, and settled on twenty-two feet.

Uffa designed *Britannia* originally with an inflated rubber self-righting chamber seven feet long at either end which afforded shelter, and a self-baling deck, so that the rowing boat became a self-righting lifeboat. In the final analysis technical and financial difficulties prevented the incorporation of the inflatable rubber chambers in the short time available, and rigid permanent structures were substituted which proved a great advantage in all respects except the very important one of windage.

Beneath the deck were watertight hatches for stowing food and gear, only one to be opened at a time. The sliding seat had sixteen inches of movement, and the rowlocks were square as used in racing, thus eliminating considerable strain, as the oar is held square to its work by the rowlock, and the blades, when swung forward and feathered, remain flat to the water by themselves.

John's experience of rowing had been confined to the odd comings and goings in dinghies, mainly from ship to shore. In an endeavour to get himself into training for rowing the Atlantic he rowed for three or four hours a day, charging up and down between the ducks and geese on the Serpentine, the millpond of a lake in London's Hyde Park!

Britannia was launched from Lallows at Cowes on a rainy windswept December day in 1968. Uffa put in an appearance, wrapped up in sweaters and a huge yellow oilskin, having been taken ill with a dicky heart some weeks before and not supposed to be there at all. He proved that he was on the mend by immediately bawling out John Fairfax for stowing the oars the wrong way round. 'Most unseamanlike, John, most unseamanlike! Don't you know any better?'

Britannia looked magnificent, but also huge and unwieldy. John had never rowed in her before, and felt so nervous of making a fool of himself in front of the dozens of reporters, cameramen and television cameras that he hardly knew one end from the other. After the launching, and in his haste to man the oars before *Britannia* could be swept under the pier, he fixed the oars and locked the gates with the rowlocks swinging the wrong way round, noticing his mistake only after the first stroke: and to add to the confusion, buttons had not been fixed on the oars so that they kept skidding towards the water.

Another hazard; John had never had occasion to use a sliding seat before. In the end all he could do was splash around and hope he did not appear too much of an idiot, causing one representative of the media to comment rather caustically: 'It's going to need to be a bloody good boat!'

John found *Britannia* superb, a masterpiece of workmanship and design. On trials she proved that, if capsized, she would right herself in two seconds flat. If swamped, she was bone dry in half a minute, water sluicing down the self-baling slots almost as fast as the eye could follow. Easy to handle and a pleasure to row, her stability was so great that two men could stand on a gunwale and she would tilt but a few inches even when on ballast.

There are some three thousand six hundred nautical miles between the Canary Islands, John's departure point, and Miami in Florida; and, since he could not hope to follow a straight course, this would mean at least four thousand nautical miles of rowing for John Fairfax. To his everlasting credit, he not only set out to fulfil this Herculean task single-handed, but achieved it in a back-breaking one hundred and eighty days.

The last words in the log of John Fairfax's Atlantic Voyage were:

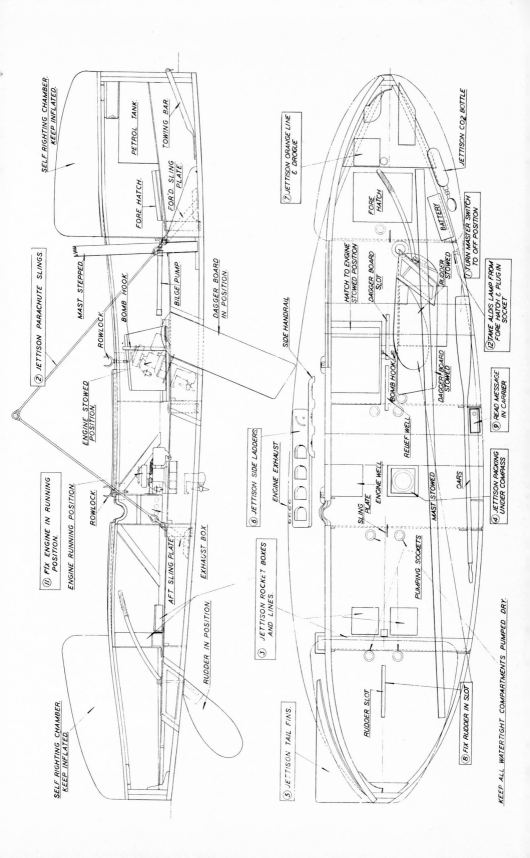

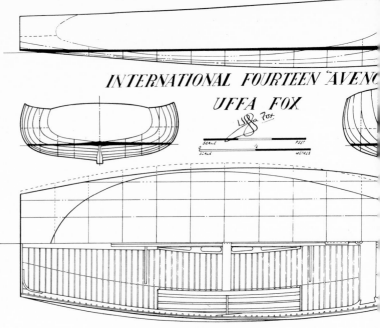

INTERNATIONAL FOURTEEN "AVENG

UFFA FOX

SCALE   FEET
SCALE   METRES

THE FIRST PLANING DROP KEEL BO

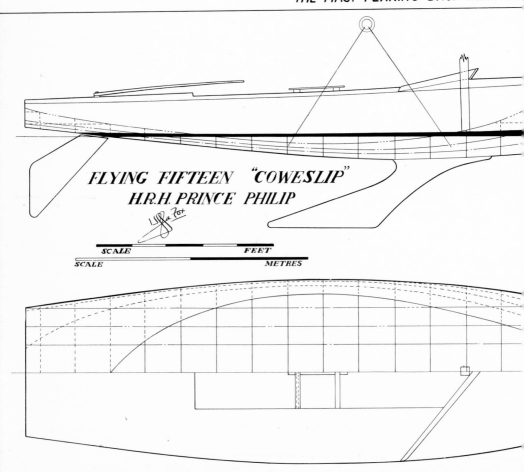

FLYING FIFTEEN "COWESLIP"
H.R.H. PRINCE PHILIP

SCALE   FEET
SCALE   METRES

THE FIRST PLANING KEEL BOAT,

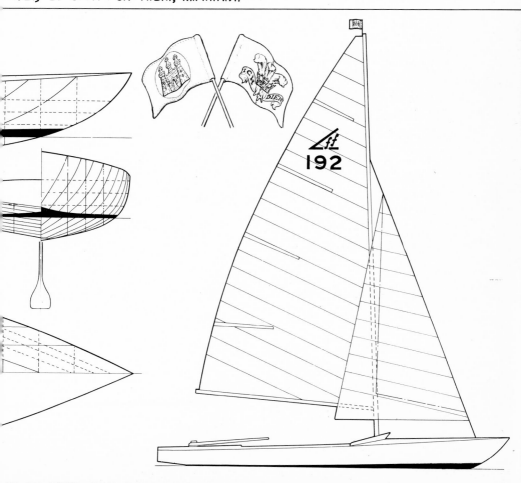

1927, BY UFFA FOX R.D.I., M.R.I.N.A.

47, BY UFFA FOX R.D.I., M.R.I.N.A.

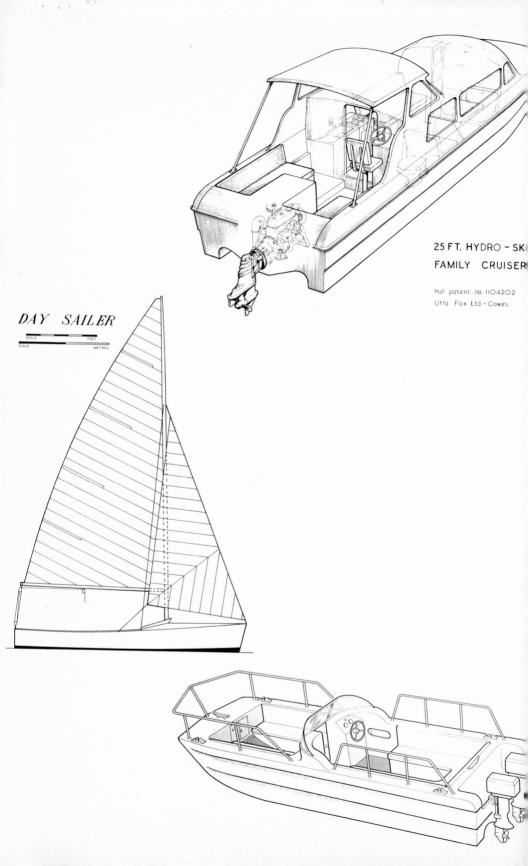

25 FT. HYDRO − SK
FAMILY CRUISER

hull patent no 1104202
Uffa Fox Ltd − Cowes.

DAY SAILER

SCALE ———— FEET
SCALE ———— METRES

'Only one thing I can say and this is to you my lovely little *Britannia* –
I salute you.'

The book of the incredible adventure, '*Britannia*': *Rowing Alone
Across the Atlantic,* bore the dedication 'To Uffa Fox, Grand Old Man
of the Sea'.

Two years later, accompanied and ably abetted by Sylvia Cook, John
Fairfax rowed eight thousand miles across the Pacific in another of
Uffa's designs, *Britannia II.*

22

With a heart that was becoming an increasing nuisance, even Uffa was forced to slacken pace eventually, not that it involved taking less of an interest in life so much as concentrating on the mental rather than the physical. Writing, designing and painting consumed more of his time, and 1968 saw the publication of *Seamanlike Sense in Power Craft*, a worthy companion to his early Peter Davies publications.

Artistically he turned his thoughts to the nude female form, startling those about him with a series of paintings with loose Rubenesque overtones. One, a rather heavy-handed version of 'The Three Graces', he hung proudly in his dining-room to the mixed delight and consternation of the diners.

Uffa won his last sailing race at the age of seventy; and when racing became too great a physical effort, to enable him to retain the freedom of the sea he designed and built a runabout launch, *Ankle Deep*. A writer in one of the national newspapers likened his home to a pink Venetian palace, with its sea and land entrances and the water lapping on three sides; but whereas the gondolas of Venice are moored to poles, *Ankle Deep* hung in davits on the outer end of the quay, from where she was easily launched at a moment's notice.

Although Uffa's pace was more leisurely he saw no reason to deprive himself of those elements of life that were dear to him, with the inevitable result that in 1970 he sustained a severe heart attack which put him out of action for several months; and the Uffa to emerge from the sick bed was an aged and enfeebled version of his former self, kept alive and tamed by a superfluity of drugs and tranquillizers.

Forbidden to fly, he was no longer able nor anxious to winter in France, and consequently had to face up to the financial burden of supporting his lifestyle on an all-the-year-round basis. The dilemma was summed up in a letter to a client when he wrote, 'If you could put a cheque in the post it would help this end as there is very little bread on the loaf.'

While accepting his limitations, Uffa was vexed by certain shortcomings, which to him were unforgivable signs of advancing age. He was especially concerned, and would bow his head in mock shame, should he catch himself in the act of committing the cardinal sin of repeating the same ribald old joke instead of treating his audience to the newest and wittiest. There were causes for gratification, though, such as the appearance of his portrait, together with Prince Philip and Prince Charles, on a postage stamp commemorating the 1971 royal visit to the Cook Islands.

Upon realizing that he could no longer clamber in and out of boats with his usual abandon, Uffa selected an old kitchen chair and designed an ingenious electrically operated hoist which lifted him from his first-floor balcony and deposited him into *Ankle Deep*. Then, with sailing over for the day, he was hoisted back onto the balcony by his ever-present and faithful band of willing helpers.

The question of broaching, which had caused Uffa deep anxiety throughout a lifetime of design, was never far from the surface of his mind. His ultimate solution, the Uffa Fox Non-Broaching, Non-Pitching and Non-Rolling Hull, was featured in his *Seamanlike Sense in Power Craft*, but never put to the test.

With Parisian winters a thing of the past and the spectrum of the whole of the year in England before him, plus the need to occupy his evergreen and active brain, Uffa believed the time was ripe to set about the construction of a prototype. He was seldom happier than when supervising and observing one of his designs as it took shape, and the construction of the non-broaching boat, the culmination of so many years of research and experiment, was no exception.

Uffa possessed a natural creative talent plus the tenacity to hold onto and develop an idea once formed, but he was no great shakes as a businessman. Had his commercial flair matched his inventive genius he would doubtless have ended his days a wealthy man, and been spared the money crises that had plagued his life and at times held back his multifarious and original thought processes.

In all probability others made more money out of Uffa than Uffa himself. Throughout the years opportunists latched onto one or other of his ideas, and with Archimedes-like cries of 'Eureka!' proclaimed them as their own.

There is perhaps nowhere more evidence of this than with the non-broaching hull. From the years following the second war when he was into water skiing and the study of suitable craft for propelling the skier through the water at an ever-increasing rate of knots, when his mind first grasped the significance of the reality that towing two persons on four skis was very much easier than dragging one skier on two skis, he had been experimenting.

In 1948 he had had the local population speculating once again, although by now they were less inclined to laugh at his antics than they had been in the days gone by, as, with two rowing dinghies lashed together side by side he stopwatched their progress while they were towed behind one of his old airborne lifeboats. His latest theory was that an air tunnel plus water pressure increases lift and gives greater stability.

His various experiments in the Solent generated considerable interest amongst fellow water skiers and yachtsmen, so much so that in the late fifties he decided he must protect his idea with a patent. However, following publication of the design of the Uffa Fox Patented Non-Broaching, Non-Pitching and Non-Rolling Hull, the water-ski hull has appeared in assorted guises. Its sea-going and shallow water potential is so great that history may well one day record that Uffa changed the shape of the workaday hull as effectively as he changed the shape of the dinghy.

When people alibi-ed the poaching of his designs with elaborate tales of how they arrived at a similar concept. Uffa likened them to huskies pulling a sled. If the team master cracks the whip overhead, it is the dog that has not been pulling its weight that does the barking.

Sadly, Uffa's deteriorating health prevented him from reaping the harvest following the outstanding performance of the prototype when it reached the trial stage, but Tony Dixon carried on the good work by adapting the theory of the design to create the highly successful Hydro Skee hull for Copland boats of Ventnor.

In the summer of '72 Uffa filled the house with his favourite people for Cowes Week, and doggedly refused to be excluded from the more exciting of the Week's festivities even should his attendance involve being propelled by wheelchair.

He was put aboard the Flying Fifteen *Coweslip*, and by a supreme effort of will took the tiller for an hour to satisfy himself personally that all was shipshape for the arrival of the royal visitors. Prince Philip, for his part, on hearing of Uffa's deteriorating health, issued instructions that his old friend should be winched aboard *Britannia* in the ship's launch so as to avoid placing undue strain on his heart while mounting the boarding ladder.

When their friendship was young Uffa had remarked of Prince Philip: 'You could put your heart in his hand and know it would be cared for.' Little did he dream that he would one day see his words fulfilled, and Uffa was moved to tears when he found himself on the receiving end of such a thoughtful gesture which added substance to his belief.

Cowes Week left Uffa so completely drained that Norman and Josephine, who had been amongst the guests at the Commodore's House, took command and transported him to the peaceful serenity of their own home to rest and recuperate. Only too aware that Uffa must avoid stairs and that his garrulous nature would be stifled in the loneliness of an upstairs room, they had a bed made up in the window of their long living-room, with its picturesque views over the open countryside, where he could be an integral part of the everyday life and bustle of the household. His drawing board, writing materials and odds and ends were assembled close at hand, allowing him to occupy himself in moments of strength.

Uffa's decision to attend the 'Yachtsman of the Year' dinner placed Norman and Josephine in something of a quandary for, should he travel by train as planned, they would need to find a railway station that could be negotiated without recourse to stairs. In the event Evesham was decided upon. Josephine driving Uffa to the station and trundling him by wheelchair to the train for the journey to London, where he was met and afforded the same caring treatment.

The dinner was to prove Uffa's last public engagement, for his batteries were running low, and on 27 October 1972, after nearly two months of devoted nursing by Josephine, the invincible force that had projected him to the summit of his chosen vocation was no more.

There could be no more fitting epitaph than the final words of *More Joys of Living*, when Uffa wrote:

> . . . and now I have learned that a quiet departure from earth is also not a thing to dread, for when it is time for mine, as I already have the sea flowing in my veins, I have only to be clothed by the heavens and crowned with light to be complete and able to enjoy Paradise.
>
> So when death's dark angel glides silently invisible alongside, to bear my innermost spirit aloft, I shall go happily and shall not flinch.

EPILOGUE

'Just a moment,' cried St Peter, hastily closing the Gates of Heaven as Uffa attempted to force a passage. He regarded Uffa's foot, still wedged firmly in the partially open door, coldly.

'I thought it would be a good idea if I nipped in smartly to avoid the rush,' smiled Uffa winningly.

'An admirable sentiment,' chided St Peter, 'were it not that our notes show you as listed elsewhere. Our own intake has already been processed for the day.'

Uffa gazed at him with crushed disbelief. 'Well, I can't fathom that,' he faltered. 'I've never intentionally gone out of my way to harm others. Whenever people have come to me for help or advice I've done my best; and I've been a regular churchgoer, particularly over the past ten years.'

St Peter allowed a slight flicker to momentarily touch his lips. Yes, he mused ironically, with passions spent and the end in sight one could almost smell the fear as they trooped back up the aisles.

'And look at that lot down there! They can't all be wrong,' continued Uffa, gathering strength. 'I can't have been all that bad when the highest in the land bother to turn up for my Memorial Service.'

St Peter transferred his gaze below to the Church of St Martin-in-the-Fields, Trafalgar Square. The church was full and bursting at the seams. Not the usual mournful crowd. More of a large happy family gathering, united in cheerful discourse as they recounted tales of the man to whom they had come to pay tribute.

And what was that music? To the left of the altar, facing the assembled multitude, the orchestra from the royal yacht *Britannia* played. An audible sigh and rustle swept through the congregation as everyone took a sharp intake of breath, and turned one to another with knowing looks. They were playing Uffa's favourite, 'Farewell and adieu to you Spanish Ladies'.

Taking time off from official engagements to honour an old friend were their Royal Highnesses Prince Philip, Prince Charles and Princess Anne, while the lesson was read by the Prime Minister, the Right Honourable Edward Heath. In the Address, Sir Max Aitken, who had put so much of himself into organizing the Memorial Service, said, 'We mourn for Uffa whose mind touches our hearts. He was pure gold.'

St Peter refused to be drawn. 'You would be quite downhearted if you knew the actual percentage we accept from the Memorial Service bracket. The majority of them can consider themselves fortunate if they as much as ascend the first rung of the heavenly ladder. At least you will be able to say that you saw the Gates of Heaven and spoke with St Peter.'

'Fat lot of good that is to me,' growled the wounded Uffa, ostentatiously fingering the rolled document he carried in his hand.

'Is that something interesting you have there?' St Peter enquired politely, in a kindly effort to ease the situation.

'Oh, this,' replied Uffa nonchalantly. 'It's the Certificate presented to me by the Goldfish Club on my *This is Your Life* programme. I just happened to have it with me, and I thought I would keep it in memory of the men whose lives I saved with my airborne lifeboats.'

St Peter extended his hand for the manuscript and studied it diligently. He eyed Uffa uncertainly. Muttering anxiously, 'This could cost me my job,' he swung the gates back fractionally. Like a streak of greased lightning Uffa was through.

'Is that it, then?' queried Uffa breathlessly, rubbing the palms of his hands briskly up and down together several times. 'Am I in for life?'

St Peter smiled. 'The answer is in the affirmative, but we prefer to call it Eternity.'

Uffa beamed. 'In that case,' he said, 'I think I can do you a favour. What we need to do is take another look at these wings. I've only had time for a quick survey, but it seems to me that we can more than double their speed if we run a Vee section from here and continue it throughout the . . .'

INDEX